Fastest Things
on Wings

Fastest Things on Wings

Rescuing Hummingbirds in Hollywood

Terry Masear

Houghton Mifflin Harcourt

Boston   New York   2015

Copyright © 2015 by Terry Masear

For information about permission to reproduce selections from this book, write to Permissions, Houghton Mifflin Harcourt Publishing Company, 215 Park Avenue South, New York, New York 10003.

www.hmhco.com

Library of Congress Cataloging-in-Publication Data is available.
ISBN 978-0-544-41603-1

Book design by Greta D. Sibley

Printed in the United States of America
DOC 10 9 8 7 6 5 4 3 2 1

To all of the dedicated wildlife rehabbers who work tirelessly to restore life and beauty to the natural world. And a special thanks to my mentor, Jean, for the invaluable wisdom and experience she has shared with me.

Surrender yourself humbly;
then you can be trusted to
care for all things.

—*Lao Tzu*

Contents

Prologue

IF DESTINY ARRIVES at times by chance and at other times by choice, for me it came through some of each. In my case, the future appeared in the form of a pinfeathered hummingbird washed out of his nest in the ficus tree just outside our house during a punishing rainstorm. Two years later, I set up a website and began devoting my summers to rehabilitating dozens of young hummingbirds brought to me by bird lovers from all over Los Angeles.

Most people who call my hummingbird-rescue hotline insist they know a lot about dogs or cats — and sometimes both — but nothing about hummingbirds. Before my waterlogged chick dropped out of his nest and into my life, I was one of those people. I could see that hummingbirds were exceedingly beautiful, extraordinarily quick, and capable of magical flight. Beyond that, I knew little about the miniature marvels I occasionally glimpsed streaking past my second-floor bedroom window like shooting stars. Later, once I'd spent a few years rescuing hummingbirds, I believed I understood them quite well, particularly after rehabbing several exceptional birds who overturned all of my assumptions. But the arrival of my rainstorm nestling set in motion a chain of events that would not come full circle until four years later, with the appearance of a special bird who unveiled deeper mysteries about these tiny forces of nature.

This is the story of Gabriel, a male Anna's delivered to my doorstep in an elegant dinner napkin by a young parking valet who'd retrieved him from the middle of a busy street in Beverly Hills during a violent windstorm. Gabriel, named after his finder, had collided with a limousine and was near death when he arrived at my rescue facility. Gabriel's recovery from a broken and defeated adult took me on a five-month-long, winding journey that brought into sharp relief how little I really understood hummingbirds. And if Gabriel represented a convincing reminder of what I didn't know, Pepper, an injured female Anna's who arrived a month later, was the exclamation mark. The events that unfolded during Pepper's recovery and her special bond with Gabriel forced me to acknowledge complex psychological and emotional nuances in hummingbirds that I had never imagined.

Gabriel's rehabilitation during the long summer of 2008 offered a powerful lesson on the trials and triumphs of rescuing hummingbirds in a bustling urban environment. Caring for him and Pepper had to be balanced with thousands of emergency phone calls and the needs of a hundred and sixty orphaned and injured birds that flooded into my facility as the nesting season progressed. Just as each bird came with a story — from chicks in nests cut by tree trimmers to fledglings retrieved by cats and dogs — the summer's array of casualties elicited emotions that spanned the spectrum from anguish to tears of joy as I nurtured recovering birds before releasing them back into the wild. This experience rewarded me with an abundance of knowledge and insights about hummingbirds, including their rapid physical development, individual personalities, miraculous flight, and awe-inspiring migratory journeys. Scientific information scattered throughout the book stems from five years of personal research and is supplemented by the findings of leading hummingbird experts and banders in the United States, all of whom have shared astonishing discoveries that seem to border on science fiction.

Ultimately, my eventful summer with Gabriel and Pepper revealed the complexities of a rehabber's connection to wild creatures and their natural environment. And the awareness I gained from working closely with such a diverse collection of hummingbirds served as both a forceful reminder of how much there is to learn and a moving plea to accept all that is still unknown.

CHAPTER 1

Out on a Limb

FEW CIRCUMSTANCES LEAD to a person balancing precariously in a pine tree a hundred feet over the Pacific Ocean at dawn on a cloudless summer day. Bankruptcy, a messy divorce, an unmanageable addiction, a broken dream. Nagging guilt over some nameless transgression that can no longer be endured. Or the doctor explaining how you've got two months and they're not going to be pretty. But Katie isn't one misstep away from certain death for any of these mundane reasons. She's on a mission. As she edges out over the rocky shoreline, the bowing branch quivers under her feet.

"What should I do next?" she whispers breathlessly into the phone. "I can almost reach it now."

"Wait, you're calling me from the tree?"

"Yeah, I'm on the branch just below them."

"You're on what?" I wrest myself from a dream. "Katie, get down and call me back. This is insane."

"Terry, listen. Yesterday afternoon before I left my house I told you I was too busy and stressed out to deal with this kind of thing now. And remember what you said? You said, 'If not now, when?'"

"Yeah, I know what I said. But not now, okay?"

"Hey, I'm out here, so let's do this."

I hesitate as the alarming image of what Katie is up to shifts into focus. From my distant, half-conscious state, I try to imagine the line of reasoning people walk themselves through before calling me at all hours: *Maybe I'll give Terry a call. After all, this is an emergency, isn't it? I hope she doesn't think I'm too weird calling her from this hookah lounge* (the caller all pumped up at two a.m.), or *gentleman's strip club* (the stripper calling, not the gentleman), or *all-night Korean spa* (while in a sweat), or *Guatemalan village* (*¿Hablas español?*). Still, despite this rich cultural variety, Katie is my first tree person.

"Terry?"

"Yeah, I'm here." I sit bolt upright in bed. "Okay, do you have the clippers I mentioned?"

Garden clippers came up purely hypothetically yesterday when a frantic Katie called me after discovering a hummingbird trapped in her home office. She had had the French doors to the backyard propped open, and the bird flew into the house in the late afternoon just as Katie had an industry event — which her entire career and life ambition depended on — to attend. Katie called me for advice but was unable to catch the terrified bird rocketing around the rafters, so she left the French doors open and went out. When she arrived back home after midnight, she didn't see the hummingbird anywhere and assumed it had flown out, so she closed up the house and went to bed, despite my warning about checking the room carefully.

Now two chicks in a nest overhanging the steep cliffs of Malibu are screaming their heads off, and their mother is dead behind the filing cabinet. It's just two tiny birds. But these little birds create big guilt. The nestlings will sit out there crying all day as they slowly starve to death. So for Katie, there is only one way out from under the crushing weight of self-recrimination.

"I have the clippers in my hand," she confirms.

"So you're holding the phone with . . ."

"I have a Bluetooth."

"Great, then reach under the nest and cut the branch at the far end first, about two inches from the nest."

An endless silence follows, punctuated by a few muted curses over the roar of wind and waves.

"Katie?"

More silence, then: "Okay, now what?"

"Now cup one hand under the nest and cut the branch on the side closest to you." I let out a deep breath, recognizing that these instructions leave no hands for holding on. "And for God's sake, be careful."

"Don't worry. I competed in gymnastics in college. I have excellent balance," a strained voice comes back.

"Good to know."

"I finished first in the state in '95 and competed in the nationals in '96," she continues, as if we're conducting a casual, precompetition interview on ESPN.

"Even better." That will be my first line of defense in court, I assure myself.

"I do a killer handstand."

"Well, let's not press our luck."

Another long silence.

"Okay, I've got the nest."

"Good, now —"

"Oh, shit!"

"Katie?"

I hear the haunting wail of the eternal wind, and nothing else.

"Katie? Are you there?"

After a deafening silence that sends me vaulting off the bed and pacing around the room in panicked circles, I hear a faint voice drift back through a crackling connection. "A pinecone just fell on my head."

Something they never prepare you for in gymnastics.

"Are you okay?"

"I think so, but . . . damn . . . yeah, go ahead."

"Okay, now, how do they look?"

"Um, well, they're tiny, green, and super-cute."

"I mean, do they look alarmed, like they're about to fly away?"

"They look a little nervous"—she pauses reflectively—"but no, they're just kind of staring at me with big eyes."

"Good. Then cup your hand over them and make your way back, slowly. And if I were you, I'd ditch the clippers."

"Got it." She breathes heavily as I hear the sound of bark scraping under sneakers and try not to imagine the lead story on the evening news.

Finally, after the longest thirty seconds of both our lives, she exhales. "Okay, I'm back, we're back to the ladder so . . . can I, let me call you back when I . . ."

"Good idea. Put the nest in a box on some crumpled Kleenex when you get in the house and call me."

"You got it."

"Oh, and Katie. One more thing." I sigh, rubbing my eyes. "Just for the record, I never told you to do this."

"Yeah, I know." I hear her smile. "Bye."

I hang up my cell phone and sink down onto the edge of the bed. It's six a.m. and my heart is already racing as if the house were being overtaken by fast-moving flames. "Unbelievable." I shake my head. "I must be out of my mind getting involved in this insanity."

Of course, I am crazy. But I'm not scale-a-tree-alone-at-dawn-a-hundred-feet-over-the-ocean-with-no-regard-for-potentially-fatal-consequences crazy like Katie. I'm a lot worse. Katie's foray into the maddening world of hummingbird rescue is over. I have a filled-to-capacity aviary sitting on the patio and fifty young birds waking up in my garage, including a dozen noisy nestlings in the incubator waiting for the first of thirty hand-feedings they will need just to get through the day. And before I can get dressed and stumble downstairs to breakfast, my phone is ringing again, announcing more crises heading my way.

CHAPTER 2

Rescue Me

NICHOLAS RACED DOWN the urgent path of hummingbird rescue with his own brand of recklessness. He had called me in a panic at nine o'clock the night before after fishing a young hummingbird out of his swimming pool in the Hollywood Hills. Tree trimmers, Southern California hummingbirds' deadliest enemy, had been in the adjacent yard that day. Nicholas wanted to know what to do with a nestling who was a few days away from flight. I ran him through the standard protocol and, it being early June and the height of an uncommonly prolific baby season that already had me on the ropes, asked him to call me in the morning.

Nicholas calls at eight a.m. as I am pursuing a fledgling who, as much to his surprise as mine, spontaneously airlifted himself out of the intensive care unit on his first flight and is now buzzing like a bumblebee around the garage ceiling in slow (for a hummingbird, though far faster than even the quickest human) circles. As I climb onto a chair and vainly attempt to retrieve the escapee with a handheld net, Nicholas explains that his bird is not looking too good and insists on dropping it off at my house immediately.

I hang up and manage to net the unintended flight risk when he alights on the wing of a cast-iron dragonfly wind chime a young couple left behind after delivering a nest containing twins two days earlier. The nestlings' mother had built a downy, intricately spun cup on the dragonfly's back and decorated its exterior with flakes of sea-green lichen to match the wind chime. When Southern California weather is calm, nesting hummingbirds are attracted to wind chimes enclosed on porches and unreachable from the ground, since nests built there protect the chicks from predators high and low. Some hummingbirds blithely build on wind spinners, forcing their human protectors to secure the devices with weights and strings so the nestlings aren't sent whirling on a high-speed merry-go-round every time the wind kicks up. Even with all of this accommodation, when the Santa Ana winds blast into the city in late spring, some of these nests are forsaken because of instability or the loud and unexpected clatter of chimes. Since female hummingbirds fiercely defend their young against all forms of crises and attacks, only the direst circumstances can drive a mother to abandon her nest. Residing on a porch is a mixed blessing for many nestlings: they are protected from the elements, but they're also exposed to the vagaries of human activity. In the case of the dragonfly twins, their mother had been fatally clipped by a wind-driven ceiling fan mounted overhead.

When the anxious young couple walked into my garage carrying the wind chime, the camouflaged nest blended so seamlessly into the cast-iron dragonfly, I could barely differentiate the two. I stepped back a few feet to get a broader view of the dragonfly, and the tiny cylindrical nest perched between its wings and two needle-like black bills poking out of the nest's top took shape. When I looked closer, the nest's creative mix of organic and synthetic materials came into focus like details emerging in an instant Polaroid.

The nest had been woven with the usual hummingbird blend of spider silk, skinny twigs, blades of grass, tree bark, leaves, moss, seed tassels, downy feathers from finches and bushtits, dog and human hair (from a black shorthair and a curly-headed brunette, respectively), and charcoal-gray laundry lint from a dryer vent. For camouflage, the exterior had been decorated with strategically placed lichen and blue strips delicately pulled from a plastic tarp the finders were using to cover a section of their patio that was under construction. I gazed in wonder at the skill and craftsmanship involved in sculpting this elegant work of art. As with origami, it would take a human being hundreds of hours of patient practice to create a structure equally beautiful and functional. Like snowflakes, every hummingbird nest is unique, its color and design dependent upon available materials and the mother's species, time constraints, and experience. Despite the hundreds of nests I have admired over the years, each new one that comes in mesmerizes me all over again. Like seeing William Blake's "world in a grain of sand" and "heaven in a wild flower," looking at hummingbirds' astonishing creations opens the door to a magical and otherworldly realm.

Seasoned rehabbers can often identify the species of a hummingbird by the shape and color of her nest long before the nestlings have matured enough to betray their identity. Nests tend toward the color of the chicks' future feathers. In Southern California species, Anna's hummingbirds construct taupe-and-ash-gray nests; black-chinned females weave unmistakable beige-to-antique-white cylindrical nests shaped like miniature beehives; and Allen's and rufous nests sport the burnt-orange and mahogany hues of the hairs on uncoiled tree-fern fronds. How nest-building females arrive at these color distinctions that match both the tree bark and the feathers of their unhatched young remains one of nature's unsolved mysteries.

In the case of the dragonfly twins, based on the nest's muted gray tones and broad circumference, I figured I had a pair of young Anna's on my hands. After I explained the challenge of coaxing the masterpiece apart from the wind chime, the finders volunteered to leave the dragonfly until I had the time and patience to detach the nest with the surgical precision required to keep it and its twelve-day-old pinfeathered residents intact. Since the chicks' remaining firmly anchored inside their nest is a matter of life and death in the wild, extracting babies after a certain age is always a risky proposition, as they dig in tightly with their claws and may suffer foot and leg injuries if removed. So caution advises letting new arrivals remain in their natural nest until they decide it's time to jump ship.

When Nicholas arrives, bleary-eyed and unshaven, half an hour after he called, he looks as if he has been up all night at the tables in Vegas. His nestling, unlike most young birds separated from their mothers for more than a dozen hours, refuses to eat and keeps nodding off. The minute we step into the garage, I lift the baby out of Nicholas's Rolex watch case and place her in a faux nest constructed by placing tightly wound Kleenex inside a plastic salsa cup.

"Is he okay?" Nicholas asks, nervously rubbing his unshaven chin as I set the nestling in a chorus line of orphaned chicks who begin peeping and swaying like bobble-heads the second I touch the sliding glass door to the ICU.

"She."

"Oh, yeah? How can you tell?"

"See how white her throat is? There's no five o'clock shadow like the young males have."

"Is she okay?" His expression softens.

"She's not as lively as nestlings usually are, but time will tell."

"Well, she was pretty alert during the night," Nicholas assures me.

"During the night?"

"Yeah, I slept in a chair with her on my chest and fed her every half hour, like you said."

"You fed her all night?" I turn and notice that, over his rumpled blue jeans, he is sporting a black silk pajama top streaked with a white residue that to law enforcement might mean a ride downtown for Nicholas but to a hummingbird rehabber looks suspiciously like dried sugar water.

He nods, staring with a pained expression at the slumbering fledgling in the ICU.

"Every half hour?"

"Yeah, I set my alarm and fed her every thirty minutes, just like you said," he asserts, crossing his arms defensively over his barrel chest.

I study his face to see if he's kidding, but Nicholas returns my gaze with a comical seriousness. "Well, that explains why she's so exhausted. They don't normally eat all night," I say.

"Oh, they don't?"

This assumption that hummingbirds stay up all night dining, carousing, and getting into trouble is a misconception I've encountered hundreds of times. I used to think it revealed an absurd lack of common sense. But then I thought about bats, which, though mammals, share some of the aerial skills and eating habits of hummingbirds and often appear in the same educational videos and nature programs.

"No. They aren't nocturnal, so they don't hunt in the dark."

Nicholas gives me a long, expressionless look. "I've stayed up all night for worse reasons," he finally says with a shrug, smiling at his folly.

"I probably should have made her eating schedule clearer when we talked on the phone," I say apologetically. "I just got so many calls yesterday."

"No, no." He waves me off. "I'm the crazy one."

"Only a sane person can afford to admit he's crazy," I point out as we make our way out the garage door. "And as crazy as you may be, you're also the hero. Your bird's chances of survival just rocketed from zero to about a hundred percent. Because of you, she'll be back out there in a couple of months, in fighting form and ready to take on the wild world."

"Oh, wait"—he reaches into his back pocket—"I wanted to give you something . . ." He trails off, fumbling around in his jeans. "I forgot. I don't have my wallet. It got soaked when I jumped in the pool."

"You jumped in the pool?"

Nicholas nods after some hesitation.

"With your clothes on."

"Yeah, I kind of panicked when I saw her floating around out there. I figured she only had about a minute before she drowned." Nicholas pauses, then narrows his eyes and throws me a sidelong glance as I suppress laughter. "That was crazy too, wasn't it?"

After Nicholas departs, I sink into a teak lounge chair on the patio next to half a dozen small flight cages humming with fledglings at various stages of development, from beginners who sit stone-still on their perches, warily observing the broad expanse around them, to the week-older pinballs bouncing confidently back and forth between perches in pursuit of greater opportunity. It's just nine a.m. As I close my eyes and melt into the warm morning sunbeams breaking over the roof of the house, the phone rings, signaling more distress waiting in the wings.

CHAPTER 3

I Can't Get Over You

WHEN IT COMES TO SAVING HUMMINGBIRDS, sometimes crazy isn't enough. Some people, like Stan, break rank and elevate the perils of rescue to impossibly dangerous heights.

Stan mistakenly locked the family cat out of the house when he got home late Friday night from his job as grill chef at Jerry's Famous Deli. The next morning, his kids found a female hummingbird dead on the front porch. The same hummingbird that built a nest outside his daughters' bedroom and that the entire family had been obsessing over for the past six weeks. Stan's kids named the chicks Minnie and Mickey and have been documenting their progress with hours of film footage for a school science fair. Now the chicks' mother is gone because the cat ambushed her as she was picking aphids off a hibiscus at dawn (the time of day when hummingbirds, like people, are most vulnerable), the nestlings are hysterical because they haven't been fed since the night before, and the kids are inconsolable because the magic surrounding the nest has become the center of their imaginative universe.

"The birds are screaming, my kids are crying, and my wife hates me," Stan reports over the phone. "What do I do?"

"You'll have to cut the nest and bring it to me. The nestlings need to go into rehab. It's the only way they'll make it," I explain as I rush a large flight cage from the patio to the garage to fill feeders sucked dry by three high-octane fledglings with bottomless appetites.

Silence.

"Stan?"

"Yeah, I'm thinking."

"Look, it's no big deal. I'll tell you how to cut the nest and give you the location of the nearest rehab facility you can take them to. Of course you can bring them to me," I say encouragingly, "or we have a network of drop-off points all over Los Angeles."

Stan breathes a heavy sigh. "I'm just not sure . . ." He trails off.

"What's the problem?" I press as my call-waiting beeps frenetically. "You just cut the nest and put it in a box. It's simple."

"It would be simple if it weren't for the Rottweiler in the yard. The nest is in the bougainvillea next to our house, but it's in the neighbor's yard, and he's out of town for the week."

"So who's taking care of the dog?"

"He has a pet-sitter, but she comes by at a different time every day and I don't have her number. The guy just moved in a couple of months ago. I haven't actually met him. All I know about him is that he loves that dog."

"Does he seem like the violent type?"

"No, he seems like a nice guy. I've never seen him angry."

"I mean the dog. What do you know about him?"

"I know he barks like mad every time I walk by the fence between our houses."

I think for a few seconds. "Can you reach the nest from the window?"

"No. It's on an adjoining wall."

"Can you reach it from the roof?"

"Yeah," a tentative voice comes back. "I think I can."

I give Stan the same nest-cutting instructions I'd given Katie, taking into account that this time, the finder will be hanging above an angry Rottweiler rather than teetering on a tree branch a hundred feet over the ocean. "And Stan," I add, "with hummingbirds, things don't always go as planned, so take somebody with you in case you need help. Okay?"

"Okay, I think my other neighbor is home."

"Perfect. Call me when you get the nest."

Stan, the reluctant hero, agrees. As soon as he hangs up, my phone signals two missed calls, and another one comes in just as I notice the hummingbirds in the aviary tussling over empty feeders I filled a few hours ago. As I rush through the security door, I tap the touchpad with my right hand while wresting two feeders from the springs that anchor them to the aviary bars with my left.

"Terry?" a panicked voice pleads from the other end of the line when I pick up the call.

"Yes," I answer on my headset as I race out the security door and back to the house for more food.

"Thank God. I have two baby hummingbirds in a bowl in my kitchen and I don't want them to die. They're so tiny and helpless and I don't know what to do. I've got them on some paper towels under a lamp," the caller sputters at breakneck speed, "but they're breathing really hard and I'm getting so stressed out." She begins hyperventilating.

"Okay, try to relax and breathe slowly," I advise as I feel my blood pressure spiking from the day's events.

"All right." She takes a deep breath.

"Now, how did they get in your kitchen?"

"My son brought them home from soccer practice. He and an-other boy took them out of a nest."

"Where?"

"I don't know. He won't tell me." The caller begins choking up. "I scolded him when he told me what he did and now he's crying and won't talk to me."

"When did all of this happen?"

"He got home about twenty minutes ago."

"What about the other kid?"

"He's got a lot of issues," she says, exhaling with disdain. "He can't think about anything but himself and he's —"

"Did you —"

"I don't like my son hanging out with him because he's so self-centered and dysfunctional, always in trouble —"

"Okay, I get it," I interject. "Have you tried to reach the little so-ciopath?"

"I left a message at his house but nobody called me back. The poor little things. They hardly have any feathers. I don't know what to do . . ." She trails off tearfully.

"Try asking your son one more time. It's not too late to get them back to their mother."

"Okay, hold on." She sniffles and I hear quick heels tap down a tile hallway and then a door squeaking open. "Noah, honey, the hummingbird person is on the phone —" A muffled conversation followed by the child's tearful protests erupts in the background. "He just cries every time I ask him," she says, her voice coming back. "Noah, look, we can —" She fades away again. "He just keeps crying." She sighs with resignation. "My husband and I separated recently so there are a lot of other things going on right now."

There are always a lot of other things going on. Hummingbird rescue is rarely simple and straightforward. Young hummingbirds' helpless vulnerability draws out raw emotions that unleash our deepest insecurities about our humanity, mortality, and place in the natural world. And those uncertainties threaten to blow the lid off any other unresolved anxieties that might be boiling just below the surface.

Still, I recognize that some parents would drag the information out of a defiant youngster in a crisis like this. Some mothers would drop the hammer on the resistant kidnapper and get the nestlings back where they came from despite his tearful protests. But the human element is the biggest wildcard in hummingbird rescue. And personalities, life dramas, family relationships, and parenting styles are quantities I have to factor into the equation with every call I get.

"I feel so terrible about this. It would just kill me if they died."

"Don't worry, I can save them," I assure her and then give her my address and hang up to take another urgent call. It's Stan.

"Terry." I hear Stan shout as if from a great distance. "When I cut the nest the chicks flew off."

"Did you see where they went?"

"My neighbor says he can see them hanging on some lattice across the yard."

"The same yard the Rottweiler is in?"

"Yeah, the same one." Stan's voice suddenly pulls in closer. "And I'm not Rambo," he concedes before lapsing into silence.

I pause to reflect on the hazards of life in Los Angeles. Never mind out-of-control wildfires, nerve-jangling earthquakes, stray bullets from shooting rampages, road rage–induced street brawls, and high-speed paparazzi chases down Sunset Boulevard. With hummingbirds in the mix, Katie almost splattered herself across the cliffs of Malibu, and Stan is about to be dismembered by an irate Rottweiler in the San Fernando Valley.

"Will they be okay now that they're out?" Stan asks in a resigned tone that tells me he already knows the answer.

"No, they won't survive. They're like one-year-old children at this point. They're completely helpless without their mother. But I'm not sure—"

"We're going in after them, then." Stan cuts me off with the determination of a commando on a deadly mission.

"Wait, I'm not telling you to do that," I protest.

"I know, but this is my fault. And my family is so freaked out. If I don't fix this, it's the kind of thing my kids will never forget, you know?"

And Stan is right; they never will. Childhood crises that trigger such powerful emotions become defining moments that stick, remaining forever embedded in family narratives. Not to mention that the loss of the birds will dead-end the science project. How will the story find closure? I envision Stan presiding over the hibachi grill on his fortieth wedding anniversary, with the kids and grandkids gathered all around, laughing, applauding, and enjoying near-perfect familial harmony and happiness, except for "that thing with the hummingbirds" that still lurks in the background three agonizing decades later. And no matter how much Stan tries to erase the dark memory, the dead babies will live on, a bloody stain on his résumé and a lasting testament to his shortcomings as a caring father. So on this otherwise fine spring morning, everything is suddenly on the line for Stan.

"Yeah, I get it," I assure him. "It's not a great situation, but a provoked Rottweiler can change your life pretty fast."

This is greeted with a tense silence. And I know he's going in. No matter what I say. There's too much riding on it.

"Stan?"

"Yeah, I'm still here."

"This might seem kind of crazy—"

"I'll try crazy at this point. Crazy's better than nothing."

"Okay, when was the last time you saw the pet-sitter?"

"Yesterday morning. She always puts a ton of food out for him when she comes by, but we haven't seen her yet today."

"So your hungry Rottweiler might appreciate something fresh off the grill, you know what I mean?"

"Yeah, he's an eating machine, I can tell you that. I'm gonna try something," Stan says nervously. "I'll call you back."

I hang up and rush into the aviary with a fistful of dripping feeders. Several birds buzz me in a blur of spinning wings as I step inside the security door, and then my phone rings. A well-spoken young salesclerk named Madison is calling from Fred Segal in Santa Monica. It's the third time this month someone there has called me about a hummingbird trapped in the store.

"We have a hummingbird flying around our salon and the customers are going crazy," she reports flatly.

"Where exactly is the bird?"

"He's up in the skylight. We tried putting a hummingbird feeder in the doorway, but he won't come down."

Hummingbirds don't come down. They are programmed to fly toward the light in the sky, no matter what, and they won't come down until exhaustion forces them to descend to lower altitudes.

"Okay, this is a challenging situation," I caution her before launching into the lengthy and complex logistics of retrieving a hummingbird from a skylight. I dispatch Madison with instructions on how to manufacture an arsenal of improvised rescue equipment and supplies, and as soon as I hang up, my phone rings again. It's Stan.

"Terry? I got 'em!" he announces proudly and breathlessly.

"Both of them?"

"Yeah, both. It was edgy for a minute there, but my signature bacon-cheddar cheeseburger worked like a dream. He downed four in under a minute. That dog's gonna be my friend forever."

"Well done, Stan," I congratulate him, applauding his new heroic status within the family. "Or maybe I should call you Rambo now."

"Maybe you should call me lucky," he countered flatly.

"Can you bring them to me?"

"We're on our way," Stan announces after taking down my address.

I hang up just in time to break up a wrestling match between a pair of male Anna's twins who aren't wasting any sentiment on brotherly love. The phone rings. Madison from Fred Segal is on the line again.

"We got the hummingbird down but he's breathing really hard and his eyes are closed," she reports uneasily above a cacophony of agitated voices in the background.

"Give him sugar water from the feeder and set him in a shallow box on some tissue in a safe place outside, off the ground, in the sun, and near a tree. He should fly off within half an hour or so. If he doesn't, call me."

"Got it."

"And, Madison, one more thing. Do you have any plants or brightly colored curtains hanging by the door of your salon?"

Madison pauses. "Yeah, we have some. Hey, what are those plants called?" she shouts to someone across the room. "Coral what? Yeah," she says, back to me again, "some coral honeysuckle hanging on the veranda outside the front doors."

Honeysuckle. Irresistible to hummingbirds since the beginning of time. The two are so intimately linked that over millions of years, in an evolutionary process known as coadaptation, the hummingbird's bill has been shaped to match the morphology of the plant's vibrant, tubular flower, which in turn has evolved a fun-nel-like design to retain abundant nectar for the little high-main-tenance fliers. Unfortunately, this epic history of coevolution has led to a minor crisis at Fred Segal on a Saturday morning in early twenty-first-century Santa Monica.

"Well, you need to move those to another location because that's what's drawing the birds into the salon."

"Oh, it is? Yeah, that makes sense, actually. I'll move them after we close tonight. Thanks."

I hang up and take advantage of the lull in calls to place the insufferably cute fledgling who discovered the miracle of flight in the garage yesterday into a small cage with another heartbreaker who just learned the thrill of executing a 360-degree turn in midair. Watching them practice their early flight training in the starter cage, I'm touched by the look of concentration humming-bird fledglings get before lifting off one perch and buzzing slowly toward the other eight inches away. Before launching, they spin their wings rapidly while gripping the perch on tiptoes. Once they work up enough confidence to let go of the perch, they float, al-most involuntarily, across the cage. As with children learning a new sport, control is the last skill to develop, so beginning fledg-lings often overshoot the perch and end up stuck on the wire mesh caging on the other side. Until they learn how to fly in reverse, it's up to me to gently extricate them from the mesh and return them to a perch, facing inward, so they can immediately fly back across the cage, miss the perch, and get stuck in the mesh at the other end two seconds later. Like infants learning to walk, fledglings starting to fly appear deliberate and uncertain. But young hum-mingbirds are on a much tighter schedule than toddlers, and what looks strenuous and awkward today will be all grace and fluidity tomorrow.

Half an hour later, Stan arrives with a pair of beleaguered nest-lings in a Converse shoebox and two red-eyed adolescent girls in emotional recovery. Stan was right: at five six and a hundred and thirty pounds, with wire-rimmed glasses and no hair, he isn't Rambo. But he is the star of the day. Stan and I chat in the garage as I place the twins in the crowded ICU while his daughters peer with hypnotic fascination at the fifteen soon-to-be-released young adults flying blurred laps inside the aviary. It's amusing to see the girls gaping in silent awe at the hummingbirds engaged in their fast-paced bathing, sparring, flower-eating, and bug-catching rou-tines. Within minutes, both forget all about the morning tragedy that had threatened to shatter their fragile adolescent dreams.

While I'm feeding the voracious chicks, Stan recounts how thrilled the family had been watching the mother build her nest and incubate the eggs. He describes how the kids sat on the bed by the window with their digital camera for hours every afternoon while doing their homework so they could film the mother feeding her babies. His family couldn't believe how fortunate they were to have front-row seats to the unfolding of such a miracle in nature. It was the most extraordinary wildlife event the kids had ever wit-nessed, like something out of a Disney fairy tale.

"We couldn't get enough of it." Stan smiles wistfully. "But the second I landed in the yard with that Rottweiler and saw the fur sticking straight up on the back of his neck"—he whistles softly, rubbing his palm over his wet brow and shaking his head—"I prayed I'd never see another hummingbird again. Know what I mean?"

"I know exactly what you mean." I nod with a wry smile, glanc-ing at the dozen babies in their nests inside the ICU gazing up at me and following my every move. "Better than you can imagine. These are the unlucky victims in the endless string of collisions between man and nature in this overcrowded city." *And judging from the day's drama,* I think, *it's not just the hummingbirds who need rescuing.*

As Stan and the kids head out, I give them a rundown of the intricacies involved in hummingbird rehabilitation. Later on, I follow up by e-mailing them photos of the twins at each stage of their six-week journey through rehab. A month after dropping the nestlings off, the girls win family tickets to Disneyland for introducing the fascinating world of hummingbird rescue to their middle school at the science fair.

"Give my best to Minnie and Mickey," I tell Stan when he calls to report his daughters' achievement and check on the two colorful Allen's thriving in the aviary.

"Are they going to be okay when they get out?" he asks anxiously.

"No, they're going to be better than that."

"That's such great news. Can you believe it, Terry? After everything that happened, they turned out so perfect," Stan marvels.

"Yeah, it's pretty amazing, isn't it?" I agree. "It's almost like winning tickets to Disneyland."

CHAPTER 4

This Magic Moment

I RESCUED MY FIRST HUMMINGBIRD in the spring of 2003 after one of our Abyssinian cats escaped from the house and brought home a chick who had been blown out of her nest during a fierce Santa Ana windstorm. The cat, aptly named Tintin for his endless string of mishaps and adventures, rushed into the house early one spring morning and carefully placed the undamaged nestling on the hardwood floor in front of me and my husband as if he were bestowing a gift of incalculable value. While Tintin had already accomplished untold remarkable things in his young life, delivering this miniature feather duster ended up transporting us all into a mysterious and unexplored new world unfolding just outside the door.

After calling around, I located Jean Roper—the most experienced hummingbird rehabilitator in Los Angeles, if not the world—and drove the nestling to her house. Surprised at how many hummingbirds she had, I volunteered to help, took her phone number, and then forgot all about it. The following spring, in early April, I rescued a chick dangling from a nest that had been flattened by an unrelenting, torrential downpour. On the second morning of the three-day deluge, I was on my way to teach an English class at UCLA when the young hummingbird dropped, metaphorically speaking, out of his nest in the ficus tree and into my life. The moment I stepped out the door that morning with my umbrella, poised to make a dash for the car, I noticed the pinfeathered chick hanging upside down by one claw from the decimated nest. It doesn't rain much, or often, in Los Angeles, but when heavy storms do roll in off the Pacific Ocean, water comes down sudden, fast, and hard. And if you happen to be a young hummingbird caught in the fury of a coastal downpour, nature shows no mercy. Although I was already late, I splashed to the shed in my high-heeled Italian boots and hauled out an eight-foot stepladder, cursing myself through the blinding gusts for getting involved. After gently dislodging the chick from the nest in the hurricane-force wind and rain, I stumbled down the ladder and trotted back to our converted garage behind the house. Certain the ice-cold nestling was dead, I grabbed a handful of paper towels from the laundry room and was about to set him on a shelf and hurry off to class when a tiny claw rubbed almost imperceptibly against my palm. I raced back into the house, uncovered Jean's phone number from a jumbled stack of business cards and scraps of paper in the depths of the file cabinet, and called her.

"Give him some sugar water right away," Jean advised, "and keep him warm."

"Until what?"

"Until you get him here," she answered.

Glancing at my watch, I suddenly was living the recurring, anxiety-filled dream I had in which my class started in five minutes and I was over half an hour away. While hydroplaning across spilled sugar water on the kitchen floor, I bribed a colleague at UCLA to take my American culture class before calling Jean back. At the time, I didn't know anything about hummingbirds, but I had been watching the nest for weeks and was certain the baby would die if I didn't act quickly. Ten minutes later, I was in my car crawling in the fast lane along the paralyzed freeways skirting downtown Los Angeles. I had no inkling as I rushed through the morning's panicked events that I was charging full throttle into my future. After a tense commute through pounding rain with zero visibility, my now-revived patient chirping in protest all the way, I arrived at Jean's front door with the Barneys gray-flannel suit I had just bought and meticulously put on that morning soaked through. When she answered the door, Jean didn't bat an eye. She'd seen a lot worse. Awed by the number of hummingbirds she already had so early in the year, I again volunteered to help. As we were admiring the lively array of fledglings buzzing around the cages in her sunroom off the patio, Jean and I marveled at how the rare opportunity to rescue a hummingbird had presented itself to me twice in as many years. But as I would soon discover, there are no accidents in such matters.

A month later, Jean called and asked me to retrieve an adult hummingbird trapped inside a film-prop rental warehouse in Hollywood. After chasing the preternaturally fast male around beneath vaulted ceilings for an hour while tripping over Hollywood's history of surfboards, saddles, whiskey barrels, and treasure chests, I finally captured him by duct-taping an antique butterfly net to an aboriginal spear. Two minutes after downing a strong dose of sugar water in the palm tree–lined parking lot, the handsome but terrified bird shot back into the wilds of the Hollywood Hills. Impressed by my ingenuity, Jean called again the following week requesting an emergency pickup. When I arrived at her house that night toting a pair of pre-fledglings discovered by a ten-year-old who'd heard them peeping inside a neighborhood green-waste container, I inquired about the waterlogged nestling I had dropped off the month before.

"He's gorgeous," Jean said effusively. "He's a deep, dark green, which is unusual for an Anna's. But that's not all," she added cryptically. "He has something else."

"What? What else does he have?" I asked. "Can I see him?"

"He's sleeping now. But I'll show you next time you bring me a bird."

"Well, I guess that pretty much guarantees I'll bring you another bird."

"That's the idea." She smiled mischievously.

A week later, Jean called about a nest with two chicks that had been cut by city tree trimmers in Hollywood.

"Why do they trim trees in the spring when birds are nesting?" I asked angrily. "Don't they get it?"

"They don't care." Jean sighed with a world-weary exasperation that indicated she'd been through this argument with the city too many times. "It's whenever they get their funding."

Before I could disconnect my cell phone, I was in the car retrieving the nest from a young Latino tree trimmer who was waiting at a bus stop on a crowded corner of Sunset Boulevard.

"¿Sabes qué árbol?" I asked as he handed me a small takeout box containing the nest I hoped to return to the mother.

"No." The sun-scorched young man shook his bandanna'd head as he swept his hand toward a sprawling boulevard of slashed jacaranda and ficus trees winding into the Hollywood Hills. When I opened the nachos box he had tucked the nest into and met the gaze of two fully feathered, rufous chicks who were peering up at me with a poignant mix of fear and expectation, the moment froze in time. As I lingered at the traffic-congested intersection under the blazing sun with the box of twins in my hand, the stark contrast between the metallic sea of cars and the pristine natural beauty of the delicately colored nestlings tugged at something deep inside, like a memory from an earlier existence. As the harsh urban landscape fell away around us, a mournful wind whistled from the distant hills. Suddenly it seemed as though I were standing alone with the birds in a vast and uninhabited desert. A desolate feeling, at once alluring and haunting, swept over me. And for the first time, I glimpsed the importance of the work I was involved in. Without people who cared enough to call about them and a few hard-working rehabbers to take them in, hundreds of these magnificent creatures would perish under the crush of civilization every year. As I listened to the buzz of chainsaws and explosive clatter of the wood-chipper shredding tree limbs down the block, I wondered how many others had been missed. This disturbing recognition of human carelessness, along with the suffocating exhaust fumes and blistering noon sun radiating off the concrete sidewalk, caused me to stagger slightly before sinking onto a bus bench.

"*¿Estás bien?*" the tree trimmer asked with an expression so disarming he felt like an old friend.

"*Sí, estoy bien.*" I nodded as he sat down beside me and, for a fleeting moment, became my silent companion in our isolated bubble of compassion that required no explanation. "*Gracias,*" I said finally, gesturing toward the yellow box in my hand.

"*De nada.*" He bowed his head with a serious half smile before turning a reflective gaze toward the horizon. "*Son pájaros especiales.*"

"Yes, they are," I agreed softly. "Very special."

Ten minutes later I was making my way down the smog-shrouded freeway in a daze, as if driving through a dream. When I arrived at Jean's still reeling from the day's events, I tried to appear nonchalant while inquiring about my rainstorm rescue.

"Come out here." She motioned me through the house and into the backyard, where dozens of large flight cages hung from a long trellis that had served as a grape arbor in an earlier life. "This one." She pointed to a cage on the end in which two adult Anna's, a male and a female, were gracefully pirouetting back and forth between perches. The strapping young male looked darker than I had imagined he would from Jean's description, to the point of appearing almost black from certain angles.

"You're right." I nodded excitedly. "He's incredibly beautiful. I've never seen a hummingbird that dark."

"Not an Anna's anyway," Jean agreed. "But look closer. Don't you see anything else?" she prompted, as if we were playing a child's hidden-object game.

When the two birds alighted side by side on a perch, I peered more closely into the cage. Aside from his cobalt-green feathers, the male looked like any other Anna's. But closer inspection revealed something I had never seen on a hummingbird before. On the top of his head, in the very center, was a bright white spot that formed a perfect circle. I knit my brow as I studied the spot. "What's that from?"

"I don't know." Jean shrugged. "Maybe a mutation. Or some kind of albinism. Who knows?"

"It's so cool." I stared in disbelief.

Jean nodded. "I always know who he is. He's easy to recognize."

"Have you ever seen that before?" I turned and looked at her questioningly.

Jean shook her head. "Never."

"Never?" I echoed incredulously, trying to imagine the five thousand birds she had shepherded through rehab during her two-decade career of saving hummingbird lives.

"Uh-uh." Jean shook her head resolutely. "I'd remember something like that."

"Is he okay otherwise?"

"Oh, he's great," she assured me. "Healthy, strong, and really smart. He gets everything the first time."

I left Jean's house that day proud and excited that my bird had turned out so exceptional, and I flattered myself that his uniqueness had something to do with me. Speeding down an unusually empty freeway toward home, I wondered if my uncommon discovery, along with the moving encounter with the rufous nestlings that afternoon, represented some kind of culmination of events in my hummingbird-rescue efforts that had brought me full circle and would guide my hummingbird experience to a meaningful conclusion. But before I could get home, Jean called me on my cell phone.

"There's another nest with two babies at the West LA animal shelter," she reported with exasperation. "Same thing. You don't have to bring them tonight. Just keep them until you can get down here."

But Jean knew that I understood the danger of keeping young hummingbirds on a sugar-water diet for more than a day or two. Already starting to stress inordinately about each bird entrusted to me, I picked up the pinfeathered Anna's twins on my way home and was back at Jean's house the next morning. By the end of a busy month retrieving tree-trimming victims, I was onboard for the rest of the season. And the next.

After another year of driving in wide circles around Los Angeles's tangled freeways picking up hummingbirds from shelters and delivering them to Jean's rehabilitation center, I persuaded my husband, Frank, to help me build a dozen elaborately detailed cages designed specifically for educating young hummingbirds. A month later, we bought an intensive care unit and an outdoor aviary, got permitted under a local wildlife-rescue nonprofit, passed a state inspection, and took the giant leap into saving tiny lives. But while I made the leap into the unknown believing, like Kierkegaard, that faith would carry me through, it turned out to be more like jumping off a tall building convinced, like Superman, that I could fly, only to discover halfway into the free fall that I most certainly could not.

Before hummingbirds, Frank and I had spent our days going to work, renovating a dilapidated house, attending graduate school, and writing books. By the summer of 2004, we had finished a seemingly endless four-year remodeling project on our house in West Hollywood, and I had, at the same time, wrapped up five years of demanding study for my doctorate. Although I had a challenging job teaching English to international graduate students at UCLA, I felt hungry for a connection to the natural world that was more compelling than tending to half a dozen potted cacti on the patio that I always managed to destroy by overwatering. Which is about the time the hapless hummingbirds came along with Jean and her encyclopedic knowledge of rehabilitation, lending credence to the Buddhist proverb *When the student is ready, the teacher will appear*.

In late spring of 2005, just as the hummingbirds were gliding into the nesting season, with all of its attendant calamities, I had a dream. I was making my way through a dark and towering coniferous forest when I came upon a blue spruce rotating slowly on its axis, like a planet. The unusual motion captured my attention, magnetically drawing me into the tree's orbit. As I cautiously approached the mysterious evergreen, everything around me, including the tangled vines encircling the bushes, the pine needles on the trees, and the stars in the sky, began to shimmer with a silver light, like a snowy landscape illuminated by the full moon on a winter night. I peered into the darkness, and my gaze alighted on several shiny, oval Christmas tree ornaments scattered on branches throughout the tree. When I edged in more closely, a glowing white light beamed through me and onto the crystalline figures, which sat frozen and inanimate. The light did not come from within but from beyond, propelled by a powerful force channeling through me like a river through a conduit. As the light infused the figurines, their obsidian eyes blinked and they began breathing and moving on the branches before bursting to life and spinning their wings rapidly in unison. Within seconds, the tree lit up with twenty-one radiant hummingbirds adorned in sapphire, emerald, amethyst, ruby, copper, silver, and gold. When the white light streaming through me and into them brightened to the blinding intensity of the sun, the birds slowly elevated themselves from their perches and hovered in front of me for a few seconds before swirling, in an evanescent flash, into the azure sky above. In an instant they were all gone into the world of light. And I was left standing alone below, gazing up in wonder, with both a twinge of sorrow at seeing them depart and a rush of exhilaration that I had been the agent who liberated them from their dark slumber. In the dream, I didn't count the birds but instead felt the number, as one does in dreams. Later I recalled how many hummingbirds emerged from the enchanted tree only because I phoned Jean the next morning to describe the dream's vivid imagery.

"I hadn't even been drinking. That much," I pointed out.

"Impressive," Jean said.

"Twenty-one is a lucky number, you know."

"Uh-huh." She exhaled as I heard dozens of plastic feeders dropping into her sink. "We'll see how lucky it feels a few years from now."

That summer, my second one shuttling desperate orphans through the city's traffic-clogged arteries, I kept a few nestlings for myself and called Jean every day and most nights for advice. As soon as a bird fledged, I drove it to her house for the advanced stages of rehabilitation. By September of 2005, in a curious fulfillment of my neon dream, I had unwittingly rescued twenty-one hummingbirds. The number could have been a coincidence, or subconsciously orchestrated. Or it could have been the first in a series of serendipitous events that would befall me once I entered the enigmatic world inhabited by the featherweight phenoms.

Whichever it was, my early success saving hummingbirds proved nothing less than remarkable. I took the hardest cases to Jean, so I never knew the dark flipside behind my unqualified triumph. When the nesting season peaked in June, I found myself fielding three or four calls a day. Like a seasoned combat medic, I became an expert at triage, prioritizing injuries and responding with an immediacy that shocked Los Angeles residents accustomed to waiting hours, even days, for callbacks from city services. I had my emergency routine down and it worked flawlessly. I brought unresponsive birds back from the edge of death. Injured hummingbirds rushed in prone and lifeless came out flying the next day. Nothing failed on my watch.

"Is he going to be okay?" a trembling finder asked as she and her tearful teenage daughter watched me feed the fledgling they had accidentally locked in the garage the night before and then found sprawled unconscious on the cement floor that morning.

"No question," I assured them calmly, setting the awakening bird into the ICU. "It's a done deal."

Just as my confidence grew with each bird I saved, my approval ratings among friends, acquaintances, and the general public soared. Colleagues at UCLA who had barely acknowledged me for ten years began chasing me down on campus and striking up conversations about their experiences with not just hummingbirds but all forms of avian, mammalian, and even reptilian life. Everywhere I went — meetings, parties, supermarkets, the car wash — people wanted to talk. Everyone applauded my unique talent. When I strolled into shelters and humane societies to pick up orphaned chicks, the staff greeted me like a celebrity, showering me with adulation and fistfuls of free syringes. Callers to my hummingbird-rescue hotline praised me for being "a saint," "an angel," "a wonderful person," and, my personal favorite, "an inspiration." I felt like an overnight sensation; attaining this lofty stature had come quick and easy. Before hummingbirds, I had been grappling with the usual nagging fears and doubts that drive people in their midforties to impulsive and embarrassing behavior. But within a few short months, I had transitioned from that insidiously creeping midlife sense of disillusionment and lack of purpose to feeling gifted and necessary.

Everyone who starts out in wildlife rescue entertains the fantasy of edging closer to the beauty of nature and gaining an intimate understanding of other species while saving helpless lives. Since my youth in rural Wisconsin, I had been rescuing every unfortunate creature that fell into my empathetic path and, with each success, craving more opportunity. Now my lifelong dream of participating in organized wildlife rehabilitation had been realized and I was being abundantly rewarded for my charitable efforts. I woke up every morning energized and eager to work miracles. Fate had blessed me with the magic touch. I possessed a rare ability. There was no doubt in my mind that I could save anything. There was nothing I couldn't do.

And so, in my foolish naïveté, I blindly rushed into that proverbial land where angels fear to tread. And there was much to learn.

CHAPTER 5

Cry

AFTER MY HEADY ASCENT to the peak of the curve that first year, there was only one place left to go. My introduction to the unforgiving side of rescue arrived early on, in the late winter of 2006, the start of my second year in the lifesaving business. A stylishly dressed yuppie with two young children brought me a female Anna's just about to fledge; the first baby of the year. The Beverly Hills oak tree her nest had been in was cut down to clear space for a tennis court. The family, who kept her for a day before calling me, dropped off the emerald-green, newly feathered, and impossibly cute two-inch nestling around dusk on a misty evening in March.

Since the kids had been feeding her sugar water in the car before they arrived, I placed the chick, still in her original nest, in the ICU in my garage, turned up the heat, and waited thirty minutes before returning to give her the protein formula we feed hummingbirds in rehabilitation. When I opened the sliding glass door to the ICU, she chirped for food, but her crop—a small transparent sac on the right side of the neck in which a hummingbird stores food—appeared full. I waited another thirty minutes before coming back to feed her. Again she cried, more adamantly this time, al-though her crop, which should have been flat and empty by then, still looked like a bubble. I filled a 1 cc syringe with formula and tried giving her a little, but the liquid leaked out the sides of her mouth and ran down the pale silver feathers on her breast. I waited an hour and came back. This time when she cried loudly for food, she began breathing through her mouth, and her crop was bulging. When I touched her, she felt ice-cold despite having been tucked into a nest in a 90-degree ICU for two hours. A hummingbird's baseline temperature runs around 105 degrees, so when it feels cold to us, it's a clear sign of slowing metabolism. At nine p.m., I called Jean in a panic.

"It sounds like her crop is blocked." Jean sighed. "Do you know what they fed her?"

"No, but I have their phone number. I'll call them."

When I reached the woman who had delivered the bird, she as-sured me that they had given the chick only sugar water. I called Jean and reported this information with relief.

"She's not telling the truth," Jean countered flatly.

"Why would she lie?"

"Because she knows she screwed up. And now she's afraid you're going to jump all over her."

"Well, that's crazy," I insisted. "I just want to save the bird. I'll call her again."

I called the finder back and explained that I wasn't going to get angry but that I needed to know what she had fed the nestling so I could decide how to proceed.

"Nothing else, just sugar water," she said.

"Are you sure? Because I need to know if there was anything else," I pressed. With a little more prompting, she confessed the kids had fed the chick some ants.

"Ants?" I repeated in horror. "Hummingbirds never eat ants. Ants have a hard exoskeleton that won't pass through their digestive system. Why would you let your kids do that?" I demanded.

"We thought she needed some protein," the woman pushed back. "I'm sure she'll be fine," she added dismissively.

"You think so?" I scoffed, preparing to unload the last two hours of stress that was expressing itself through a brain-mashing headache. But my tone alerted her to the attack that was coming and she waved a white flag.

"I'm sorry. We didn't know." She fell silent as, despite my promise not to get angry, I upbraided her for not telling me sooner and then hung up, leaving her, I'm sure, crying guilty tears.

I called Jean and reported the disheartening information.

"People do that a lot." Jean sighed with disdain. "They think all insects are alike. Now you're going to have to siphon her crop."

"Siphon her crop?" I repeated in horror.

"It's her only chance, Terry."

"But I have no idea how to do that," I sputtered. "Why don't I just bring her to you?"

"There's not enough time for that. If she's mouth-breathing, you have to do it right away," Jean said, and then launched into instructions on how to perform a procedure that seemed to require the delicacy of brain surgery. "And be careful to position the angiocatheter in the right place and not to siphon too quickly or you'll rupture the crop and she'll die," she added flatly at the end.

Two minutes later I was back in the garage in a heart-pounding panic, holding my breath as I managed to extract a syringe full of cold sugar water from the chick's crop. Within minutes she looked infinitely relieved, so I fed her and waited. Thirty minutes later, her crop was bulging and she began mouth-breathing again. Out of desperation, I repeated the siphoning and then fed her an almost imperceptible amount of nectar. But the same thing happened, and the nestling continued to peep loudly. I called Jean, who suggested I put warm water in the syringe and try to dissolve any flinty debris obstructing the crop. I followed her directions, with the same dismal result.

"The ants are blocking her digestive system," Jean said with resignation during my third call at eleven p.m. She suggested that I try to clear the digestive tract by massaging the chick's abdomen, but it didn't sound promising. "Beyond that, there's not much you can do." She sighed. "I'm sorry, Terry."

But Jean wasn't sorry simply because she had been unable to find a way to relieve the nestling's suffering. She was sorry for what she knew was about to happen to me. Between my first inadvertent rainstorm rescue two years earlier and my twenty-one lifesaving triumphs since, I had come a long way in my education. And although Jean never said it directly, there had always been one last bridge to cross. A final test upon which all else depended. She was leaving me anxious and alone with the failing nestling, and her intent was clear: *You want the full experience of hummingbird rescue? Well, here it is, in its uncut version. Make no mistake: if you choose to pursue this dream, this is one of the nightmares you're signing up for.*

Although the hands on the kitchen clock were sweeping toward midnight and I already felt spent, I couldn't bear to leave the chick alone and crying in the incubator. I returned to the garage, took the nest her mother had artfully camouflaged with lime-green paint chips and that I had placed in a plastic salsa cup out of the ICU, and sat on the floor with her beside a small space heater. When she began thrashing and struggling to breathe, I lifted her out of the nest and held her in my hand. Using Reiki hand-warming techniques that a refreshingly enlightened hummingbird finder had introduced me to the year before, I was able to raise her body temperature a few degrees. At one in the morning, after she'd settled down and I'd started to fall asleep sitting against the brick wall, I tried to put her back in the nest, but she gripped my hand with her tiny claws and refused to let go. Each time I tried to place her in the nest, she anxiously clawed her way up onto the sleeve of my sweatshirt. So I sat holding her in the dim light as she stared up at me with unblinking dark eyes.

We remained locked in the grip of this unbreakable embrace for the eternity of an hour. It was just one tiny bird in the palm of my hand, but her disarming vulnerability and desperate desire to live coupled with my sad inability to help brought an avalanche of pain crashing down on me. By two o'clock she had me on my knees on the garage floor weeping, despite my efforts to be strong and professional. I had been fairly warned, from Jean and other rehabbers, of the danger that lay down this road. Signs of the anguish awaiting me in wildlife rescue lurked all around those first few years. Anybody could have seen it coming. Still, I had managed to deny it all, believing I would somehow sidestep the land mines. Most painfully, as I held the trembling nestling in my hand, I couldn't accept how a creature so innocent and perfect could die such an agonizing death because of a careless mistake.

"I'm sorry," I whispered as tears dropped from my eyes onto her elegantly arced wings that would never know the magical flight for which they had been so ingeniously crafted. "I wish I could do something."

By three her heart rate had dropped from the hummingbird's usual resting rate of two hundred fifty beats per minute to less than one hundred. When it slowed to around sixty I could no longer tell if the light pulse I felt in my hand was hers or mine. As I sat gently stroking her head with my index finger and watching her miniature white eyelashes blink heavily, I felt as if something inside me was slipping away with her. Finally, her tiny vibration diminished to almost nothing. Ten minutes later, her eyes closed for the last time, and she was gone. And I no longer was, or ever again would be, that unflappable genius who could miraculously save anything that came her way. It was not that I hadn't seen something die before. I grew up on a Midwestern farm where death was everywhere and often, to my unending horror, intentional. But this was the first time I had been entrusted with saving a life and failed completely. All of my self-assurance and bravado shattered to pieces on the hard concrete floor that starless night in the middle of March. And something else crept in and took its place: a gnawing anxiety tugging at the edges of my psyche that I couldn't quite bring to consciousness and that I wouldn't come to grips with until two years later.

Eventually it happens to everyone. Every rehabber suffers an early loss that won't let go. This young Anna's was mine. But losing her didn't make me brick up my heart and run for the exit. Instead, watching her die so unnecessarily hardened my resolve and made me promise, as I watched her tiny spark fade into the darkness, to save hundreds of unlucky victims like her. It was a vow I would make good on that summer, and the next, and the next several years after that. But my smooth-sailing confidence had run aground on nature's rocky shoreline, and the recovery would prove a long one.

I got involved in saving hummingbirds because their delicate beauty and poetic flight spoke to my soul. I had no understanding of the thousand ways they could tear your heart out. Creatures die randomly and uneventfully in nature every day. But uncommon pathos surrounds the passing of hummingbirds. Their deaths hit hard. And you don't have to be a sentimental slob to be floored by them. I have seen jaded filmmakers, hardheaded corporate executives, and calloused construction workers cradling nestlings like fragile glass figurines in their Paul Bunyan hands shed serious tears over these little birds. I've seen everybody cry. I even had a crime scene investigator break down in my garage one night when her rescued fledgling died on arrival. Although she had become accustomed to wading through unspeakable horrors in gritty neighborhoods crouched in the shadows of downtown Los Angeles, watching a young hummingbird fade away with a distressed beat of his tiny wings cracked her professional armor wide open.

"I see people with their heads cut off"— she grimaced through tears as she stared at the unresponsive young male lying on the counter in front of us after my attempts to revive him had failed—"I don't get emotional." Only after fifteen minutes of soft talk and fistfuls of Kleenex was she able to her pull herself together enough to drive home.

That same spring, a heavy-metal guitarist's roadie delivered a nestling to me, one of two that survived after being knocked out of a bottlebrush tree while people were stringing lights around the musician's patio for a party. The guitarist later tearfully confessed he felt responsible for the death of the young bird's sibling.

"You won't tell anybody I cried, will you?" he asked during his second follow-up call. "It would destroy my image." He laughed nervously.

"Everybody cries about hummingbirds," I assured him. "But don't worry. Your secret is safe."

Few are immune to a hummingbird's misfortune, regardless of the form it takes. Callers often come unglued over nests that contain only eggs. Every time I advise someone to let a nest of eggs go because the logistics of saving it from housepainters, termite tenting, tree trimmers, and nursery tree purchases prove too complicated, I get the same response, spoken in the resolute tone of someone refusing to give up on a lifelong dream: *If it were another kind of bird, I might. But these are hummingbirds.*

With all of the distress that unhatched eggs create, it's the loss of the young that really tears people up. In the spring of 2007, during my third year of rehabbing, an ex-Marine came apart in my garage one rainy afternoon as his nestling took its last breath a few minutes after he arrived with her in a Macanudo cigar box. He blamed himself because he'd cut the nest while trimming the rosebushes and then put off bringing me the surviving chick until the next day. After the nestling died, he described, with a distant look in his eyes, how his young son had been killed in a freak accident a few years earlier and how his death had precipitated a bruising divorce that left him feeling hopeless and alone.

"I don't know why I'm telling you all this." He brushed away tears as I handed him a Kleenex from the pile of tissues I construct faux hummingbird nests with.

But I knew why.

"That doesn't seem quite right," my neighbor observed a few days later when I described the events leading up to the meltdown of the emotional Marine he had seen pulling out of our driveway. A retired federal agent who had worked for the government all his life, my neighbor learned early on not to let the misfortunes of others affect him because, as every good bureaucrat knows, sentimentality is the most ordinary sign of weakness. "A grown man crying over a bird." He shook his head derisively as we chatted on the sidewalk outside my house. "There's something really wrong with that," he insisted.

Until it happened to him. My neighbor had agreed to keep his cats locked in the house on release days, but a few weeks later, his cat snagged a young adult I had just freed from the aviary as she was mining nectar from a fuchsia in his backyard.

"Is she going to be all right?" he asked with trepidation as he handed the motionless young female over to me at the front gate just before dusk. After several hours of emergency care in the ICU, I was able to coax the quiet beauty back to life.

"I'm so relieved to hear that, Terry," he said when I called him after her second release a week later. "I don't know why it got to me so much."

But someday I would know why, although it would take me a while to nail it down. The trauma of that cold winter night with the young Anna's stayed with me, like a wound that wouldn't quite heal. Reflecting on that loss, the details of which sharpened to a piercing point with every recall, I felt I had gone as far as I could with a wild animal. But it was not the last time my reach would exceed my grasp with a hummingbird. A larger lesson, more moving and incomprehensible in its meaning and complexity, was thundering my way.

CHAPTER 6

Angel Flying Too Close to the Ground

YOU CAN LEARN A LOT about someone by his reaction to a helpless hummingbird in need of rescue. In fact, you can find out just
about everything you need to know about a person. Most magnani-
mous souls who call hummingbird rescue are willing to exert themselves in some way. Maybe not by going out on a limb like Katie or
confronting a Rottweiler like Stan, but they'll usually make at least
some effort. A few callers, though, refuse to do anything, even
when they created the problem and circumstances require little of
them. They call only to angrily demand that somebody else spring
into action. Some people won't take five minutes to save a life, regardless of the minimal investment it requires. Philosophers refer
to this kind of myopic narcissism as "unenlightened self-interest."
Nothing good can come of it, though many who suffer from this
failing won't discover the truth until it's too late.

Nonetheless, most callers to hummingbird rescue rearrange
schedules, postpone well-laid plans, and go out of their way to get
injured and orphaned birds into rehab. Some people will do anything they can to set things right.

Gabriel was one of these shining stars. In an anxious call one afternoon in early April, the young parking valet breathlessly reported that he'd seen a bird collide with a stretch limousine outside an Italian restaurant in Beverly Hills during a gusting windstorm and had raced through traffic to retrieve the inert bird from the middle of Rodeo Drive.

"I'm not sure he's alive," the young man whispers in a lyrical Spanish accent as he hurries through my front door cradling a white cloth dinner napkin. "I'm Gabriel." He flashes a million-dollar smile and extends a rain-dampened hand.

"Terry." I shake his strong hand firmly. "Thank you for bringing him in."

"Of course." Gabriel glances at me from under his baseball cap with bottomless brown eyes flooded with compassion, curiosity, and all kinds of other attractive things. "I would never leave him out there like that." He shakes his head.

Gabriel, who has taken the Metro bus to deliver his hummingbird, lays the napkin on the table and unfolds it carefully. At first glance, I can't tell if he has brought me a hummingbird or a wet cigar butt. The bird is so caked in Los Angeles road grime, it doesn't look as if it could ever have been a living creature. I reach down and touch the waterlogged tangle of feathers, and the body feels as cold as ice and doesn't flinch. I take a deep breath.

"Is he dead?" Gabriel looks at me in alarm.

I pick the bird up and place him in the palm of my hand, trying to feel a vibration. "I can't tell." I frown, certain he is dead.

But Gabriel, who doesn't miss a thing, breathes heavily and knits his brow as though he is about to cry. "I got him here as soon as I could. And I tried to give him some sugar water like you said," he says in a protest against life's unfairness.

"You did everything you could," I assure him as I gently lay the motionless bird down on the napkin. "And that's what matters. It's tough out there for these guys. Especially in this kind of weather."

"Yes, all of a sudden the wind blew so hard," Gabriel tells me. "I was watching him flying down to another hummingbird sitting in the top of a tree across the street. He kept flying over the other bird four or five times. I don't know why. But he was going really fast and—"

I start to interrupt and explain how his hummingbird was involved in a common courtship ritual, but Gabriel can't wait to finish his story.

"Just as he came down, the wind made a . . . a big . . ." Gabriel waves his hands in the air like a magician.

"Gust?"

"Yes, gust, and he went straight down."

"Did he hit the car?"

"Yes!" Gabriel nods vigorously. "He bounced off the top of the car and fell into the street. So I ran out and got him before the other cars hit him."

"I guess you're lucky, then."

"I know." Gabriel rolls his eyes and shakes his head in disbelief. "I didn't even look before I ran out there. I was so scared for him." As Gabriel is detailing his death-defying rescue, I glance down and think I see the bird's foot twitch slightly.

"Wait a second." I raise a palm toward Gabriel and then cup the icy bird in my hands and blow warm air onto him several times. I discovered the miracle of this technique after retrieving a fading hummingbird from a city shelter on a frosty winter night the year before. The fledgling was so cold when I picked her up that I feared she would die before I could get her home to the ICU, so as soon as I got in my car I cranked up the heater, cradled the frozen bird in my hands, and blew the life back into her. Within minutes she revived and began gulping formula from the syringe I had brought along. I administer this same heat therapy to Gabriel's bird, and just as I am about to give up, a tiny claw rubs almost imperceptibly against my palm, triggering a memory I can't quite recall.

"He's alive." I turn toward the back door.

"Really?" Gabriel's eyes widen with childlike wonder.

"I'll be right back." I race the bird into the garage and place him in a natural nest inside the ICU with several babies who, out of habit, begin bobbing for food even though they ate less than ten minutes ago. Using my rubber-tip dental tool, I wedge his bill open slightly and inject one-tenth of a cubic centimeter of nectar into his mouth. The shock of the food causes him to sway backward involuntarily before collapsing on his side. I right him in the nest and crank up the heat before returning to the house.

"Is he alive?" Gabriel asks excitedly when I come back in.

"So far." I nod.

"Oh, I'm so happy!" he exclaims, clenching his fists in celebration.

"But it will be a while before I know for sure if he's going to make it," I caution. "Injuries like this can take a long time to recover from, and you never know which way they're going to go. They can really drive you crazy." And in that moment I could not have imagined how prescient my words were. "I'm taking care of quite a few birds right now, but I'll do my best."

"I don't mean to . . . to . . ." Gabriel begins. "I mean, I know you are a good person. But if there is someone else who can help him more or who . . ." He trails off uncertainly.

"No, I can do whatever it takes," I assure him.

"Terry, please." Gabriel pulls back apologetically. "Don't misunderstand me. I mean, if you are too busy. If there is somebody else I can take him to, I will do that."

I think of Jean, who, with fifty rescues at her house already, needs another hummingbird right now like she needs a hole in her head. "No, the other rehabber lives south of downtown and it's a long way."

"I don't mind," Gabriel jumps in. "If you are too busy."

When I gaze into Gabriel's soulful brown eyes and realize he really would ride the bus four hours to Jean's house and back for a battered hummingbird that has little chance of surviving, I almost cry. "No, I can save him," I promise Gabriel, as if saying so will make it true.

"Thank you so much, Terry." He smiles with relief. "Here"— Gabriel reaches into his back pocket and takes out his wallet —"I want to give you this." He pulls out eight one-dollar bills, all that he has.

Rescuing any kind of wildlife is a costly enterprise. In the case of these hummingbirds, except for the food and feeders provided by the nonprofit with which Jean and I are affiliated, every dollar comes out of our own pockets, and it can add up to thousands when you take into account equipment and supplies. Still, I'm not about to accept Gabriel's last eight dollars.

"Thank you, but no." I wave him off. "His expenses are taken care of, so he can focus on his recovery."

"Ah, Terry, you are so great." Gabriel shakes my hand effusively. "I know you will save him."

"Hmm." I purse my lips as the image of the young Anna's who drove a knife through my heart two years earlier comes creeping out of its dark night. The memory of her death has altered my frame of mind, informing my interactions with every bird that has come through the door since. And in that sense, my long-lost fledgling will never die.

Ever since that agonizing night on the garage floor, the specter of failure has been hanging over me like the sword of Damocles. Although most injured and orphaned birds that have come into rehab fly out healthy and robust a few months later, a certain number — those with broken wings or concussions, the newly hatched — don't make it. And each hummingbird that dies bruises and toughens me a little more. After two years of easing suffering birds to their final ends, I have not become hardened. But I have not regained my early confidence either. Instead, the heady self-assurance I once paraded around like the belt of an undefeated champion has been replaced by a fearful anxiety, punctuated by moments of sheer terror, at the enormous responsibility I have taken on.

Like all rehabbers, I endure periodic meltdowns that fill me with a withering sense of frustration and hopelessness. Psychologists refer to this phenomenon as compassion fatigue, the mental and emotional trauma caregivers experience as a result of empathizing with the pain and suffering of those who cannot be saved. For doctors and nurses who reach the limits of their empathy, this can lead to flipping the switch and turning off emotions completely. With rehabbers, this feeling of hitting the wall arrives like clockwork at the same time every year, in late June, as broken and young rescues continue flooding into already overcrowded facilities.

"I can't do this anymore," I complained to Frank late one afternoon the summer before as I sank into a kitchen chair after a punishing day spent sweating over six new intakes: two irreparably injured adults, two badly damaged juveniles from a yard-clearing incident involving an electric bush trimmer, and a pair of unpromising, day-old hatchlings with eggshells still stuck to their lumpy bald heads. "Everything coming in is almost or already dead. I'm running a damn morgue."

"What did you expect?" Frank asked philosophically as he slid into a chair beside me. "If only healthy and lucky hummingbirds were flying around out there, they wouldn't need you. Why do you think they call it rescue?"

"It's just so depressing." I sighed as I feverishly stuffed rolls of tightly wound Kleenex into stacks of plastic salsa cups.

"It's always going to be that way," he told me. "'And while the sun and moon endure / Luck's a chance, but trouble's sure. / I'd face it as a wise man would, / And train for ill and not for good.'"

"Who said that?"

"A. E. Housman."

"Well, thank Professor Housman for the reality check." I blinked up at Frank dejectedly. "But tell him I still never thought it would be this hard."

"Nobody does," Jean consoled me later that evening when I recounted our conversation to her over the phone. "If you'd known, would you ever have started?"

At the time, her question seemed rhetorical. But gradually, along with the heightened angst created by helpless hummingbirds, came a larger understanding of the nature of existence. One that demanded accepting the inevitability of death. Not in coldly rational terms, but in a mature, tempered way that involved learning to absorb the anguish, both my own and that of others, that comes with life's hardest of realities. Because if one lesson had sunk in over the past few years, it was that nobody wants to watch a hummingbird die. That's where rehabbers come in. We take the pain for everybody.

The unanticipated sorrow that came with rescuing wildlife drove me to another recognition as well. Staring death in the eye every day gets tough after a while. As in war, there's a cumulative drag on the psyche as the bodies pile up. Especially when you find birds on their backs in the ICU at five in the morning before you're really awake, or ready to face anything. Losing three or four in a day is excruciating. It's impossible to imagine the spiritual drain until you've been through it. So you can't just brush it off and go to bed like nothing unusual happened. Because if they don't kill you in the daylight, they'll creep in and get you in the dark. So you have to find a way to cope. Or get out. But joining wildlife rescue is a little like getting involved with the Mob: once you're in, it's for life. When you're a rehabber, you can't quit and walk away. Too many things depend on you. So you begin searching for something that makes it all possible. Drinking is not a long-term solution. I have to get up before dawn every morning. Drugs are worse. Because if you don't stay focused with birds who require special diets, need to eat every thirty minutes, break like glass, and move quicker than the eye, things can go very wrong, very fast. Western philosophy, which trained me in logical analysis while I was studying for a master's degree during my restless youth, was far too rational for hummingbirds. So I turned my gaze east, to my old standby Lao Tzu, whom I had often consulted during times of hard luck and trouble. One night, I randomly opened the *Tao Te Ching* in response to the stress and pain brought on by too many hurt hummingbirds. Lao Tzu's advice was simple: *Practice nonaction.*

"Easy for you, Lao Tzu," I scoffed. Maybe if you're meditating beside a bubbling brook on some scenic bluff out in the middle of the forest with nothing else to do but contemplate the meaning of life. But what about when you're juggling fifty hummingbirds in rehab with the phone ringing day and night and more casualties rolling in every hour? How about when hundreds of birds walking that thin line between life and death are depending on you every minute of the day for six months straight? And what about when desperate parents with children in tears show up at your door at nine o'clock at night pleading for help? Then what do you do, Lao Tzu? Say, *Sorry, I'd love to help, but I'm practicing nonaction right now*?

Rescuing young hummingbirds from the overheated streets of Los Angeles is about as far from nonaction as you can get. Most wildlife centers won't even let them through the front door. Every rehabber will tell you that immature hummingbirds are the most demanding, high-maintenance, and stress-inducing birds under the sun. Why do you think so few agree to take them on? Concluding that I might not be ready for Lao Tzu's wise counsel yet, I tossed the book on the nightstand and resolved to revisit enlightenment at a later date.

Apart from the suffering I witnessed every day, there was another problem. Because it wasn't just about the birds. As much as I agonized over the misfortune of the hummingbirds I couldn't save, I would be disingenuous if I didn't admit that I spent some of those long nights with dying birds crying for myself. My first year, when I couldn't lose, I was dancing on top of the world. But gradually, with each disheartening loss, I began to feel more and more sorry for myself. *Why would anybody do this with her Friday nights?* I wondered when two handsome film-industry couples from London on their way to a celebratory dinner at Spago dropped off a young adult who had slammed into a Beverly Hills office window and sustained a serious concussion. When I greeted the jaunty, impeccably dressed foursome at the door in my navy blue scrubs and nectar-streaked T-shirt that I had put on at six o'clock that morning, before twelve hot and sticky hours managing hummingbirds, the contrast between their fashionable attire and my grubby uniform, as well as our respective prospects for fun that evening, did little to lighten my mood.

Of course, once again, I had been forewarned. Years ago, when I first expressed interest in rehabbing hummingbirds to Jean and remarked on how thrilling it must be, she turned, looked me dead in the eye, and said, "Oh, trust me, you don't want the thrill of this much misery." Admiring the collection of elegant fledglings buzzing around her cages, I laughed it off at the time. Three years later, standing in the doorway clutching the Tiffany box containing the wobbly hummingbird as I watched the carefree partygoers bounce back into their air-conditioned, jazz-pumped Audi coupe, I wasn't laughing anymore. *Who in her right mind would invite this kind of agony?* I could be out with clever and literate colleagues from UCLA for an end-of-the-quarter Mexican buffet and margarita fiesta at happy hour. Or drinking French champagne and savoring takeout from the best Italian restaurant on the west side with my ironic international friends next door amid easy laughter about nutty neighbors, bumbling politicians, and the insufferably bad movies coming out of Hollywood that summer. After so many protracted nights spent reviving dying hummingbirds over the past few years, I had begun questioning whether the thankless work I did served any real purpose.

"You will save him, Terry." Gabriel nudges me from my reverie, as if sensing my misgivings.

"I hope so." I smile wistfully as my smartphone announces a new voicemail. "Sorry," I apologize to him as I glance at the message marked *Urgent!* "Can you excuse me for a second?"

"Of course." Gabriel nods graciously while he tries to accommodate the three Abyssinian cats that have emerged from the bedroom and begun crawling all over him. Our cats possess that sixth sense that directs them to disappear when certain personalities come into the house. But they greet Gabriel like catnip, climbing into his arms and affectionately licking his tanned face and shiny black hair.

After listening to the anguished message, I press the call-back button and get Mia, who is sobbing as she describes a pair of nestlings who are dying outside her house in Hollywood. "I found the mother dead under the nest this morning, and the babies are almost gone," she says, weeping. "It's killing me because I've been watching them for a month. I even bought a feeder and hung it by the nest so they'd have enough to eat, but she died anyway."

"Can you send me a picture of the nest?"

"Sure," Mia answers with faint hopefulness.

"Okay. Take a picture from a distance using a zoom and no flash and send it to me," I instruct her.

A minute later I get a photo of two bright-eyed, two-week-old Anna's nestlings with their bills up and no signs of distress. When I call Mia back, she is still in tears.

"It's all right, Mia," I console her. "The dead hummingbird you found is not the mother. She's still there."

"I don't think so." Mia sniffles. "I haven't seen her all day."

"Trust me, she's still there. But just so you can rest easy, I want you to sit out of sight and watch the nest until you see her come in and feed the chicks. And as soon as you do, call me back because there's something else we need to talk about."

Mia agrees.

When I get off the phone, Gabriel is still wrestling with the cats. "Thank you so much," he says emphatically before rushing off to catch the bus.

"My pleasure," I tell him as the phone rings and Mia's number pops up again.

"Terry, she came back the second we hung up!"

"She was never gone," I assure her as I wave Gabriel out the door.

"Thank you so much!"

"You're so welcome. Now, Mia, one more thing. Move that sugar feeder you put by the nest as far away as you can. Hummingbirds can fly very far, very fast, so the mother doesn't need a juice bar two steps from her front door, okay?"

"Okay." Mia starts giggling.

"All right. And on a more serious note"—I adjust my tone—"the dead hummingbird you found was killed by the mother because it tried to use the feeder and got too close to the nest. Female hummingbirds defend their babies fiercely, and the feeder is causing unnecessary tension and stress."

"Oh my God," Mia gasps. "That was my fault, then." She begins crying again.

"Hummingbird lessons can be tough, but at least you know now. So move the feeder right away and bury the dead hummingbird somewhere else so we can get things back to normal around that nest, okay?"

"Okay." Mia pulls herself together. "I'm so sorry, Terry."

"No apologies. It's great to know there are people like you out there who care so much."

"No, Terry, it's you who are great." Mia sniffles. "You've been so helpful, and I love you so much. I mean"—she pauses for a second—"I hope that didn't sound too weird."

"No, I'll take love. It's a lot better than some of the other sentiments I get from people."

While caught up in addressing Mia's drama, I had forgotten to get Gabriel's contact information. I bolt out the front door, but he is already gone. I race back to the garage and find his hummingbird leaning on his side in the nest, barely breathing. I load another syringe and touch the top of his head, but he doesn't respond, although the seven nestlings in the ICU pop up on tiptoes and begin swaying and peeping loudly for food. Nestlings in rehab have to be fed every thirty minutes, but they'll eat every ten, five even, if you invite them to. I go down the line and give each gaping mouth a shot of formula before returning to Gabriel's bird.

"Come on," I coax, rubbing the top of his head lightly with my index finger, "open up." But he lays stone-still with his eyelids drooping heavily. I pry his bill open again and give him another dose of formula. This time he pulls back weakly, swallowing slow and hard, the way hummingbirds hanging in that uncertain balance between life and death do. I wait and watch. A few minutes later he wobbles back and forth slowly before righting himself in the nest. Seeing him respond this way is all the encouragement I need. I lift him out of the nest, wrap his still-damp body in a tissue in my hands, and exhale warm air onto him again. After a few minutes of this revitalizing therapy, he opens his eyes, looks up at me weakly, and blinks.

"Welcome back, Gabriel." As I'm tucking him into an especially thick, natural nest in the warm ICU, a vague recollection like déjà vu tugs at the edge of my consciousness. A familiar feeling that I have been through all this before. Then again, I *have* been through it, dozens of times, and maybe that's all there is to it. And before I can grab hold of anything specific, I start mentally tallying feeders that need to be filled and cages that have to be cleaned, and the memory slips away like a dream upon waking.

CHAPTER 7

Hypnotized

SINCE I BEGAN rescuing hummingbirds in Hollywood, in 2005, both the number of birds and the variety of species coming into rehab has been growing. While some 330 species of hummingbirds exist in the Americas, 95 percent reside south of the United States–Mexico border, and only sixteen breed in the United States. Of these, the Allen's, Anna's, black-chinned, broad-tailed, and rufous now nest in the Los Angeles area. Rufous and broad-tailed nestlings have begun showing up in Southern California rehab facilities only recently. Occasionally a calliope (at an endearing three inches from head to tail, the smallest breeding bird in the United States) or a Costa's (a dazzling, violet-adorned desert denizen) finds its way into rehab from the far-reaching eastern outposts of Greater Los Angeles.

Allen's hummingbirds, once nearly nonexistent on the mainland in Southern California, made their way here from the Channel Islands off the coast of Ventura in the early twentieth century and now represent the most common species in Los Angeles. Jean's mentor, Helen Bishop, the godmother of Southern California hummingbird rehabilitation, began rescuing birds in Anaheim in the early 1970s, and she didn't see an Allen's her first ten years. Allen's didn't begin appearing in Jean's records with any regularity until the late 1980s. But once the Allen's population gained a toehold on the mainland, there was no turning back. In 1990, Allen's represented roughly 20 percent of Southland rehab intakes; in 2000, 40 percent. By 2012, Allen's accounted for 60 percent of rescues admitted to Southern California hummingbird-rehabilitation facilities.

The public's growing awareness of the rescue option has resulted in more hummingbirds landing in rehab every year. Over the past two decades, annual intakes of Anna's and black-chinned at rescue facilities have tripled, while the number of Allen's have increased nearly tenfold. Although I suspect some young rescues reported as Allen's may in fact be rufous, there is no way to determine how many are misidentified. At the same time, studies indicate that a certain number of hybrids appear in areas where nesting species overlap. And the occasional preference among female Allen's for the phenomenal speed and glamorous iridescence of the rufous males may be creating a new species as a result of hybridization. Since juvenile Allen's and rufous appear nearly identical in size, shape, color, and wing structure, without sophisticated genetic analysis, it would be almost impossible to determine how many hybrids are coming into rehab. But hummingbird rehabbers unanimously agree that the explosion of rust-hued Allen's showing up in Southern California facilities points to interbreeding.

Whatever the case, nobody is certain why the Allen's numbers are expanding so exponentially. It may have something to do with their ramped-up breeding season, which starts earlier in the year and extends later into the summer than that of other Southern California species. Additionally, whereas females of some species have just one nest per year, Allen's females seem predisposed to nesting two or three times, known as double- and triple-brooding, each breeding season. Every summer, dozens of concerned Angelenos call hummingbird rescue to report an Allen's female starting a new nest immediately after, and sometimes even before, the first clutch has fledged.

Over the past century, the Allen's — smaller and quicker than the second most common Los Angeles species, the Anna's — has migrated from its nesting territory in Southern California to its wintering grounds on the west coast of Mexico. In recent years, however, many have elected to remain in the city year-round, breeding from January through May. Every year as the Southern California air warms in late winter, I hear the unmistakable whirring of the males performing their courtship display just outside the house. Unlike many birds — including species as varied as red-tailed hawks, crows, ducks, doves, robins, finches, and swifts — hummingbirds don't pair-bond; they breed. And their breeding, like everything else they do, is quick and to the point.

Allen's and rufous males have perfected a lightning-fast courtship ritual referred to as the shuttle display. The male buzzes thirty feet into the air and then swoops down toward a perched female, creating a metallic whirring sound with his feathers in the process. The male then swings in front of his potential mate in a series of shallow, ten- to twenty-foot arcs before executing a higher arc that ends with him shaking his rust-colored tail feathers rapidly from side to side at the apex, producing a high-pitched tinkling sound like the ringing of tiny bells. Having witnessed this display on numerous occasions, I can testify to its hypnotic effect on females, even those of the featherless variety.

I've spent years observing the antics of hummingbirds in Hollywood, and the mesmerizing jingle of these bells ringing in the spring has become hauntingly familiar; it fills me with both eager anticipation and a vague sense of dread. Because once nature's bacchanalian celebration of renewal begins, things are bound to go wrong, and some of the misfires invariably end up at my front door.

While male hummingbirds produce sound with their wing feathers to draw female attention, their tail feathers play the most significant role in attracting the opposite sex. Whereas females and young birds sport rounded tail feathers that allow them to fly in the safety of silence, the adult males' tail feathers, with their spiky tips, have been designed to create a musical attraction. After their first-year feather molt, Allen's and rufous males can be distinguished by the color of their backs, which runs toward green on the Allen's and rust on the rufous. And unlike the Allen's, the mature male rufous has notches at the tips of the second pair of tail feathers (counting from the center), which ornithologists use to identify the species.

After observing rufous and Allen's males in the wild for several years, I had an epiphany: since males create music with their tail feathers during courtship, these tiny notches must give the rufous a unique sound designed to appeal particularly to females of their species. I had this breakthrough after years of listening to the Allen's males in Los Angeles ring their tails in courtship and combat. But it wasn't until I spent a summer in Portland, Oregon, that I noticed the rufous males at my feeders seemed to produce a buzzier zing while courting than the Allen's, whose tail feathers whistle like the wind rushing over stabilizer fins on a falling bomb. Research indicates that the shape of the male's tail feathers determines the pitch produced in courtship displays. Since the tail feathers of the Allen's and rufous males appear nearly identical, the notch likely plays a key role in differentiating the sound each creates.

This musical distinction also explains why, in places where the breeding territories of these species overlap, like Southern California, rufous females may be unimpressed with the overtures of Allen's males, who serenade at a different pitch. That this barely visible notch on the rufous male's tail feathers could, over millions of years of evolution, play a pivotal role in delineating one species from another attests to the powerful influence the most subtle distinctions in nature can exert on the physical world.

During courtship, male hummingbirds of every species use their dazzling iridescence to increase their attractiveness. When a male dances in front of a prospective mate, he flares his gorget, or throat feathers, which reflect various colors like a disco-ball strobe depending on the angle at which the sunlight hits them. In the rufous and Allen's, the male's sequined gorget can shift from gold and copper to orange and a brilliant scarlet. A male will sometimes spend days courting the same female in his territory, with varying degrees of success. As is the case with humans, the female's reactions to the male's sexual advances range from annoyed indifference to hypnotic fascination.

The Allen's high-voltage, in-your-face courtship display is nearly indistinguishable from the war dance males execute when seeking to intimidate rivals in their territory. It's an impressive commotion that, from a distance, looks like a miniature green-and-orange pendulum swinging wildly in midair. Although callers consistently describe the hummingbirds they rescue as cute and sweet, people who have observed hummingbird shootouts around sugar feeders recognize their mean streak. When two hummingbirds are grounded and one flies off, callers often speculate that the mate or partner was trying to help the bird that couldn't get up. When I explain to the callers that they witnessed two males engaged in mortal combat, and the one that fled the scene of the crime was the victorious assailant, people gasp in horror that hummingbirds can be so barbaric.

Hummingbirds fight over the same three things — food, sex, and territory — as all competitors in the wild. Watching them tussling at sugar feeders, you might think that hummingbirds inhabit a pure Hobbesian state of nature. But like Lemurian crystals, these intrepid birds are multifaceted creations with complex dimensions that imbue each with a unique, dynamic energy. In rehab, no two hummingbirds are alike. Among aviary rehabs and new releases, I have witnessed as much acceptance as contention. That said, when males are breeding and competing for territory in the wild, it's a war of all against all. And these winged warriors are hardwired to fight to the death.

As with human beings in Southern California, the greatest threat to a hummingbird's survival is not other animals but members of its own species. No small number of adult males land in rehab after losing battles to faster, more experienced, or more aggressive challengers. A shocked caller recently reported seeing a male broad-tailed antagonist driving his rival to the ground and violently whacking him over the head, killing his victim before the woman could get outside to chase him off. Sparring males wield their rapier bills with samurai precision, using them like sabers to spear the skulls and impale the hearts of adversaries in combat. Despite hummingbirds' violent impulses, most people continue to regard them as adorable, proving that if something is small and pretty enough, it can get away with murder.

Some species, like the Allen's and rufous, can be especially belligerent. During the spring breeding season in Los Angeles, Allen's males are regularly found locked together on the ground in a deadly embrace that often has fatal consequences for one, if not both, opponents. Allen's males sometimes employ these same violent tactics when pursuing females. Watching their raucous performance from afar, you might find it difficult to tell if Allen's are engaged in courtship, combat, or some combination of the two.

Anna's males have a somewhat grander and more spectacular approach to the courtship game. From my patio, I see the male spiral high in the sky over a female preening her feathers at the top of the thirty-foot ficus tree overhanging the driveway. When the male reaches the apex of his ascent at one hundred feet, he dives fifty miles per hour in a U-shaped arc. The moment he reaches the bottom of his descent, directly over the female's head, he spreads his tail for one-twentieth of a second and emits a high-pitched *schoop* as the downdraft causes the inside edges of his tail feathers to vibrate like a guitar string. Wind on the downdraft amplifies sound, so the faster the dive, the more resonant the tone, helping the female make her decision. At the same time, the male, who has positioned himself to maximize reflection from the sun, flares his magenta gorget in a blinding iridescent flash. After a dozen repeat performances, this explosion of color, along with the rush of whirring wings and the seductive thrill of his one-note "song," has a hypnotic effect that drives the female into a breeding frenzy.

Chris Clark has documented this stunning juxtaposition of sound, color, and velocity using cameras with shutter speeds of five hundred frames per second. A zoology professor who has spent the past several years researching the mechanics of hummingbird flight, Clark has filmed male Anna's on courtship dives traveling at an unfathomable 385 body lengths per second. (This is the equivalent of a six-foot human dropping nearly eight hundred yards per second.) Although diving peregrine falcons can reach a higher speed in miles per hour, when measured in body lengths per second, hummingbirds travel almost twice as fast, making them the fastest things on wings.

When a female is sufficiently impressed with her suitor's sky-diving prowess, she levitates a few feet off her branch, and the two lock together and spiral to the ground in an aerial ballet. Though both appear dazed and exhausted after their brief encounter, no time is wasted on the tender touches of romance. Each has to get on with the business at hand: he to locating other willing females and she to finishing the demanding task of nest-building she began before her quick impregnation.

This whirlwind breeding ritual goes on across neighborhoods throughout Los Angeles from midwinter to early summer, turning backyards into extended speed-dating venues, with males tirelessly pursuing every female in sight and ambushing unsuspecting targets at the sugar feeders. During the early-spring months, female Allen's can expect to be sexually harassed and assaulted whenever they drop in for a drink at the local sugar feeder. Not all females prove willing participants in the courtship game, however. Occasionally, a nesting mother will turn her feminine fury on an intrusive young male and reverse the chase, angrily banishing him into the wild blue.

Given the speed and determination with which they pursue their chosen targets during breeding rituals, ardent male Anna's like Gabriel can easily be injured while engaging in dive displays. Just as large birds and aircraft can fall victim to wind shear, an amorous hummingbird redlining a high-speed dive to impress a female can be driven to the ground by a sudden downdraft. Because of the risk of injury, hummingbirds normally refrain from engaging in courtship displays during stormy weather. So in the case of

Gabriel's death-defying overture, I can only conclude that his Beverly Hills romantic interest must have been one irresistible female.

Gabriel came into rehab just after I started the Los Angeles Hummingbird Rescue website, setting the wheels in motion for what would for me become a transformative summer saving hummingbirds. A few months after I posted the rescue hotline, what had started as a hobby ballooned into a fifteen-hours-a-day, seven-days-a-week way of life. I had spent the past spring and summer feeding and cleaning up after hummingbirds from dawn to an increasingly late bedtime. Three months of hummingbird rehab lengthened to six, and the previous season's average of four calls a day mushroomed into twenty. By 2007, after fielding five hundred calls and rehabilitating more than one hundred hummingbirds, I had been drawn into so many implausible rescue scenarios that it took a lot to surprise me.

In the year before Gabriel's arrival, some of my more challenging rescues included a pair of breeding hummingbirds stuck together in an elementary-school soccer goal during a game; a fledgling trapped and floating around with tourists inside a skydiving wind tunnel at Universal CityWalk; three grounded hummingbirds that had crashed together into the Walt Disney Concert Hall downtown (because of its undulating, mirrorlike panels); a nest with a pair of day-old hatchlings inadvertently transported to a Pasadena Rose Parade float in a Japanese maple bought from a San Diego nursery; a young adult darting in and out of an indoor film set at Paramount Pictures; and a three-day-old nestling the size of a bumblebee retrieved at the La Brea Tar Pits by an English bulldog with formidable jaws.

The four-year-old female bulldog had been brought to an adoption event at the La Brea Tar Pits on Wilshire Boulevard, seven miles west of downtown, where flawless skeletons of mastodons,

camels, jaguars, saber-toothed cats, and dire wolves had been recovered after the animals got stuck in asphalt pools in Ice Age Los
Angeles ten thousand to forty thousand years ago, during the Late
Pleistocene period. The bulldog located the hatchling in some tall
grass under a coral tree, wrapped it up in her mammoth tongue,
and deposited the miniature pink dinosaur at the feet of adoption volunteers in the middle of their picnic lunch. The naked and
barely inch-long female Allen's, which a rescue volunteer brought
me in a sheared-off Starbucks coffee cup, arrived unscathed, made
it through rehab, and was released into early twenty-first-century
Los Angeles three months later. The bulldog, volunteers proudly
informed me, was adopted immediately after surrendering her
near-microscopic discovery to the authorities.

Near the end of that same summer, an older gentleman called
about an adult female hummingbird that had been hit while in
flight by a golf ball on a fairway in Bel Air.

"I got two of those in the same year," Jean marveled when I
called to report the golf-course collision. "You could spend a lifetime trying to hit a hummingbird with a golf ball and never accomplish it."

"They're such fast-moving targets," I agreed. "It seems like
you'd have a better chance of winning the Mega Millions."

Hummingbirds were so quick, we speculated, that they rarely
encountered anything traveling faster than themselves, so they
might be interested in and caught off guard by golf balls hurtling
by at a hundred miles an hour. In any case, Jean and I are always
convinced we've heard it all. Until the next unbelievable call.

In early April of 2008, the annual dancing, chasing, hooking,
and sparring commotion that accompanies hummingbird breeding
had reached its frenzied climax just as a spring storm was churning
its way through the city. So I was not surprised when Gabriel called

from Beverly Hills to report a hummingbird thrown off course by an unpredictable wind. With the explosion of spring's restless energy, Gabriel's was one among several anxious calls I received that day reporting nests blown out of trees and adult birds injured. But Gabriel did not deliver just another hummingbird in need of rescue. Gabriel presented a mystery that would upend everything I thought I knew about hummingbirds. A tiny force that brought sharply into focus the limits of reason, underscored the subtle and complex rhythms of the natural world, and affirmed the enigmatic forces governing life itself.

CHAPTER 8

Going Out of My Head

A FEW HOURS after Gabriel's ill-fated romance with the enticing female led to his encounter with a stretch limo in Beverly Hills, I come out to find the defeated suitor sprawled flat and listless on his nest with his wings splayed. When I lift his salsa cup from the warm ICU, Gabriel doesn't flinch. I gently fold his wings back against his body and rub his head lightly, prompting him to open his bill just enough for me to slide the angiocath into his mouth and inject some formula. Gabriel swallows slowly, though with less effort than when he first arrived, and then lists onto his side and lapses into unconsciousness. I try to wipe the oily dirt off his head and back with a Q-Tip soaked in warm water, but he is so encrusted it will have to wait until a later time, if there is such a thing for him. Although I have seen a few birds that looked worse than Gabriel beat the odds and make it back, his beleaguered condition does not inspire optimism. Watching him drift away, I do what I always do whenever I get a bird as debilitated as he is: pray for a miracle and prepare for the opposite.

As I'm returning Gabriel to the warm ICU, I hear my phone ringing dimly somewhere in the garage. Before I can extricate the phone from a mound of plastic syringes and paper towels, a voice-mail pops up marked *Urgent!* I hear an extended, rambling plea that makes no sense, and I hit the call-back button halfway into the message that threatens never to end. Some callers are so neurotic and stressed out that I can't fathom how they get through a day in a city like Los Angeles, where life is spinning out of control at a maddening pace. A few have already gone off the rails by the time they call, and they blather on so unremittingly that I can't get a word in edgewise. Sometimes I just sit and listen to their free association in speechless silence.

In this case, when a panicked voice answers halfway through the first ring, I identify myself and ask how I can help.

"Yeah, I have this bird and I don't know what the best course of action is because he—I mean, I think it's a he, I don't know how you can tell—but I have this injured hummingbird, I mean, I don't know if he's injured or sick or just young or what, but anyway I found him on the sidewalk by my neighbor's house while I was walking my dog, and he was lying on his side so I picked him up and, I mean, I know you're not supposed to touch them or anything because you leave your DNA on them—"

"It's okay to touch them," I correct him, trying to imagine how hummingbirds might go about detecting human DNA on their feathers. Maybe they check themselves into the crime lab for analysis and put a team of investigators on the case.

"I mean, I know if it's a young bird you shouldn't touch him because then his mother will reject him—"

"That's an urban myth."

"Well, I know, I mean, I read you're not supposed to keep them because they're federally protected but then it doesn't seem like the government cares about them anyway because it makes all these laws and then does hardly anything to help them —"

I have to give him that one.

"So that's why I called you, and, anyway, I picked him up and brought him home, well, first I put him in the grass by the sidewalk but then he just laid there and when I came back, I couldn't leave him on the ground because it's raining and a cat might get him and I don't like to see anything suffer, not even people, even though they're not my favorite species, so I put him in a box on the porch but then I wasn't sure what to do because he didn't look too good so I brought him in the house and put him on a towel but he's just sitting there all wet so —"

"Can I —"

"So then I read on your website I should give him some sugar water so I made some but I'm not sure I have the right kind of sugar, I mean, is organic all right? Because that's all I have and I didn't want to wait too long because I know they need to eat every thirty minutes. Actually, I didn't know that before I looked it up but that's what I read on your website, well, not just on your website but on several of them, which is why I tried to feed him with a syringe so —"

"Could I —"

"So I tried to give him some sugar water but he wouldn't eat any, he just sat there shaking his head and —"

"Shaking his head?"

"Yeah, I mean, not like he was saying no to the sugar water but like back and forth a couple of times, not constantly, but every time I pass my finger in front of him to test his vision he tries to follow it, and then his head goes back and forth really fast like he's watching a Ping-Pong game."

"That's a head injury. It's serious."

"Well, that's what I thought but I'm not an expert and I don't know anything about hummingbird neurology so I can't say for sure what's wrong with him but he looks really messed up and I'm going crazy, I mean, I don't know what to do with him because even though he doesn't look that good I want to save him but I have no idea how so—"

"You have a couple of choices," I jump in assertively, to no avail.

"My neighbor told me I should take him to the shelter but that's why I called you because I hate going to the hospital myself and really freak out when I have to go to the emergency room so I can only imagine how he would feel, but anyway I know going to the hospital is terrifying even when you have comprehensive health insurance and he'd probably be really scared."

"He's already scared, but I don't think he would know he's going to the hospital."

"Well, I hope not, because I had to be rushed to the ER once and it was the most horrific experience ever and I still have nightmares about being trapped in an ambulance, but I won't kill you with the details."

"I'm already carrying my own full load of nightmares, so I appreciate that."

"So maybe I should take him somewhere, or maybe I should wait awhile because I can take care of him twenty-four/seven and I don't want to stress him out more than he already is so I think I'll just keep him until he stabilizes and maybe he'll be okay."

"It's unlikely he'll recover from a head injury that quickly, but if you don't want to drive him somewhere right now"—*Given that it's rush hour,* I say to myself, *and even if you manage to get on the freeway at six p.m. in Los Angeles, you're not going anywhere for a long time*—"you can keep him a few hours and then bring him to me in West Hollywood."

"Yeah, because it's rush hour right now and I'm in Santa Monica and there's a Sig Alert on the Ten East so I don't want to sit in traffic for three hours if he's not going to make it anyway, because there's no point, is there?"

"Maybe not."

"But then I thought maybe there is some magic potion that might cure him, you know?"

"Maybe."

"I mean, maybe he just needs some time or food, even though he doesn't want to eat anything, but maybe a professional could help him more than I can."

"You can bring him to me anytime."

"Because I'm a Kevorkian so I don't believe in letting him suffer needlessly if he's in pain and terminal anyway, but if he has a chance and the shelter kills him then I'm responsible for wrongful death just like well-intentioned rescuers aren't protected under the Good Samaritan law."

"Well, I think—"

"Because I don't know if anybody can save him. I mean, I don't think the prognosis is good but then I'm not an expert and I don't know what I'm doing at all, so I'm pretty hopeless."

At last we arrive at the truth. Despite this frank admission, the tangential young man decides to call me back in a few hours. I hang up and wonder what just happened. In any business or institution that deals with the public, callers run the spectrum and you have to be prepared for anything. And so it goes with hummingbird rescue in Southern California, where people from a dizzying array of social classes, ethnic backgrounds, professions, educational levels, criminal histories, states of mental health, and degrees of sobriety call at all hours of the day and night in search of help and understanding.

The summer before, three rail-thin, black-leather-clad Goths who reeked of whiskey, weed, tobacco, and some unidentifiable pharmaceuticals brought me a fledgling in a breath-mint box. Even though their bloodshot eyes looked more like a hard Sunday-morning sunrise than an early Saturday night, they somehow, through their chemically induced haze, recognized the value of the tiny life they had stumbled upon on a crowded sidewalk in West Hollywood. The instant they found the grounded fledgling that dozens of others had indifferently passed by, they took time off from their busy club-hopping schedule to look me up on their smartphones, stroll down to my house from Sunset Boulevard, and deliver the patient, after which they quietly returned to the mad party carrying on just a few blocks away. I gained a lot of respect for the Goths that night. Despite the abuse these three emaciated rebels were subjecting their own bodies to, they wouldn't dream of standing idly by while a helpless hummingbird starved his way to an early death.

The poker-faced Goths, who looked hard as nails when they first appeared at my door, turned out to be unusually sensitive and thoughtful. But other, more questionable residents I've dealt with through hummingbird rescue have given me pause. I've taken in birds from drug dealers, gangbangers, the morally bankrupt, the criminally insane, and other degenerates lingering on the periphery that nobody has bothered to report. But the atrocities damaged humans commit against one another do not translate into ill intentions toward the orphaned and injured hummingbirds these lost souls rush to my door. In fact, it's quite the reverse. Hummingbirds provide an avenue for some of the walking wounded to express the empathy they are unable to extend to members of their own species, who are collectively implicated in the anger and pain these hardened cases carry around with them in an unforgiving city. In short, hummingbirds, perhaps more than anything else in their tortured lives, give them something easy to love.

Still, some of the conversations I have over the phone make me wonder. The odd tone of voice, the off-color remarks, the dark secrecy some finders have about where they are. You never know who is going to show up at your front door with a box in his hand. One recent exchange I had about a fledgling pulled out of a storm drain just after sunset went something like this:

"Where are you?"

"Whadaya mean?" a gravelly voice comes back.

"I mean, what part of the city are you in?"

"Does dat matter?"

"Well, only insofar as I can give you the location of the nearest rehab facility."

"Well, why don'tcha tell me where you are."

A little uneasy, because I fear that I am about to invite a Mob boss to my house after dark, I tell him I'm in West Hollywood. "Near the Beverly Center."

"I can do dat."

"But, well, how far away are you? Because it's nine thirty already and I have to get up at five, so if you're more than a half an hour —"

"Everything in LA is twenty minutes, depending on traffic," he interjects. "I'm in Pasadena. I'll be der by ten. Okay?"

"Well, actually there's a humane society in Pasadena you can take him to tomorrow if —"

"I'll be der by ten," he repeats adamantly.

"But if you're in Pasadena there's no way that . . . Hello?" I say as the line goes dead.

At 9:59, a six-foot-two, two-hundred-pound, rock-solid, heavily tattooed mixed-martial artist shows up at my front door cradling a perfect Anna's fledgling tucked into a sparkplug box.

The bright-eyed young male pops up like a jack-in-the-box and cries for food when I open the top. "He looks great," I say with a shrug.

"Good, 'cause my girlfriend was freakin' out he was gonna die," he grumbles.

"I can't believe you made it here so quickly," I marvel, peering after him as he lumbers off my porch toward the street.

"Carpool lane." He flashes me a crooked smile before throwing a leg over his Kawasaki Ninja, dropping the visor on his helmet, and roaring into the dark city.

I close the door and glance down at the fledgling staring up at me silently with huge eyes and his mouth gaping like the figure in Munch's *The Scream*.

"I don't blame you for being scared. You may be fast some-day"—I shook my head—"but you're never gonna move like that again."

Over the past decade, I've talked to twenty thousand random callers from all over Los Angeles on my precarious journey down the byzantine path of hummingbird rescue. How could I not have encountered a little bit of everything? But one thing all callers—the good, the bad, and the scary—have in common is a desire to restore light and equilibrium to the artificial Los Angeles landscape that we share with our flying urban jewels. And by saving nature's treasures, with each rescue, compassionate finders return this rough-edged metropolis to the City of Angels, whose tiny winged envoys offer the opportunity to celebrate the best of our humanity by participating in their preservation into the distant future.

CHAPTER 9

We're in This Thing Together

THEY THRIVE because of, and in spite of, us. Over the past fifty years, Americans have increasingly flocked to urban centers, and hummingbirds have followed closely behind, taking advantage of our lush backyards planted especially for them and mesmerizing us with their captivating beauty and grace. But as I quickly learned on my early tree-trimming expeditions, for them, living alongside us is a mixed bag. Sharing space with people is never easy, even for creatures as universally loved and admired as hummingbirds. Human carelessness, indifference, and sometimes blatant disregard for their winged companions in the natural world are the reasons rescue has become such a big business in the Greater Los Angeles area, where thousands of hummingbirds struggle to coexist with eighteen million people concentrated in the most densely populated metropolitan sprawl in the country.

Southern California ranks as the hummingbird-rehabilitation capital of the United States, if not the world. State-sponsored and private nonprofit wildlife organizations admit more than one thousand hummingbirds into Southland rescue facilities every year.

Southern California's impressive rehab volume prompts wildlife centers from all over the country to call Los Angeles Hummingbird Rescue for advice. Rehabbers from facilities in New York, Michigan, Missouri, Texas, Florida, and Washington have contacted me about the nuts and bolts of hummingbird rehabilitation. During our extended conversations, I can't resist asking staff members how many intakes they had the year before. Most report between five and fifteen. When I visited the Audubon Society in Portland, Oregon, a few years ago, a volunteer proudly described taking in a dozen hummingbirds.

"I mean in a year," I said to clarify my question.

"That's a year," she confirmed.

"That's a day in June," Jean said with a laugh when I called to report the diminutive statistic.

"A slow day in June," I added.

If we include all of Southern California's rehab facilities, we've had spring days in which over thirty young hummingbirds were rushed through rehabbers' frenzied doors. And we keep that many more alive out there every day during the nesting season by coaching callers through "soft" intervention strategies that require long experience and quick thinking. Telephone-assisted rescues, which run the gamut of possibilities, include telling callers how to liberate trapped birds from houses, offices, schools, and garages; retrieve and feed window-strikes; head off human interference; repair nests damaged by weather and human disturbance; construct faux nests for fledglings grounded in precarious circumstances; and dust mite-infested nests.

The proliferation of cell phones has made it faster and easier to answer questions that defaulted to sheer conjecture several years ago. When I first started doing rehab, I had to rely on the caller's description, often imprecise and distorted by personal perceptions and anxieties, to determine a bird's age and condition. Now I ask callers to send me photos of the birds so I can assess their age, gender, metabolic condition, and general health before taking action. After rehabilitating hundreds of hummingbirds, I have learned to read their posture, demeanor, and the look in their eyes, even from a photograph. Observing them closely every day, I've come to know them inside and out and can interpret the subtle messages they send intentionally or inadvertently through their body language. Every detail offers clues about their present situation and physical condition, enabling me to address problems with swiftness and accuracy.

When a caller attending a Make-A-Wish Foundation picnic in Griffith Park finds a black-chinned nestling grounded on a public walkway, he looks up Los Angeles Hummingbird Rescue on his iPhone and calls me within minutes.

"Twenty kids are circling, insisting we rescue him," the caller warns. "What should I do?"

"Send me a photo of the bird," I tell him, "close up, from his right side."

"His right?"

"Right."

When I get the photo a minute later, I notice the nestling's crop is bulging. The image is so crisp and sharply detailed I can see the dark outline of fruit flies inside the bird's crop. I call the young man back immediately. "His mother is still feeding him. So shear off a paper cup about two inches from the bottom and line it with Kleenex. Have the kids help build the nest so they are invested in the outcome. Then secure the cup to a tree branch nearby, in the shade and out of the kids' reach, and watch from a distance to make sure the mother locates the new nest. If you see her feed the chick once, you're good to go."

"Got it," he answers confidently.

But while cameras can be a positive force in rescue, they create their share of trouble as well. In this digital age when no experience is meaningful unless it is photographed, uploaded, and shared on social media sites, hummingbirds, being spectacularly photogenic, suffer the dual consequences of their exotic beauty and people's need for validation. Each year dozens of calls to rescue are the result of amateur photographers using flashes to capture images of active nests. Older nestlings get spooked and plunge to the ground when a camera flashes close by. The reason for their terrified reaction, I have speculated, may be that adult male hummingbirds flare their iridescent throat feathers and angle them toward the sun to maximize light reflection when confronting adversaries during battle. Conceivably, then, brooding females and feathered nestlings instinctively interpret a sudden flash of light as a hostile male approaching with deadly intentions. Whatever the case, aside from the potential for sustaining fatal injuries from the fall, a nestling has a seriously reduced chance of survival once he is grounded, even with the mother still present. After the damage is done, the careless photographers often become frightened and embarrassed, and they appoint others to do damage control.

A young hummingbird lover named Skye calls on behalf of a neighbor who is insisting she rescue a baby he scared out of the nest with a flash the day before and that he is convinced has since been abandoned. Both the perpetrator and his wife have called Skye several times from work and urged her to get the chick into rehab immediately.

"They're driving me crazy, calling every twenty minutes," Skye reports with exasperation.

"Were there two babies in the nest before he scared them out?"

"Yeah, there were two."

"So what happened to the other one?"

"She flew up into the tree. But this one is smaller and can't fly."

"He's a little younger. They hatch a few days apart, so he's not quite ready yet."

"No, not at all. He fell to the ground, so I put him back in the nest, but nobody has seen the mother since yesterday. My neighbors are afraid he's going to die. I don't know what to do."

"Take a photo of the nestling from a distance using a zoom lens and no flash," I instruct her, "and send it to me."

Two minutes later Skye sends a photo of the young male Allen's resting comfortably in his nest, bright-eyed and abundantly fed.

"The husband says he knows from being a Boy Scout that if anybody touches the baby, the mother will abandon it," Skye volunteers when I call her back.

"That's a myth," I inform her. "Hummingbirds don't abandon their babies just because somebody has touched them. So his Boy Scout education was a little thin. Maybe they should have taught him not to get too close to nesting birds with a camera flash," I suggest.

"Exactly," Skye laughingly agrees. "What a waste, all those long summers of Boy Scout training."

"So next time he calls, ask him to renew his Smokey Bear pledge to use caution and common sense before lighting a fire. Or taking a flash photo."

"I will," Skye answers gleefully.

But not all camera calls are so lighthearted. Another caller who got too close to a nest with a flash threw the alarmed mother into such a panic she darted off, slammed into a picture window, dropped to the ground, and died instantly from a broken neck, leaving a pair of week-old Allen's babies in the nest.

"I feel like such an idiot." Jasper weeps over the phone as he describes the tragedy. "I'm seventy years old and I should have known better. I've been watching her at my feeder every day for two years. She was so perfect, so beautiful. And she trusted me. She let me get close. And I killed her. And I don't know what to . . . how to . . . oh God," he sobs.

Desperate calls like this arrive without warning, at any time of the day or night. And I empathize with each hapless casualty, avian and human, as I struggle to keep my own emotions in check while everyone else comes unglued. Callers like Jasper are so devastated by a hummingbird's death that I have extended postmortem debriefing sessions with them over the phone. I spend hours every year comforting guilt-ridden callers as they cry over birds that have been accidentally maimed or killed. Because, as a veteran of the rescue wars, I've put in my time. So when it comes to finding someone who gets how it feels to cry like a baby over a dead or dying hummingbird, callers have come to the right place.

"Cut the nest and bring the chicks to me. Everybody screws up sometimes," I console Jasper, "so stop beating up on yourself. Bring me the babies and I'll get them back out there, healthy and strong. And life goes on."

Agonizing scenarios like Jasper's unfold every day during the nesting season. With telephone rescues, rehabbers function as dei ex machina, gods that magically appear from the machine to resolve hummingbird entanglements and advance otherwise tragic stories toward happy endings. Most window-strikes, birds trapped in houses and garages, babies falling from nests, and victims retrieved from spider webs can be saved with advice given over the phone. And though the conversations often prove long, emotional, and exhausting, the extended hours spent coaching callers through this deluge of emergencies during the breeding season save hundreds of hummingbirds annually.

The paradox of running a hummingbird rescue is that our primary goal is to keep jeopardized birds in their natural environment and out of rehab. Orphaned, injured, and otherwise compromised birds that can't be preserved in the wild are brought to us as a last resort. Despite efforts to keep them in nature, half the birds we get calls about end up in our care. Jean and I together admit four hundred hummingbirds to our facilities every nesting season and send another three hundred to other rescue centers in Southern California. And each year, more keep coming.

Stepped-up planting of nectar-producing vegetation and the growing use of sugar feeders have led to population explosions in crowded cities like Los Angeles, where hummingbirds have become year-round residents and the most treasured backyard visitors. Some Angelenos go to extreme lengths to attract hummingbirds to their properties by maintaining staggering numbers of plants and sugar feeders for the guests who never leave. A recent caller informed me that she and her husband cultivated one thousand potted plants aimed specifically at attracting hummingbirds to their property in Orange County.

"How many plants?" I ask, thinking I misunderstood.

"A thousand," she repeats.

"A thousand potted plants?" I exclaim in disbelief.

"Yes!" She giggles.

"Just for hummingbirds?"

"Yes. It's insane, isn't it?"

"Well, it's no crazier than what I do. But how do you take care of them all?"

"It's all we do." She laughs, with a clear recognition of her mad obsession.

Still, I don't quite believe her about the thousand plants. Until she e-mails a photo that shows an undulating sea of epiphyllum and clivia suspended from trellises and stacked on tiered planks across a patio extending into what seemed like eternity.

Other committed enthusiasts hang corridors of sugar feeders, filling them year-round to accommodate the burgeoning number of fast-flying beauties visiting their balconies and backyards. A repeat caller named Paul phones me every summer from the hills above Burbank to report the dizzying number of hummingbirds dining in his yard. Based on the volume of the twenty feeders he hangs out every morning and the metabolic requirements of hummingbirds in the wild, Paul is feeding between three and four hundred hummingbirds a day most months of the year.

"I have to fill them all every day," he laments. "I can't leave LA. I can't go anywhere. I would feel too guilty."

"I know the feeling," I say sympathetically every time he calls. As much as anyone, I understand how people surrender their souls to hummingbirds.

Angelenos' devotion to monitoring what many perceive to be their divinely assigned nests weaves hummingbird and human life together into the fabric of urban existence. Besides having to cope with intrusive backyard photographers, nesting hummingbirds get caught up in international social media pressure. Callers who put webcams on nests report receiving hundreds of texts and chat comments from viewers alarmed about inclement weather, the distressing appearance of the babies, the disturbing angle of a nest, or a mother's deficient parenting skills.

In the heat of the summer baby season, a hummingbird enthusiast who has a live webcam running on a nest with a pair of two-day-old hatchlings calls me in a panic after receiving dozens of chat comments criticizing the mother for not feeding her babies often enough.

"What should I do?" Pam asks pleadingly. "Everybody on the

chat is freaking out because the mother isn't feeding the babies. People are writing every two minutes urging me to rescue them."

"There are way too many helicopter moms hovering around this nest," I caution her. "Hatchlings have a yolk sac and don't need to eat every thirty minutes until they get a few days older. The mother knows what she's doing. You just need to let her do her job."

"But the babies are opening their bills and begging for food every time she comes back to the nest and she just sits down and ignores them. Can't we do something to help?"

"I know what we can do," I say. "Let's take a vote on YouTube and have people give the mother's parenting competence a thumbs-up or thumbs-down. If her disapproval ratings are high enough we can call the state and ask social services to intervene. Then they can come out and arrest the mother, confiscate the chicks, and put them up for adoption so they can be placed in a more stable home environment where the parent isn't such a slacker."

After a moment of silence, Pam bursts out laughing so hard she cries. "Thank you, Terry. You've just made me realize how ridiculous we're being with all of our anthropomorphic second-guessing."

Two weeks later Pam calls me about the same nest, which is now tilting precariously to one side after an explosive windstorm. By the time she calls, the nest is seriously compromised, with the older chick clinging desperately to the outer edge.

"The nest is falling and one of the babies is almost upside down. They're getting thousands of views and everybody is going crazy. What should I do?"

"I'm in the supermarket right now," I tell her as I load my basket with white sugar and Q-Tips. "Can I call you back?"

"No, Terry, can't you tell me now?"

"I'll just be ten minutes."

"Please, Terry, this is an emergency. The oldest baby could fall any second," Pam persists. "Can you just give me some quick advice for now?"

But there's no such thing as a quick conversation about a nest repair. "Okay," I relent, sitting down at the blood pressure machine by the pharmacy before launching into a long discussion on how to mend a broken nest. "You'll need some pipe cleaners."

After a twenty-minute tutorial, I dispatch Pam and check my watch. During hummingbird season, I take the summer off from teaching at UCLA and turn my life over to the birds. Once orphaned nestlings start arriving, I can't go anywhere for very long. Frank and I have no summer holiday because hummingbird babies flood in over the Fourth of July weekend. There is no such thing as a day off or a vacation. Leaving town is out of the question. I can't leave home for more than thirty minutes during daylight hours. I can't even go out for lunch. My friends collectively write me off for four months. I eat my meals, if you can call them that, while standing in the kitchen talking on the phone. Or, more frequently, on the run between the house and the garage. If I need to go to the doctor or dentist, I put it off until September. I can't even get a haircut. Never mind that by the end of the summer my unruly auburn curls make me look positively Paleolithic. The birds in the ICU need to eat every half hour, and I've been gone too long already.

I grab a small bunch of rotten bananas from a discard box tucked under the display and hurry to the checkout counter. Fruit flies love decaying bananas, the stinkier the better. When summer temperatures head into the eighties, a few decomposing bananas in a Tupperware container can incubate and produce hundreds of fruit flies daily for growing birds in the aviary. This abundance of arthropods gives the young adults ongoing opportunities to hone their bug-snatching skills. Though it might seem that catching fruit flies comes naturally to hummingbirds, young birds' first attempts prove uncertain and off the mark as fruit flies have developed erratic flight patterns to evade capture.

I know from my own experience that although fruit flies appear slow when buzzing around a glass of wine in the summer, they are nearly impossible to catch with your hands. A young man from the city of Diamond Bar found a fledgling on a Wednesday, and since he could not bring her to me until the weekend, he wanted to know how to supplement the bird's diet in the meantime. I explained to him that if he put rotten bananas on a plate outside, fruit flies would appear in a day or two. But when I warned him about the difficulty of capturing the wily insects, he boasted that he had been training as a boxer since he was a teenager and insisted he could catch enough for the young bird to thrive on until he got her to rehab.

"I came back with two the first time," he admitted sheepishly the morning he delivered the hungry fledgling to my house. "And even though I tried for an hour every day, I didn't get much better with practice. But they sure did." He laughed.

To get sufficient protein in the wild, hummingbirds have to eat two to three hundred fruit flies a day. When a hummingbird is hunting insects in flight, its elastic lower bill pivots as much as 25 degrees to create an expanded open surface. Once the bill is bent to its limit, it snaps shut in less than one one-hundredth of a second. When first learning to hunt, young adults in rehab plunge straight into a swarm of fruit flies with their mouths wide open but fail to flex or snap their bills, causing them to miss what appear to be laughably easy bug grabs. After their initial failed attempts, the young trainees learn to twist their lower mandibles when pursuing the crafty insects. Still, their first catches are awkward and comical as they wrench and shake their heads wildly in midair to subdue squirming fruit flies clinging to their tongues and the sides of their bills. With practice, young hummingbirds learn to anticipate the fruit flies' defensive maneuvers and flex their bills accordingly. After mastering these basic techniques, they further hone their hunting skills by darting in swift vertical and lateral trajectories to head off escapees.

Without a mother to supplement his protein intake while learning to hunt, a young hummingbird will quickly perish in the wild. Newly fledged birds that get separated from their mothers starve to death within a day or two. Because of this risk, no bird leaves the aviary until he has become a mad hunting machine that can effortlessly nail fruit flies with pinpoint accuracy.

When I get to the counter with my Q-Tips, white sugar, and four sticky brown bananas, the checker looks at me searchingly, as if wondering whether I'm blind, and then offers assistance.

"Let me get you some fresher bananas." She winces as she picks up the store phone to call Produce.

"No, that's okay." I stop her. "I like them that way."

She glances at me, then at the putrid bananas oozing out of their skins and leaving a stream of sticky yellow slime down the conveyor.

"Are you sure?" She grimaces.

"Yeah. They're for my birds."

"Oh, what kind of birds do you have?" She brightens.

"Hummingbirds."

"Oh." She throws me a puzzled look and then glances at the handful of mush flowing like kids' Gak through her fingers. "I didn't know hummingbirds ate bananas."

"They don't." I smile.

"Oh." She looks at me uneasily as she stuffs the gooey fruit into a plastic bag and I hear her thinking: *Just let this one go.*

Later that afternoon, Pam sends me a photo of her nest renovation. She has fortified the circumference with a piece of a rubber rug pad and re-anchored the updated structure to the branch with pipe cleaners in the same light brown hue as the tree bark.

"Brilliant work," I tell her in a follow-up call that afternoon. "The best I've ever seen."

"Thank you so much, Terry." She lets out an exaggerated sigh of relief. "The pressure was so intense. Webcam viewers were commenting at all hours, from Europe and Canada, saying they couldn't sleep because they were so worried about the babies."

"Well, they wouldn't have made it without you," I congratulate her. "They should fledge within a week, so don't hesitate to call if you have any other questions or concerns."

"Don't worry," she exclaims, "I've got you on speed dial."

Several days later, Pam sends me a webcam clip of the twin female Allen's, who are thriving, to the infinite relief and delight of fifteen thousand emotionally invested spectators from one hundred countries.

"They're an international media sensation," I tell her after viewing the poignant clip of the fledglings cautiously taking their first flights out of the nest and then circling back around to check on each other.

"Thank God they're out," she rejoices. "I'm so exhausted from all of the drama."

"Well, everything turned out beautifully, because of you."

"Yeah, but now I'm kind of worried about the mother," Pam says nervously.

"Why's that?"

"Well, for some reason she's tearing the nest apart. She's got it ripped to pieces. Is she doing what I think?"

"I'm afraid she is." I exhale. "So take a deep breath and prepare for the summer sequel. She's building another nest."

CHAPTER 10

Help Me Make It Through the Night

DURING GABRIEL'S FIRST NIGHT in the ICU, I get up every few hours and shuffle down to the garage in my pajamas to feed him. Hummingbirds don't need to eat at night, but the metabolism of a seriously injured bird can drop so low that a little food in the early-morning hours may mean the difference between life and death. Since he arrived just as the nesting season was ramping up, I already have, in addition to Gabriel's seven bouncy companions in the ICU, eight fledglings in starter cages, six in large flight cages, and five young adults in the outdoor aviary. With the exception of the young adults, who are in the advanced stages of preparing for the real world, hummingbirds in rehab have to be housed in a heated room to ensure protection from the cold, wind, rain, and other natural threats to which they are not yet accustomed.

To avoid waking the slumbering fledglings, who dart off their perches and begin banging around madly in their covered cages if disturbed, I creep into the garage with ninja stealth and keep the dimmer switch low when checking on Gabriel. The nestlings in the ICU gyrate excitedly for food whenever they see me during the day, but they pile on top of one another in a single nest like drunken sailors and sleep soundly at night. When I get up at three a.m. to check on Gabriel, he is cold to the touch and appears so beleaguered, slumped over in his nest, that I can almost feel him slipping away. When I come back at five thirty to put feeders in the aviary and move the flight cages outside for the day, Gabriel has lapsed into torpor.

Because of their diminutive size and large ratio of surface area to volume, hummingbirds lose body heat rapidly. In order to maintain a warm-blooded temperature and pull off fantastic feats like hovering and executing 360-degree rotations in midair, hummingbirds have the highest metabolism and largest hearts relative to body mass of any bird on the planet. Their heart rate, which can reach 1,200 beats per minute in flight, can be slowed to less than 50 when cold weather, lack of food, or injury forces them to conserve energy. Once they go into torpor, their metabolism diminishes to 5 percent of its active state. No small number of hummingbirds, particularly injured adults, enter rescue in this condition. When their body temperature plunges, sometimes as low as 40 degrees, they fluff up like cotton balls to retain as much heat as possible while sitting stone-still on the perch with their eyes closed and bills pointed at a sharp angle in the air. Contrary to popular belief, hummingbirds do not go into torpor every night unless they need to conserve body heat in colder climates. And though birds in torpor appear unconscious, they are dimly aware of what is happening to them, as they peep softly, with the most plaintive and disarming cry you will ever hear in your life, when moved. Most can be coaxed out of torpor with food and heat in twenty minutes to a few hours. When an adult awakens inside the ICU, you can almost see him wondering, as he looks around with a bewildered expression at the unruly piles of babies peeping and jostling on either side, *Where the hell am I and how did I get into this mess?*

Watching hummingbirds emerge from their deep slumber after an injury or traumatic experience always fascinates me. Torpor is an ingenious evolutionary adaptation to a constantly changing world. Life in the wild is chaotic, unpredictable, and, occasionally, downright terrifying. Torpor acts as a natural sedative that buffers hummingbirds against the harshest conditions. Rather than enduring the threat of bitter cold, debilitating injury, or piercing hunger, when the going gets tough, they check out and drift away to a more tranquil place. While humans seek to avoid the unpleasant realities of the physical world by managing external circumstances, hummingbirds take a more primal approach. They turn inward and regulate themselves. In their retreat from inhospitable conditions, they enter a dimension beyond thought, feeling, and memory. This predilection to create an altered mental and physical state in response to outside adversity betrays a profound connection to the rhythms of the natural world that humans, in all of our rational knowledge and efforts to manage the environment, are sorely lacking.

Once Gabriel enters the land of sleep and forgetting, I leave it up to him. Two hours later he emerges, though he remains lying motionlessly in his nest with his eyes closed. When I touch the top of his head, he opens his bill weakly, and I continue to feed him, along with the insanely ravenous bobble-heads, every thirty minutes. I spend the day working to coax him back, and when I come out the next morning, I find Gabriel sitting up straight and calm in his nest with his eyes wide open. Heartened by his sudden turnaround, I move him into a starter cage used for fledglings in basic flight training. But Gabriel doesn't try to fly. He doesn't try to do anything. He just sits bolt upright on the paper towel I have laid out on the bottom of the cage. I pick him up and place him on a low perch an inch from the cage's bottom. Gabriel grips the perch with his tiny feet and immediately begins eating from the syringe anchored with electrical wire in the corner. His quick grasp of the syringe's purpose surprises me since I have been hand-feeding him with a long-tipped angiocath that looks nothing like the feeder in the cage. Although it's the first time I have seen any hummingbird, juvenile or adult, identify a new feeder so effortlessly without instruction, I dismiss it. Perhaps the color of the syringe's tip, which I have painted with red nail polish for the younger birds, attracts him, I reason. But then other things happen.

Although the breeze is chilly on this early April morning, the brilliant Southern California sun is streaming down onto the patio, creating pockets of warmth near the house. The sun has tremendous restorative powers for hummingbirds. My first year doing rehab, I discovered that fledglings who struggled unsuccessfully to take flight in indoor cages made rapid progress when placed outside in the sun. Young birds that had been thrashing around the bottom of the cage for days inside the garage would magically appear on the top perch after spending a few hours absorbing sunlight. Seriously injured adults, while less likely to regain flight from a little sunshine, not only derive great psychological benefits from natural light but respond in fundamental ways to the sights and sounds of the wild world around them.

After Gabriel's cage has been outside for a few hours, I decide it's time to wash the road grime off his feathers. Badly injured hummingbirds cannot tolerate the stress of a bath when they first arrive and need to wait a few days until they have stabilized. Like little kids, young hummingbirds love a warm bath. Adult birds, in contrast, while fond of bathing in fountains and bubbling brooks in the wild, resist being washed by human hands. So I let all but the worst cases go until they can bathe themselves after they make it into a large flight cage. But Gabriel, whose feathers are so dark and crusty I can't determine his species, is in no position to negotiate. I fill a shallow Tupperware container with an inch of warm water and carry his cage back into the garage.

"Okay, Gabriel, time for a bath," I announce, reaching into his cage. Rather than sitting stone-still, like seriously injured birds do, or fleeing into the corner to escape my grasp, like healthy adults, Gabriel leans into my hand. "Oh," I say with surprise, "a cooperator. Not something you see that often in hummingbirds." I lift Gabriel out of the cage and lower him into the warm water. He immediately spreads his wings and begins paddling around contentedly in a circle.

"Excellent, Gabriel," I applaud. "Most hummingbirds freak out their first time in the tub." Gabriel gazes up at me calmly and continues paddling around like a domestic duck out for a casual afternoon swim in the backyard pond. I sprinkle water on his head and back as he floats by, then gently rub the oily dirt off his wings before letting him go back to swimming laps. While Gabriel is lounging in the tub, Larkin, who has contacted me about hummingbird crises in the past, calls to inquire about a nest that is disintegrating outside her house in Laurel Canyon.

"The mother didn't build a very good nest," Larkin laments after sending me a video in which one chick is hanging upside down from the bottom of the decimated nest and the second is clinging desperately to a torn-off side.

An expertly constructed hummingbird nest is designed to stretch like elastic as the babies mature, which is why spider webs are the material of choice. The ideal nest expands just enough to accommodate its rapidly growing chicks while at the same time keeping them tightly contained and insulated. But younger mothers fail to exhibit much foresight and tend to select inferior construction materials, ending up with shallow, rigid nests. And unlike the creative décor of nests fashioned by more experienced mothers, the décor of teenage mothers is minimalist, with little or no external embellishment. I have seen a few dozen of these substandard nests over the years. Built by females that fledged in the winter or early spring of that same year, the nests have clearly been thrown together in a slapdash manner, as if the whole experience of getting pregnant and having babies has come as a complete surprise.

"This is probably a teenage mother," I explain to Larkin as I carry large flight cages in and out of the garage to replenish formula that seems to vanish into thin air. "And young hummingbirds, like human teenagers, are ill-equipped for parenthood. They shouldn't even get pregnant because they're so unprepared for the responsibilities that come with taking care of a baby. And then, to make matters worse, they end up with twins."

"It's so funny you say that because I was thinking before I called that she looks very inexperienced." Larkin begins laughing. "Like she doesn't know what she's doing. She built the nest in a day and it's kind of flat. And now she's picking at the outside like she's trying to fix it but doesn't really know how. So do they get better with age?"

"Of course, just as with humans, there is a learning curve. So the nests of older, more practiced mothers are well designed, stable, and beautifully decorated like works of art. And the babies thrive, get a good education, and end up leading successful and productive lives."

"So what's the prognosis for my underprivileged children?"

"I'm not going to sugarcoat things here, Larkin. Without intervention, these kids are doomed. This clueless teen mom is screaming for help."

"Maybe there should be some social services center to call in cases like this," she says giddily.

"Yes, that's me. I'm the hummingbird CFS. So let's join forces and fix this broken home." Then I launch into a tutorial on how to build an improvised nest that will support the chicks until they are up and out.

When I get off the phone with Larkin, Gabriel is still circling around his bathtub like a motorboat with no driver. "I'm pretty sure you're clean now," I say, lifting him from the chilled water. When I set him on the paper towels on the floor of his cage, he again crawls onto the perch and begins drinking from the syringe as if he has been doing it all of his life.

"They should all be as easy as you." I shake my head in disbelief before setting him back out in the sun to dry off.

But I didn't understand Gabriel yet. And he was going to be anything but simple.

CHAPTER 11

Everybody Wants You

EVERYBODY LOVES HUMMINGBIRDS. It's one of those universal clichés, like "Everything you do comes back to you," or "The more you learn, the more you realize you don't know." Almost all the people who call the rescue hotline go on about their affection for hummingbirds with groupie adulation. Of the some ten thousand avian species flying about the earth, members of the Trochilidae family manage to seize the heart and spark the imagination to a disproportionate degree. In a world filled with things on wings, hummingbirds refuse to be dismissed, taken for granted, or upstaged. Cute, charismatic, and supernaturally quick, they have, during our handful of human millennia living alongside them, demanded our attention and respect.

Early Spanish explorers to the New World called them *joyas voladores*, flying jewels, for their brilliant, iridescent feathers. The colors of the *beija flor*, or flower kisser, as Brazilians refer to hummingbirds, span the shades of the rainbow, from a flamboyant, fire-engine red to a deep, luminous violet. Their iridescence comes from tiny air sacs in the feathers that reflect different colors of light, like soap bubbles. While Southern California hummingbirds shimmer brightly in the summer sun, their plumage can't compete with the dazzling neon colors seen in some of their southwestern and South American counterparts. Male desert and mountain hummingbirds sport especially brilliant hues — matching the vibrant flowers they feed on — on their crowns and gorgets. As in other bird species, the feathers of the female and young run toward more muted earth tones, to maximize protection and ensure camouflage during nesting.

Hummingbirds have always been regarded as sacred in Native American cultures. Aztec legends depict them as messengers between worlds. In Apache and Hopi lore, shape-shifting is a common theme. In Southern California, more than a few callers are convinced the spirit of a departed relative dwells within a hummingbird buzzing around outside the window. Mothers are the most frequent spiritual visitors, followed by grandmothers and dead lovers. But callers with deceased children identify most intensely with hummingbirds as spiritual ambassadors, perhaps because bereaved parents continue searching for what is lost the rest of their lives. I can't say exactly how many callers have related stories of deceased friends and relatives descending in the form of hummingbirds from the immaculate heavens above to the gritty city below, but the number is high.

Although hummingbirds exist only in the Western Hemisphere, some European, Middle Eastern, and African immigrants living in Los Angeles who call the rescue hotline describe the hummingbirds they believe they used to see back home during their early youth. Sometimes callers' accounts are so vivid and elaborately detailed, they almost convince me of their veracity, and I marvel at how people can have such enduring memories of seeing creatures they could not possibly have seen.

Soon after I place Gabriel's cage outside in the sun, a tourist from Germany arrives with an injured adult Anna's he found on the beach in Malibu. While admiring the fledglings in cages on the patio, he effusively recounts how, as a child, he used to watch hummingbirds buzz around the grapes on his grandparents' vineyard outside of Stuttgart. Although I gently explain to him that hummingbirds don't live in Germany, he maintains that they certainly do and that he has seen plenty of them.

"Are you sure they were hummingbirds? Because they don't live in Germany," I repeat more firmly.

"Well, perhaps they escaped from the zoo or otherwise mysteriously made their way to Stuttgart, then," he defensively insists, because, as a boy, he had watched them flitting about the rolling vineyards on numerous occasions.

While recently discovered fossil evidence of two-inch skeletons unearthed in southern Germany indicates that modern-type hummingbirds once lived in that region, it was over thirty million years ago. The two tiny skeletons, finely etched in stone, have long bills and wing bones designed for hovering. Oddly, the Old World hummingbird-like fossils were uncovered several years ago in a village less than fifty miles, as the crow flies, north of Stuttgart. Gerald Mayr, the German zoologist who discovered the ancient look-alikes, named them *Eurotrochilus inexpectatus* —"unexpected European version of Trochilus." Citing coevolution, Mayr theorizes that these ancient pollinators may have, over tens of millions of years, helped design the tubular flowers of some Asian and African plants living today. After the Old World hummingbirds inexplicably disappeared, bees and other long-tongued insects moved in and assumed the task of pollinating the same nectar-laden flowers.

Given the tension of dissent hovering over our conversation, I do not trouble my time-traveling German acquaintance with this archaeological news flash, even though he proceeds to recall his tiny winged visitors in elaborate detail. Regardless of contemporary hummingbirds' history of being confined to the New World, and despite my doubts about his recollections, my Continental friend adamantly sticks to his story of enjoying a childhood surrounded by the enchanting birds. By the time he leaves my yard, he almost has me convinced Stuttgart secretly harbors hundreds of undocumented hummingbirds. And, as it turns out, the German is not alone in his flight of fancy.

On the heels of my encounter with the steadfast German, a young production assistant originally from France calls seeking advice on how to rescue a bird that has gotten trapped in his Hollywood condo. When we first begin talking, he mentions that he had to look up the English designation before calling since the French word for hummingbird is *colibri*, which, as it turns out, is derived from an extinct indigenous language of the French Caribbean.

"You have a name for them, but you don't have hummingbirds in France, do you?" I prod, dropping my voice on the tag question to indicate I already know the answer.

"Well, we don't have so many in France," he concedes, "but my roommate says there are a lot in Spain."

Upon hearing this surprising news of hummingbirds inhabiting Western Europe, I recall a Senegalese documentary filmmaker who had immigrated to Los Angeles excitedly describing hummingbirds she had seen as a child in West Africa, making me wonder if there aren't imaginary hummingbirds flying all over the world. Ever since I began hearing these accounts, early on in my rescue work, I have allowed finders' recollections to run freely without questioning their authenticity. And over and over, colorful childhood stories from my international acquaintances continue to demonstrate that the mythology surrounding hummingbirds extends far beyond their reality.

Psychologists refer to this puzzling phenomenon of recalling events that never happened as *false memory*, which stems from fantasy and wish fulfillment, as when children describe encounters with hobbits and extraterrestrials. If memories are supposed to be what is left over after we forget everything else, when it comes to hummingbirds, they may be what is imagined when experience falls short of our desires. People who call the rescue hotline attach all kinds of special significance to their hummingbird encounters. While we are stumbling through mundane work, relationship, and family problems, hummingbirds, it would seem, feel compelled to zoom down magically from above and set us straight. The human imagination knows no limits when it comes to envisioning the extraordinary feats the tiny shooting stars are capable of performing. Portrayed as inhabitants of the fairy realm, these free spirits, who dwell somewhere in that rarefied air between the beautiful and sublime, spiral into our weary human world from a parallel dimension to shake things up and remind us of larger possibilities.

Occasionally, a caller describes how an expressive hummingbird dropped out of the sky and landed on his shoulder for no apparent reason other than to display affection. Some people excitedly recount hummingbirds perching on their heads and hands out of the sheer delight of getting close to them. Seasoned rehabbers ascribe these anecdotes to fantasy, since hummingbirds, unless young and helpless, badly injured, or starving for the sugar water in someone's hand, are not interested in carrying on affectionate relationships with humans. Still, tales of interspecies adoration abound, perhaps because, like unrequited lovers, we desperately want hummingbirds to be as enamored of us as we are of them.

Humans do ridiculous and comical things to get close to hummingbirds. I have seen videos of people with sugar feeders dangling from rods attached to bicycle helmets they're wearing so they can get an intimate view of the hummingbirds as they come in to drink. Residents of the Gulf Coast sit in their yards all afternoon cradling saucers of sugar water on their laps to attract ruby-throated hummingbirds preparing to fly five hundred miles across the Gulf of Mexico during their fall migration. Other admirers who live on migratory routes in Alaska remove their feeders and stand in the same location cupping sugar water in their hands so hummingbirds will come down and perch on their fingers.

Many callers to the rescue hotline elaborate on the valuable messages hummingbirds have delivered in times of grief or crisis. People frequently report hummingbirds accosting them in their backyards to deliver messages of love, hope, or forgiveness from deceased family and friends. Neurotic callers who project their own traumatic experiences onto hummingbird behavior present the greatest challenge to rehabilitators, as they abandon all reason in their quest for private justice.

A week before Gabriel's arrival, a distressed, middle-aged social worker in the High Desert northeast of Los Angeles called insisting that a hummingbird nest in the date palm beside her house had been abandoned by a bird that was "not a responsible mother." Mistaken reports of abandoned nests are the most common calls hummingbird rehabbers receive. Jean and I get up to five a day during nesting season. The caller was agitated and eager to cut the nest, so I warned her off and then patiently guided her through our educational tour.

"Ninety-nine percent of the calls I get about abandoned nests are false alarms," I assured her. "When the nestlings are a week to ten days old the mother stops sitting on the nest, so people get confused. But this is the hummingbird's natural behavior."

"But this is not a good mother," she objected. "I've been watching her and she's just not around as much as she should be."

"She's around. You just don't see her."

"No, I've been watching the nest constantly and she hardly ever comes back," the caller persisted.

"She comes back every half hour, but she's really quick and may stay only a few seconds to feed the chicks, which is normal."

"I don't think so. I hardly ever see her."

"But the nestlings are strong and healthy, right?"

"Well, yeah, so far, but I don't think she's doing such a great job. My own mother abandoned me when I was little, so I know how it goes. She starts being around less and less and the next thing you know, she's gone. And that's what I see happening here."

"This is a little different than your experience. The mother's absence is simply the hummingbird's instinctive behavior. She stops sitting on the nest about a week after the chicks hatch and becomes more elusive in order to keep from attracting attention to the nest, which reduces predation. So if you're not seeing her that often, it's because she's being a very good mother."

"That's what people said about my mother," she fired back. "But I knew the reality. She wasn't there when I needed her."

"Well, all you can do is sit and watch the nest for an hour without taking your eyes off it. If you see her feed the chicks every thirty minutes or so, she's doing her job and you need to let it be."

The distraught nest monitor grudgingly agreed to follow my advice but called the next day to deliver another account of the mother's neglect. Again, I assured her of the hummingbird's competence and urged her to leave the nest alone. Though still insisting I was missing the point, she agreed to keep her distance. But the next morning she cut the nest and, to my immeasurable exasperation, called me with a pair of healthy, two-week-old Costa's nestlings.

"I was up half the night crying. I just couldn't take it anymore," she reported defensively. "I know how it feels to be left alone all of the time."

When I first started doing rehab, I dressed down nest robbers like this, demanding they reattach the nest and find something else to do with their time for the next few weeks. But I have learned the hard way that people who call rescue aren't necessarily interested in doing what's best for the wildlife involved. Self-absorbed callers can be volatile and become so incensed by rational argument that they hang up and disappear. No matter how logical my reasoning might be, some people can't be talked down from their high-strung emotional tightrope. So I play along, for the birds' sake.

"Get them to rehab right away, then, so they get the care they need," I insisted, giving her the number of a rescue facility in her area. I get two or three of these off-the-map calls every year. Each time, I comfort myself with the recognition that although the chicks would be better off in their natural environment, and the last thing we need are more babies in rehab, our nearly 100 percent success rate with healthy nestlings far exceeds the estimated 30 percent chance of survival they face on the red-in-tooth-and-claw streets of Southern California.

Just like humans' imaginary medical emergencies, false alarms over abandoned nests throw entire families into crisis mode. When domestic drama devolves into emotional pandemonium, the rehabber is often cast in the role of shrink in managing the family feud.

Not long after the nest cutter's meltdown in the High Desert, Spencer from West Los Angeles called at eleven on a Saturday night, twelve hours after his five-year-old son shook the branch of a potted tibouchina on the front porch that a hummingbird nest was attached to, sending the mother darting off in terror. The pervasive misconception that touching a nest or chicks will lead the mother to reject and abandon her babies accounts for no small number of frantic calls to hummingbird rescue.

"Sorry to call so late, but we just got home from a dinner party and the mother still hasn't come back. Nobody has seen her since this morning," Spencer related dejectedly over the phone. "At first I was angry at my son because I warned him several times to stay away from the nest. But now I just feel sorry for him because his sister is furious and calls him a murderer every time she passes him in the hallway."

"Your daughter sounds really tough. I'd recommend law school."

"I'm an attorney," he responded playfully.

"I went to law school for a while."

"What on earth possessed you to do that?" he asked with exaggerated disbelief.

"I don't know. I guess I got tired of trying to make an honest living. No offense."

"None taken," he replied lightly. "So you took up hummingbirds instead."

"Well, they're a passion, not a profession. And they definitely keep you honest. So, getting back to your daughter, it sounds like the apple didn't fall far from the tree."

"Unfortunately, no."

"How old is she?"

"She's eight." He sighed. "Very smart and really into animals. My wife is trying to be strong but she's freaking out inside because she's convinced the babies are dying. And my son senses her fear, so he's been hiding in his bedroom. The whole family is losing it.

I've spent the entire day trying to run interference, but now nobody can sleep. I don't know how much longer we can take this stress."

"Okay, Counselor, let's break down the facts of this case," I said, and then I walked him through my usual round of questioning about the chicks' age, appearance, noise level, and behavior.

"My wife says they looked really lethargic this afternoon," Spencer told me after submitting to my interrogation. "Could I just bring you the nest so we can get past all of this?" he pleaded with the weariness of a family-court judge after a long day on the bench.

"I don't think that's the right move. Based on the nestlings' age and your description of their behavior, I think the mother is still there and the chicks are fine. They might appear lethargic because they're at the age when their eyes are just starting to open so they look kind of squinty. But when the chicks can thermoregulate and don't need their mother's body heat anymore, she moves off the nest. So her seeming disappearance at this point is actually just part of a hummingbird's natural behavior. It's an unfortunate coincidence that she stopped sitting on the nest the day your son shook the branch. But she's still on the job and will zip in to feed the babies every thirty minutes during the day. So maybe you can explain this to your family in order to calm things down a little and get some sleep."

I instructed Spencer to have someone get up at the crack of dawn and watch the nest closely for thirty minutes to determine if the mother was still present. He reluctantly agreed. When I checked my voicemail the next morning at seven, Spencer's message was the first of three.

"Terry!" an exuberant voice boomed. "The mother came back at dawn and fed the babies. It was amazing. What a tremendous relief," he shouted as the family celebrated in the background.

Later that week, Jean called me after hours of dealing with traumatized hummingbird lovers who were psychologically imploding for reasons entirely imagined.

"I've spent the whole morning on the phone counseling people about crises that aren't even real," she lamented with frustration. "Then a woman calls and is hysterical about a fledgling flying around inside her house. It took me ten minutes to calm her down enough so she could listen to what I was saying. I should put out a shingle."

"Why bother?" I asked rhetorically. "The line at your door is already snaking around the block."

The following day, Willow, a textile artist in West Hollywood, called me to describe how she communicated telepathically with a hummingbird in her yard and had connected with the bird through divine intervention. I get this a lot. People assume that since I rescue hummingbirds, I travel through portals and am privy to all kinds of paranormal information unavailable to regular human beings. Callers often confide that hummingbirds represent their spirit animals or totems. Others describe their hummingbird shrines and tattoos and report bonding spiritually with them. During my first few years of doing rescue, I shared laughs with other rehabbers over such accounts, since we viewed bonding with hummingbirds, like falling in love with the town playboy, as strictly a one-way street. But I had something to learn about this too.

In Willow's case, the emotionally starving artist placed a potted lantana on her dining-room table to lure the hummingbird into the house with the goal of forging a stronger connection. Predictably, the bird flew in, became panicked and disoriented, hit the glass trying to get out, fell, and, in a bizarre twist, ended up tightly sandwiched between the two lower panes of the kitchen window. Given my impossible schedule during hummingbird season, I don't normally do house calls, but I happened to be driving near her neighborhood on Melrose when Willow called and frantically informed me that the trapped bird had chicks in a nest in the pepper tree just outside. When I got to her house, with its walls draped in loud artwork indicating she had drifted into a few too many hippie-dippy Melrose yard sales, Willow was sitting red-faced at the kitchen table trembling with fear.

"She doesn't love you the way you love her," I admonished the weeping Willow as I carefully extracted the petrified hummingbird from between the windowpanes with chopsticks. "Don't ever invite her in again."

By the end of that mad week, in an entirely different but equally unforgettable scenario, Shannon, a graduate student from Riverside who brought me a spider-web victim, described how a hummingbird had diverted her from a potentially deadly encounter as she was hiking alone in the San Bernardino Mountains. Just as Shannon was about to descend the trail into a ravine, an adult male Anna's appeared out of nowhere and hovered directly in front of her, flashing his magenta gorget like a stoplight in the bright sun. When she approached the bird, he took off in the opposite direction. Assuming he was gone, she continued down the trail, but the bird zoomed up from behind and hovered just to her left. A moment later, to Shannon's astonishment, the hummingbird buzzed in wide circles over her head several times as she was making her way down the trail, then, like Lassie, signaled her to follow him in the other direction by flying a few yards ahead and hovering at eye level. Intrigued by his friendly behavior and armed with a new high-speed digital camera, Shannon turned and followed the dazzling male up the trail and along the ridge for several hundred yards, snapping photos all the way. After taking dozens of pictures, Shannon descended the trail on the other side of the ridge and went home. Two days later, she read a news story reporting the body of a young hiker at the bottom of the ravine the hummingbird had guided her away from. A month after the incident, when Shannon made the sixty-mile drive from Riverside to deliver the female hummingbird she had found entangled in a spider web inside a parking garage, the cause of the hiker's death remained undetermined.

"My dad sent that bird up in the mountains," Shannon asserted unequivocally as she watched me manipulate a watercolor paintbrush soaked in warm canola oil to remove the sticky spider strands binding the adult female Anna's wings to her body like a mummy's wrappings. "He died a week before it happened. And he loved hummingbirds. He used to take hundreds of pictures of them in his yard." She hesitated for a moment and shook her head, as if wrestling with her own disbelief. "He was right there, shielding me. I could feel it. That bird was trying to tell me something."

I glanced over at Shannon with a knowing look. Before rehab ran up on me and hijacked my life, I had a similar experience of feeling that a hummingbird was attempting to communicate with me in some supernatural way. He accosted me at the break of dawn when I stepped out onto the front porch one glorious spring day to get the newspaper. After hovering a foot in front of my face and looking me straight in the eye for what seemed like an eternity, he suddenly executed a sharp vertical and then vanished into the wispy pink clouds overhead. Like Shannon, I sensed my bird was trying to relay a special message from beyond. But in my case, the hummingbird, also a male Anna's with a shimmering magenta head and gorget, was not telegraphing how much I was loved and missed by dearly departed spirits or steering me away from some unknown catastrophe. Instead, my decorated soldier arrived at the front door like the selective service recruiting for the armed forces. And his message from the hummingbird branch was clear: *We want your life.*

When I first began rehabbing hummingbirds, my reaction to stories like Shannon's near-death encounter always inclined toward skepticism. *They're just birds,* I wanted to say. But then that's foolish, because they are not. Other small birds like chickadees and nuthatches are nearly as quick and almost as cute. But they don't possess the hummingbird magic that resonates so deeply inside the human spirit that it drives people beyond the limits of sanity. There is something dreamlike and unreal about the fabulous little fairies. And there is a reason for the mythic proportions these miniature birds have assumed historically and continue to enjoy in popular culture today.

After hearing so many mystifying stories like Shannon's over the years, all I could do was concede that hummingbirds were capable of extraordinary things. But even with this recognition, I did not understand how deeply their meanings run. Despite the abundant factual and scientific knowledge I had acquired during my close encounters with hummingbirds over the previous few years, I was about to discover far more subtle and complex mysteries spinning within their legendary wings.

CHAPTER 12

Brown Sugar

IF ANYONE HAD TRIED TO EXPLAIN the range and complexities of the hummingbird temperament to me before I started doing rescue, I would not have believed it. We expect our dogs and cats to have unique personalities, and individual differences in higher mammals like elephants and great apes have been well documented. But when we regard a creature as small and seemingly indistinct as a hummingbird, we don't usually reflect on whether a particular bird is fundamentally aggressive or shy, friendly or aloof, confident or insecure. And yet these variations exist. Even after several years of rehabilitating hummingbirds, I continue to be fascinated by the sometimes slight, other times immeasurable, differences in their dispositions.

While Gabriel is getting recharged by solar power, I check on the feeders in the aviary where twin female Anna's from West Los Angeles and three other young adults are jockeying for position around the pink and purple blossoms of a potted fuchsia hanging from the ceiling. The two female Anna's had been illegally cut from a tree by a well-meaning nature lover named Shinobu who had come from Tokyo, where there are no hummingbirds, to Los Angeles, where hummingbirds seem to be falling out of the sky. Shinobu had been watching the nest's progress in a juniper tree in his front yard for four weeks. One day in February, Shinobu wrongly assumed the mother had gone missing and cut the nest containing the week-old twins.

Although I am forever reminding callers of the reasons females appear to vanish a week after their eggs hatch, unfortunately, as with Spencer and his high-anxiety family drama, the mother's sudden absence throws nest watchers into a panic. I get a hundred calls a year about this abrupt change in behavior. Before I set up the rescue hotline, well-meaning bird lovers cut these nests in a misguided attempt to save the babies, who then died from being fed sugar water for too long. Now I tell alarmed residents to sit out of sight and watch the nest for half an hour until the mother comes in to feed the chicks and to call me back if she doesn't. I never hear from 90 percent of these callers again, unless it is to celebrate the mother's unexpected "return."

Unlike most concerned hummingbird enthusiasts in Los Angeles, however, Shinobu did not call before acting. Certain the mother was missing in action, he removed the nest from the tree and brought the chicks into the house. Possessing the Japanese fascination for netsuke, Shinobu fell in love with the intricate details he saw in the baby hummingbirds and decided to raise them himself. So, despite his good intentions, Shinobu managed to do everything wrong, first by neglecting to call before deciding to become the hero and then by keeping the nestlings and feeding them an unidentifiable, sticky dark liquid that thoroughly gummed up their crops. One chilly morning about a week after he cut the nest, Shinobu called me from Sony Studios. When I got the chicks from a volunteer driver who picked them up from Sony and delivered them to my house in a decorative Japanese teacup, both nestlings were ice-cold. They had stopped eating because their crops were blocked (which was the reason Shinobu had finally called) and were stretching their necks out and gasping for air. I put them in the ICU, cranked up the heat, and called Shinobu immediately.

After saying hello and reminding him who I was, I cut to the chase.

"So, why did you cut the nest?"

"Because," Shinobu began confidently, "Mother was gone."

"Well, you know the mother does not sit on the nest all of the time after the chicks are a week old," I explain.

"No?"

"No. She flies in to feed the chicks every thirty minutes, but she doesn't sit on them during the day or at night after they are about a week old."

Silence.

"So she probably was still there . . ." I trailed off.

More silence.

"So you should have called me before you cut the nest," I finished.

Deafening silence.

"Shinobu?"

"Yes," he answered with the urgent tone of a soldier being reprimanded by a superior officer.

"What have you been feeding them?" I asked as that stubborn memory of my cold night in March with the young Anna's came hurtling out of the past.

"Sugar water," Shinobu said quickly.

"And how long did you keep them?"

"Just a few days."

"How many days?"

"Maybe four," he replied uncertainly.

"Maybe more?"

"Maybe a week," he admitted.

"And you fed them only sugar water?"

"Yes, sugar water only."

"Are you sure? Because I need to know if there was anything else."

"Just sugar water." Shinobu stuck to his story.

"What kind of sugar, then?"

"Brown sugar."

"Brown sugar," I repeated. *Terrific,* I thought to myself. Brown sugar is made with molasses, a thick syrup that sticks to a hummingbird's crop like glue.

"And you didn't feed them ants?"

"Yes," he answered.

"Yes, you did feed them ants?" I tried to clarify, recalling that a cardinal rule in English as a Second Language classes was never to ask a question with a negative in it because many foreign-language speakers answer the opposite way an American would.

"Yes, I did not," he asserted.

"Ah, okay. So no ants."

"No, I did not know," he said defensively.

"Know what?"

"They should eat ants."

"No, they should *never*"—I emphasized each word—"*eat ants.*"

"Oh." Shinobu sounded perplexed.

"So at least in that respect, you're off the hook."

"Hook?" he asked innocently. "What hook?"

"*Daijobu desu yo,*" I finally assured him.

"*Ah, hai, arigato gozaimasu!*" Shinobu laughed with relief.

"You're welcome," I answered lightheartedly. "Now, Shinobu."

I assumed a more serious tone and began my standard lecture. "Hummingbirds are wild animals protected by federal law, so it is illegal to keep them."

"Uh-huh."

"And they need to be cared for by experienced rehabilitation experts who are licensed by the state."

"Uh-huh."

"So you will call me right away if you ever find a hummingbird that you think needs help."

"Uh-huh."

"And you will never keep another hummingbird, or any other wild animal, in your house again. Okay?"

Silence.

"Shinobu?"

"Yes!" he finally exclaimed resolutely. "I will not."

As soon as I hung up, I raced back to the garage and took the teacup out of the ICU. The nestlings' crops were bulging with coagulated lumps of brown sugar they had no hope of digesting. Both were a few hours away from starving to death. Fortunately, in the two years since my first unforgettable loss, I had become a master at siphoning crops. Since then I had taken in hummingbirds fed prune juice, Gatorade, protein powder, soda pop, wheat bread, boiled eggs, Fig Newtons, and, in one bizarre instance, human breast milk. Needless to say, hummingbirds eat none of these things in the wild. I donned telescopic surgical glasses and quickly went to work extracting spoonfuls of gooey brown liquid from the chicks' crops, flushing them with warm water, and then siphoning again. After repeating this daunting procedure three times, I fed the immeasurably relieved nestlings a protein-enriched formula I had warmed in the ICU before calling Shinobu.

After one uncertain day, during which the chicks shied away from the angiocath whenever I offered food, both miraculously recovered from their brown-sugar overdose and began growing with science fiction speed, as if making up for lost time.

The brown-sugar twins turned out to be among the sweetest hummingbirds I had ever encountered. Although birders are not inclined to use such endearing terms to describe hummingbirds in the wild, once nestlings enter rehab, distinct personalities emerge. To label all hummingbirds as mean and combative misses one of the most fundamental truths every rehabber quickly comes to recognize: hummingbird dispositions are as varied and diverse as those of any domestic pet. Some are tough as nails, others fragile; some show high intelligence and learn everything immediately, others take more time; some rush in and boldly take charge of every social situation, while others are fearful and shrink away from confrontation. And, finally, some display childlike dependence, while others are fiercely self-reliant and can't wait to get away from their caretakers.

From the beginning, the brown-sugar twins fell into the category of the bright, quiet types. Although rehabbers discourage close contact with rescued wild animals who are destined for release, the brown-sugar twins had little interest in obeying the rules. Both craved the personal touch, exploring my fingers with their translucent tongues every time I fed them in the ICU. After they fledged and moved up to the starter cage, they danced in tandem on their perches, fluttering their wings and seeking words of encouragement whenever I walked by or came around to fill their feeders. In the large flight cage, they darted over and landed on the back of my hand when I reached in to hang freshly picked lantana and honeysuckle or change their bath water. After graduating to the aviary, they greeted me at the door and commenced mining the lavender and passionflower in my hand before I could get it fastened to their perches inside. My hummingbird attire consists of old T-shirts from scuba adventures Frank and I had pursued over the years, and the twins zeroed in on the PADI dive flag stitched onto the chest pocket, repeatedly drilling their bills into the decal in search of the sweet succulence that the color red always promises in their world. They also slept close together, side by side, every night on the same perch in their cages and later in the aviary's ficus tree. Neither ever displayed a trace of aggression toward the other or any other hummingbird. Still, there was no doubt in my mind they would thrive in the wild because of their high IQs.

Hummingbirds have a reputation among avian researchers for their mental acuity. Like songbirds, hummingbirds possess the largest brains in relation to body size of all the birds on the planet. Because of hummingbirds' considerable intelligence, most fledglings in starter cages require just a day of instruction before learning to feed themselves. But tremendous variation exists among young birds. A few learn the first time and race ahead. Some sit on their perches day after day, crying for food even though the syringe is positioned directly in front of their bills and I have directed them to it dozens of times. Some just can't seem to get it. Others choose not to.

The brown-sugar twins, despite being deprived of their mother at an early age, went through rehab confident and self-assured. They picked up everything—how to self-feed, maneuver between perches, mine nectar from flowers, catch fruit flies, bathe, and use a sugar feeder—without delay. Just as important, once they joined other hummingbirds in the aviary, they knew how to get out of the way when trouble started.

Placed in the aviary with a small group that included a wild and fiercely aggressive rufous male I'd dubbed Chucky, the twins displayed admirable composure in the face of chaos. Whenever Chucky—who liked me even less than he liked other humming-birds—flew into one of his violent rages and began assaulting everyone in sight, the brown-sugar twins instinctively retreated to the perimeter until the dust settled. Chucky, who sported bright tangerine tail feathers, had been rescued by Charles (hence the nickname) from the side of a road in the sparsely inhabited hills north of Claremont after a Santa Ana windstorm. I don't know how Chucky ended up unconscious and face-down in the gutter, but the punishing gusts that swept him out of his soft nest and onto the hard pavement that merciless night in March somehow transformed him into the angriest hummingbird ever to come through rehab (though later experience with other offenders that came into rescue suggested Chucky had likely been born a tyrant). Chucky's cage mate was a smaller Allen's male who had had the misfortune to arrive from the Pasadena Humane Society at the same time as Chucky, and the two of them, as well as a sturdy pair of Anna's (a male and a female confiscated from an eight-year-old nest robber who was detained by a neighbor while he was carrying the chicks down the sidewalk and who ran off upon questioning) graduated to the aviary with the brown-sugar twins.

As with classes in school, every cohort suffers its bully. But Chucky gave fresh meaning to the stereotype of the pugnacious hummingbird. To his credit, Chucky was not insufferable when he shared a flight cage with the diffident Allen's male and had everything under control. But the second he moved into the aviary with four larger, unknown quantities, Chucky went bad fast. Within minutes of entering his new and uncertain domain, Chucky began launching preemptive strikes against opponents both real and imagined. The Allen's male, who had accepted his subordinate status early on and therefore sat on a perch out in the open as if the pecking order were already established, bore the brunt of Chucky's murderous wrath. Annoyed that his former flunky neglected to grasp the new world order and head for cover when battle erupted, Chucky would make an example of him by hooking his legs and driving him to the cement patio with an audible thud. The male Anna's, though considerably larger and stronger than the rufous, was less developed mentally and therefore managed to lose every fight to Chucky, who would dive-bomb him from above and then circle back and torpedo him into the aviary bars. The Anna's older sister, even bigger and less inclined to back down, didn't fare much better. I came out to the aviary their first afternoon together to find Chucky hovering over the female and resolutely plucking feathers off the top of her head whenever she tried to eat from a feeder.

All hummingbirds require training in conflict resolution, and the experiences they have in the aviary can, like boot camp, provide invaluable lifesaving skills they'll use once they enter the wild. But Chucky's lessons in survival crossed the line. After a day of random flybys, I called Jean to report the flaming terrorist.

"He's such a little shit," I complained in frustration.

"What's he doing?"

"Anything he wants. He's in perpetual attack mode. I don't know what to do with him. He's been in the aviary only a day."

"Throw him out," Jean advised. "If he's that mean, he doesn't need you anymore."

"I've never had a bird this aggressive."

"He's the perfect hummingbird," she said. "Nobody's going to push him around out there."

"That's for sure. He even buzzes me and clicks behind my back whenever I change the feeders. Sometimes I get this eerie feeling he'd take me out if he could."

"He would," Jean assured me. "If he were big, you'd have to shoot him."

The next morning, just after breakfast, I ejected the little orange fireball, who shot over the house like a bullet and disappeared into the rising sun on his way out of town, never to be seen again. After Chucky's early departure, the relief in the aviary was palpable, and Zen calm prevailed for the remaining two weeks of the brown-sugar twins' stay in rehab.

Watching the platinum-colored sisters snapping up fruit flies in the aviary that sunny afternoon in April, an image of the dark ice cubes they had been when they arrived in the teacup comes back to me. It seems impossible these robust beauties can be the same birds that arrived frozen and near death two months earlier. Rather than applauding myself, I am impressed with the resilience of nature in the face of so much human error and interference. Now, despite their unpromising beginning, the brown-sugar twins are about to return to the wild, where they will thrive and perpetuate their extraordinarily attractive genetic heritage into the foreseeable future.

After checking the feeders in the flight cages on the patio, I head back to the garage. As I pass Gabriel's cage, I notice him running his bill up and down his wing feathers, a clear sign that a hummingbird is feeling relaxed. I hurry into the garage, go down the assembly line of gaping mouths in the ICU, then return to examine Gabriel. When I step outside, I can see Gabriel on his low perch resting quietly in the sun. But his feathers still appear black.

"Damn," I whisper under my breath as I approach him. "That's some serious road grime. We'll have to bathe you again." But when I lift his cage, I see Gabriel's deep green feathers and brilliant magenta gorget flash brightly in the sunlight. "Ah, you're an Anna's. But you're so dark," I observe. And then I notice something else.

Surprised and confused, I grab my cell phone, which is attached to me day and night during hummingbird season, like a fifth appendage, and call Jean. When she answers on the eighth ring, I don't waste any time.

"Have you seen a lot of those cobalt-green Anna's like the one I brought you during that rainstorm four years ago?" I ask her.

"Not a lot." She pauses reflectively. "Just a couple every year."

"How about hummingbirds with white spots on their heads? How many of those have you seen?"

Jean thinks for a moment. "Just that one."

"Are you sure?"

"Uh-huh," Jean says in a strained voice that indicates she's lifting something far too heavy.

"Are you absolutely sure?"

"Yeah, I'm sure," she answers impatiently. "Why?"

"Because he's sitting in a cage on my patio."

CHAPTER 13

Hello Stranger

IT'S WHAT YOU LEARN once you think you know everything that makes all the difference. After working closely with hummingbirds for two years, I imagined I understood them pretty well. But in this naive assumption, I was a lot like a college student who comes home for winter break her freshman year spouting a world of new ideas without understanding the true meaning behind any of them.

"The magenta has come in on his crown and gorget but he still has a white spot on his head. Do you think it's the same bird I brought you as a nestling four years ago?" I ask Jean excitedly as I crouch beside the cage admiring Gabriel's cobalt-green feathers and bright white spot glistening in the sunlight.

"No," Jean answers flatly. "I know it is."

"Really? You think he flew all the way back up here after you released him?"

"Well, let's see." Jean speculates. "If he flew north in a straight line, it would take him all of about thirty minutes to get to Beverly Hills."

"Doesn't that kind of shock you, though? That after I rescued him from that rainstorm he would end up back here four years later under the same circumstances?"

"Nothing they do shocks me anymore."

"But why here? I mean, of course, for a lot of people, Beverly Hills tops the list of desirable places to live, but why would he come here when he could go anywhere he wants?" I wonder, envisioning the appealing landscape and picturesque small towns sprinkled up and down the rugged and spectacular California coast.

"Because they return to their birthplace to breed," Jean points out, as if explaining something obvious to a slow child.

"But he was just a baby when I brought him to you. How does he know where he was born?"

"Don't have a clue," Jean replies, "but obviously he does or he wouldn't be there."

Although I have read about the remarkable homing abilities displayed by other birds, I never thought Los Angeles hummingbirds would be so driven to return to a specific location in such a tangled urban sprawl. In a city crammed with a million houses and apartment buildings that appear as an endless mosaic when you're flying over in a jumbo jet, how can hummingbirds determine which neighborhood and in some cases, even more unbelievably, which particular yard to stop at?

Anecdotal accounts of hummingbirds returning to their birthplaces to breed have been around forever. But it wasn't until avian aficionados began banding hummingbirds thirty years ago that these stories got the weight of solid scientific evidence behind them. Since then, banding groups have reported almost unimaginable discoveries from their investigations. Among other amazing things, banding studies have revealed the astonishing migratory flights some of these micro-marvels undertake annually.

While many Los Angeles hummingbirds don't go anywhere anymore, and their most demanding flights are between sugar feeders on the block, others make the trip to Mexico and back each year. George C. West, a professor emeritus of zoophysiology at the University of Alaska, banded over fourteen thousand humming-birds in Arizona during a decade spent tracking the migratory hab-its of the fifteen western species. Professor West cites research by the North American Breeding Bird Survey estimating the global population of Anna's hummingbirds at five million. Ninety-six per-cent of Anna's breed in the United States, and 15 percent spend their winters in Mexico. Black-chinned hummingbirds are also estimated at five million, with 86 percent breeding in the United States and 100 percent wintering in Mexico.

According to Professor West, each autumn large numbers of Southern California Anna's and black-chinned migrate east to Ari-zona's sky islands — high-elevation forests surrounded by low-ele-vation desert — before continuing south into northern Mexico for the winter. In the spring, these birds complete their circular migra-tion route by returning to California west of the sky islands at lower elevations that host a sufficient supply of edible insects. In addition to the large sedentary population of Anna's living in Southern Cali-fornia, millions of others nest up and down the West Coast. Some migrate as far north as British Columbia and more recently Alaska, where they have extended their distribution over the past few dec-ades thanks to abundant sugar feeders and introduced vegetation.

Impressive as these international flights may seem for a bird that weighs less than a pygmy mouse, hummingbirds from other parts of the United States complete long-distance migratory jour-neys that border on the supernatural. Ruby-throated humming-birds migrating north to Canada to breed and nest fly five thousand miles a year on a journey that includes a nonstop eighteen-hour, five-hundred-mile flight over the Gulf of Mexico each spring and autumn. Not all of the estimated seventeen million ruby-throated hummingbirds that breed in the United States make this trans-Gulf flight — some prefer to follow the coastline — but the intrepid voyagers that do double their weight, from three grams to six, before departing land. Hummingbirds preparing for this strenuous crossing sometimes put on so much weight, they lose their capacity to fly for a short time. Every September, callers from Alabama and Florida report finding the squishy butterballs splayed on the ground under sugar feeders, waiting up to thirty minutes to burn off enough weight so they can get airborne again.

Researchers believe the ruby-throated travelers depart land at dusk and make most of their trans-Gulf journey at night. Lying in bed on cool September nights, I try to imagine these miniature marvels gliding through the silent darkness, spinning over an opaque ocean with nothing but the moon and stars to guide them on their overnight flight. They are propelled by forces beyond themselves, across five hundred miles of flat and featureless water, with no room for error. Since hummingbirds fly low when they migrate, fishermen occasionally report seeing them whiz by in the early-morning hours. Some seek a temporary resting place and have been spotted perched on the masts of boats in the Gulf hundreds of miles offshore. Although it's assumed most hummingbirds make this flight straight through or perish if they fall into the ocean, we can't be certain.

In Southern California we get dozens of calls every year reporting hummingbirds floating around in swimming pools. Most of these downed drifters are new fledglings that have fallen into the pool and do not have enough strength to fly out. But on several occasions, people have called about an adult hummingbird floating in the pool only to discover five minutes later that the bird has flown off.

The legendary trans-Gulf flights made by waves of ruby-throated hummingbirds are the stuff dreams are made of. But other marathon fliers like the rufous are capable of completing a seven-thousand-mile round trip when migrating from Central America and the U.S. Gulf Coast to Alaska and back. As reported in Bob and Martha Sargent's quarterly research journal *NetLines*, a female rufous banded in January of 2010 in Tallahassee, Florida, was recaptured in Alaska's Prince William Sound in June of the same year after completing a 3,500-mile flight. Six months old when banded, as determined by the diagonal grooving on her bill, the young rufous weighed in at 3.7 grams. Banding researchers speculate the year-old female had been born in Alaska in June of 2009 and was returning to her birthplace to breed, clocking 7,000 miles her first year out. Such phenomenal migratory feats make Gabriel's thirty-minute, twenty-mile commute from Torrance to Beverly Hills appear pretty unremarkable, even if he did have to navigate several formidable skyscrapers on his trek through downtown.

Migratory species like the ruby-throated and rufous spend much of their lives on the road, heading to northern breeding grounds from March to May and returning south from August to October. Rufous hummingbirds that do not elect to make the easy stop in Southern California migrate north up the coast before nesting in forests from the Sierra and Rocky Mountains to south-central Alaska. Rufous remain in their northern habitats only a few months to breed and nest. By August, adult males spearhead the wave back south through the Rocky Mountains and the sky islands, reaching central Mexico in October, where they spend the winter molting their feathers before commencing their long flight north in March. To accomplish these mind-boggling journeys, hummingbirds rely on the wisdom of their genetic history and the information stored in tiny brains the size of silver cupcake beads. Envisioning these near-weightless fliers braving the formidable obstacles posed by wind, fire, rain, and snow to adjust to the seasons of the earth is nothing short of awe-inspiring.

Some hummingbirds suffer what rehabbers refer to as migration fatigue. In early April of 2007, I got a call about a Costa's that had fallen from the air onto a third-floor balcony at a chiropractic hospital in Los Angeles. According to the two interns who were taking a lunch break there, the adult male dropped out of the sky and landed flat at their feet. When they handed the spectacular, violet-hooded adult to me in a sterile-glove container, he was so listless, I feared he was about to die. But after a few hours of refueling on formula while sitting in a flight cage on the patio in the sun, he exploded to life and soon was buzzing smoothly back and forth between perches. I kept him overnight and by morning he was so energetic that when I opened his cage, he rocketed over the house in less than a second and headed straight east toward the desert.

A few weeks later, when I came out to fill feeders in the aviary at midmorning, I noticed an adult male rufous sitting motionless on a low-hanging sugar feeder I had attached to the underside of the patio umbrella. His eyes were half closed and he appeared exhausted and disheveled, as if he had kept his foot on the accelerator to reach his destination despite running low on fuel. When I reached for him, he didn't blink, and as I closed my fingers around him, he went limp in my hand. I slid him off the sugar feeder—always slide a hummingbird off a perch; never lift straight up—and placed him on a low wooden perch inside a large flight cage in the sun. We do not band our releases in Los Angeles, but the minute he regained consciousness, I suspected I had rehabbed this rufous when he was young. Adult hummingbirds initially reject the formula we use in rehab because the sugar content is lower than that of the nectar they are accustomed to in the wild. But this weary traveler took to the syringe as if he had been drinking from it all his life and began gulping formula without being coaxed or coerced. More surprising, unlike most uninjured adults, he exhibited no fear or agitation when I examined him in my hand. And rufous males are not known for their relaxed acceptance of the human touch. By midafternoon, the feisty flier had burst back to life, and the next morning expressed a clear desire to get back on the road. After eating an impressive breakfast, he began gliding back and forth between perches impatiently. When I opened his cage twenty minutes later, my rufous revisit shot fifty feet into the air; within two seconds, he had cleared the Pacific Design Center a block away and was heading into the hills north of the city to fulfill his destiny.

Migration fatigue is considered unusual, occurring only in older birds or those that are in some way physically compromised. But the natural and manmade hazards awaiting hummingbirds on their long-distance flights over land and sea are random and limitless. And there is no way to determine how many of these fearless fliers encounter life-threatening bumps in the road during their extended journeys.

Marathon flights are not hummingbirds' only fantastic migratory achievements. In addition to having a GPS that guides the bird home each spring, each hummingbird possesses an internal clock capable of directing him to the same sugar feeder on the same day, year after year. Same-date recaptures — banded birds captured at or near the same location on the same day in successive years — are surprisingly common. Members of the Bob and Martha Sargent's Hummingbird Study Group have documented a ruby-throated female banded on August 18, 2009, and recaptured on August 17, 2011, at the same nature center in Nashville, Tennessee; a female rufous banded as an immature bird in Alabama in 2002 and recaptured at the same feeder for nine consecutive years during her spring migration north; and two ruby-throated females that had been banded hours apart on August 11, 2005, recaptured in the same trap on August 11, 2012, at the same location in West Virginia.

Researchers attribute hummingbirds' ability to return to the same feeders after migrating thousands of miles to their exceptional spatial memory. Migratory hummingbirds can remember to within inches the precise location and height of a sugar feeder they frequented before heading south for the winter. If a feeder hanging on a long wire in the fall is attached to a shorter wire the following spring, a returning hummingbird that has completed a several-thousand-mile journey will initially hover at the lower height the feeder was hanging at six months earlier. Nobody knows how they do this.

Ironically, because of hummingbirds' precision in spatial memory, when tree trimmers and weekend gardeners in Los Angeles replace cut nests near their original locations, the mothers are often unable, or perhaps unwilling, to return to the nests. One caller who accidentally cut a nest of two-day-old Allen's twins from a bamboo stand in his yard in Silver Lake reattached the branch a few feet from the original location less than an hour later. Zach called me several times to report the mother flying around unable to locate her nest with the pair of hatchlings. He finally sent me a video showing the nest tucked into the bamboo with the mother buzzing around a few yards away. I called him back and advised him to move the nest to the exact spot at which she was hovering. Since a layer of outer branches had been trimmed off the bamboo,

Zach could not get the nest precisely in its original location, but he was able to attach it closely nearby. An hour later, he sent another video that showed the mother searching within a few feet of the nest, which was positioned deeper in the hedge than it originally had been. I instructed Zach to sneak in and feed the hatchlings sugar water every thirty minutes while the mother was conducting her reconnaissance. The distressed female continued to fly off and return dozens of times during her protracted afternoon search.

"I just want to run out there, point to it, and say, 'Look, it's right here!'" Zach exclaimed after watching the mother search in vain for three hours.

"If only you could, right?" I agreed.

Finally, as darkness descended and it became clear the naked hatchlings had no chance of surviving the night without their mother's body heat, I had Zach deliver the twins to rehab.

This scenario plays out several times each year with accidentally cut nests. In the case of young hatchlings, callers often report the mother searching within a few feet of a repositioned nest. Rather than being unable to find it, some nesting females may be wary of sitting on a nest that has been moved to a new location. Interestingly, when the same situation involves nestlings or grounded fledglings that are old enough to cry audibly, the mother quickly falls back into her maternal routine. Even when I have callers place feathered chicks into faux nests in a tree several yards from where they were discovered, the mother easily locates them and resumes her feeding duties, suggesting that hummingbirds rely more on sound than sight when locating their displaced young.

With all of their mysterious abilities, hummingbirds never cease to astonish even the most experienced experts. How do these miniature fliers make such epic journeys year after year in their quest to return to their ancestral birthplace? Zoologists, ornithologists, and natural historians speculate and marvel at hummingbirds' miraculous capacities from their different scientific perspectives. But perhaps only the imagination of the poet can envision these tiny bundles of contradictions as they navigate their way over arid deserts, sprawling plains, alpine forests, fog-shrouded plateaus, rolling hills, windswept bluffs, snowcapped mountains, wetlands, rivers, lakes, and a vast ocean. Venturing into the unknown each day, moving on to new places or in search of others to which they have already been, hummingbirds live the life of pure adventure as they navigate their way through ever-changing though not entirely unfamiliar surroundings in the natural world.

City residents often express envy of the freedom and exhilaration that hummingbird flight symbolizes. In Los Angeles, while we struggle to extricate ourselves from freeway gridlock that takes two aggravating hours to escape, hummingbirds zoom off to distant horizons somewhere on the margins of the earth, places the wild heart flees to when the city limits our power to break free. In their global excursions, hummingbirds ignore humans' unnatural and artificial borders. To them there are no states or countries, only clouds, wind, and the open sky. Departing from shared urban communities, they venture to far-flung destinations we cannot know but can well imagine. And our yearning to tag along and share vicariously in their enigmatic travels captures the essence of the hummingbird's allure.

CHAPTER 14

She Blinded Me with Science

FOUR WEEKS AFTER Gabriel's arrival, on a balmy night in early May, Pepper shows up at my door at eight o'clock in a white cardboard takeout box. Hayley, a statuesque, dark-haired beauty with arresting hazel eyes, was working on a film set in Los Feliz next to Griffith Park when she discovered Pepper stranded in the jalapeño dish (hence the name) during a catered outdoor lunch. Pepper's bright green back blended into the jalapeños so seamlessly that Hayley nearly scooped her up onto a plate before noticing the wounded Anna's flailing around in the stainless-steel chafing dish.

"What do you think happened to her?" I ask after Hayley laughingly describes the culinary confusion.

"There are a lot of tall trees around the set," Hayley says with a shrug, "so maybe she fell out of her nest."

I lift Pepper out of the box and examine her carefully. "She's not a baby, though," I point out.

"Oh, she's not? How can you tell?"

"See the length of her bill? Juveniles have a shorter bill. But there's still a lot of grooving," I observe, examining her with my surgical loupes, "so she's a teenager who has been out on her own, probably for about a month or two. So something happened to her."

Hayley frowns. "Like what?"

"Ah!" I exclaim, noticing a few contour feathers missing from the back of her head. "Did you see another hummingbird around?"

"Yeah, actually, one of the grips said he saw another hummingbird buzzing around the set after I found her. Then when we were going over some footage later, we noticed them zipping through a scene together."

"She should be in the credits, then."

"Absolutely," Hayley agrees. "I'll make sure of that."

"What did the other hummingbird look like?"

"Kind of like her, but with a bright red head. We figured it was her mother."

"No, it wasn't her mother. It was an adult male, probably trying to breed with her." I point to the missing feathers on her head.

Hayley looks at Pepper closely, then glances at me in horror.

"But she's just a teenager, so she isn't ready. Still, the adult males can be pretty aggressive toward young females," I explain.

"What is it with males anyway?" Hayley clicks her tongue, turning her palms upward in a gesture of disbelief and disdain.

"Right?" I say in a tone of agreement. "It's the same all over the world."

"I've actually met a few like that myself," she mumbles in a low, confidential tone.

"Who hasn't?" I ask as we both laugh.

"Oh, the poor thing." Hayley groans sympathetically. "Well, I fed her sugar water all afternoon like you said. I'm sorry about bringing her so late but we just wrapped up an hour ago and I'm leaving for Italy tomorrow morning."

"Don't worry, this isn't late." I set Pepper on a faux nest in the ICU, but she hops off and begins buzzing around the bottom of the incubator in a circle. I must betray my disappointment because Hayley glances at me in alarm.

"What's wrong?"

"Her right wing. See how it's not rotating as high as the left?"

"Yeah." Hayley nods. "Is that bad?"

I don't want to say what I'm thinking. I never do in cases like this. Because a broken wing is the saddest thing. For a hummingbird, it's the end. With larger birds, particularly hawks and owls, broken wings can often be surgically pinned and will heal over time. But a hummingbird's light bones and complex shoulder joints fracture easily. And they cannot be put back together again. Nobody wants to hear this. Still, I try to aim for honesty because a lot of finders call weeks, sometimes months, after dropping off a bird to check on its progress.

"She has a chance." I turn to Hayley, who is already starting to tear up. "I'll give her time."

"What happens if she can't fly again?" she asks anxiously.

I look at Pepper in silence, trying to find the right words to deliver such hard news. But Hayley reaches the grim conclusion on her own.

"She just looks so perfect." She glances at me pleadingly.

"It's way too early to give up," I say encouragingly as I hand her a tissue from my Kleenex pile. "These little guys can really surprise you sometimes." *In a lot of terrifying ways,* I think.

"Thank you, Terry." Hayley embraces me before pulling back self-consciously. "I don't know what I would have done without you to take her. At least I know she's getting the best care, even if . . ." She trails off.

"I'll do everything I can. But it may be some time before I know for sure."

Hayley nods bravely. "Can I call you?" She sniffles.

"Well, I'm not going to Italy. For a while." I motion to the collection of nestlings in the ICU whose number has climbed to fifteen in the past two weeks. Hayley laughs and then thanks me again and hurries off into the night.

After she leaves, I lift Pepper out of the ICU and set her on a low perch in a starter cage. Pepper doesn't head for the feeder the way Gabriel did. And unlike Gabriel, she doesn't sit calmly on the perch. Instead, she flaps around in agitation, and I can tell by the strained look in her eyes that she's in pain. Each time I return her to the perch, she hops off and tries to spin her wings. As she scuttles around the bottom of the cage in a circle, her rotation does not appear as limited as a broken wing. In fact, Pepper's damaged wing tucks flush against her body when I place her on the perch. And although the rotation of her right wing is considerably slower, the range of motion is only slightly lower than the left. Although I have seen hummingbirds just like this that never recovered even after weeks of therapy, it gives me hope.

As I watch Pepper flop around in the cage, I contemplate the wonder of the hummingbird's wing, a miracle of micro-engineering that separates it from everything else on the planet. Other birds have wing bones that resemble those of the human arm: a long bone, or humerus, connected to two "forearm" bones attached to "finger" bones that have welded together into the manus, from which the feathers extend. The hummingbird's wing, in contrast, has a truncated humerus and forearm bones and consists mainly of finger bones to which the feathers are attached. The wing rotates off a shortened humerus bone, which points down toward the tail and functions like a drive shaft. Most birds can morph, or bend and change, the angle of their wings while flying, but hummingbirds have stiff wings that enable them to hover for extended periods.

Because of their capacity to brake in midair, hummingbirds inhabit a rich evolutionary niche between insects and birds. To secure this special place in the natural matrix, hummingbirds have developed aerodynamics similar to the high-frequency wing motion displayed by insects. Flying insects have nearly flat wings that travel in a figure-eight pattern, enabling them to gain altitude by using two half-strokes that produce equal lift during the downward and upward motions. When hunting in flight, hummingbirds exhibit the same agile mobility as dragonflies because they have a similar wing motion. But just as their unique wing beat distinguishes them from other birds, the hummingbird's avian body and wing structure prevent them from flying exactly like insects.

Over the last several years, technology has advanced enough for zoologists to transition from decades of educated guessing to verifiable scientific conclusions in their efforts to unravel the fascinating dynamics of the hummingbird wing. Using digital particle image velocimetry — which atomizes a fluid into microscopic droplets that are then illuminated with a pulsating laser as they move through the air while being captured by digital cameras — zoologists have been able to deconstruct the elements of hummingbird flight into comprehensible parts.

While other birds produce lift with the downstroke, the hummingbird's ball-and-socket shoulder joints allow the wings to swivel 180 degrees. This flexibility gives hummingbirds — who generate 75 percent of their lift on the forward, or downward, stroke and 25 percent on the back, or upward, stroke — the unmatched advantage of being able to remain stationary in midair for long periods. Adding to their brilliance, hummingbirds invert their wings on the backstroke, curling the leading edges upside down to gain lift. By inverting the inner edge of the wings, hummingbirds scoop air in the same way humans can get a slight lift with an upstroke under-water. And by rapidly spinning their wings in the same figure-eight pattern as insects, hummingbirds generate the high-wattage flight power necessary for sustained hovering, giving them access to nec-tar-laden flowers unavailable to other birds.

But sometimes a creature's greatest strength can also be its greatest vulnerability. And for all of the remarkable maneuver-ability the complex wing structure affords the hummingbird, it is also an Achilles' heel that makes the bird highly susceptible to in-jury. While we cannot determine whether hummingbirds are more prone to wing injuries than other birds or if they just seem that way because adoring humans choose to rescue many of them, broken wings account for a large percentage of the calls coming in to rehab.

After years of admiring hummingbirds' surreal flight capaci-ties, I contacted Douglas Altshuler, a professor of zoology at the University of British Columbia who has spent a dozen years study-ing all things hummingbird. Professor Altshuler measures power output by attaching a rubber harness to a hummingbird and film-ing it as it lifts a string with small weights in the form of color-coded beads. Through extensive research, Altshuler has discovered, among other fascinating things, that hummingbirds possess the highest mass-specific power of all birds. Simply put, a humming-bird's power output relative to its size is greater than any other bird's on the planet, including the mighty albatross that, with its ten- to twelve-foot wingspan, can fly thousands of miles without landing, brave formidable ocean winds, and circle the globe in less than two months.

Altshuler's studies also reveal that hummingbirds with shorter wings and higher wing-beat frequency have a competitive edge at lower elevations. Rufous hummingbirds normally flap their wings at a mind-bending sixty times per second, giving them superior burst power. As astonishing as that seems, smaller species like the gorgeted woodstar in Venezuela and the Esmeraldas woodstar in Ecuador have been filmed spinning their wings over one hundred and twenty times per second for short periods. This supernatural quickness allows them to execute vertical motion and gain advantage in battle by flying above bigger birds. It also explains how a diminutive rufous like Chucky is able to dominate larger, longer-winged Anna's in low-lying regions like the Los Angeles Basin. But once hummingbirds move to higher elevations, the laws of physics prevail, and the rufous loses his advantage for the same reasons helicopters strain above certain altitudes: decreased oxygen leads to a loss of engine power and lower air density limits rotor lift. Above several thousand feet, the rufous surrenders his dominance over larger Anna's and broad-tailed competitors as he struggles with decreased muscle-contraction frequency and less lift. In other words, when hummingbirds head for the hills, size matters, and Chucky is no longer king of the mountain.

Since a substantial hummingbird population lives and nests in Pasadena, several professors from Cal Tech have consulted me over the years. They all speak like textbooks. The academic formality of the messages they leave on my voicemail kills me. They start out saying something like "Based on my preliminary investigations, I calculate the fledgling's approximate age to be . . . ," or "In researching the nutritional requirements and regional food availability, I have concluded that . . . ," and so forth. I love chatting with these large-brained scholars. I plunge right into their high-flying diction, throwing out phrases like *relative power output required for ascension* and *aerodynamic limitations based on oxygen availability.* My cerebral bird fans eat this stuff up.

A young research engineer from Cal Tech who called me about a fledgling some students found grounded on campus excitedly pointed out that the motion of the hummingbird's wingtips produced the infinity symbol. He and a colleague filmed the fledgling in flight and then viewed the footage in slow motion. Of course, this investigation had already been conducted by zoologists who specialize in avian flight, but the temptation to analyze the details of a hummingbird's poetry in motion proved irresistible to a couple of high-domed professors stuck in a cramped computer lab all day.

"Her wing-beat frequency is unparalleled. And we're in awe of her maneuverability," the professor marveled.

"So what do you think?" I asked. "Can you replicate her wing movement to design some cutting-edge, high-tech aircraft?"

"That's what we were hoping at first," he answered pensively. "But after reviewing the footage in slow motion"— the professor sighed with resignation —"we realized we're not even close."

"They are amazing, aren't they?"

"Unsurpassed flight ability," he agreed. "She's so far beyond anything I have ever seen."

"And she's just a beginner," I point out. "Get her to me so she can learn to execute more advanced maneuvers that will really blow you away."

Hummingbirds' unique wing design enables these flying acrobats to hover, do straight verticals, barrel-roll and somersault, rotate 360 degrees in midair, and accelerate from zero to sixty in a few seconds on a dive. When going about their daily rituals of feeding and sparring, hummingbirds can fly backwards, sideways, and upside down. Because they love fast-moving food, this diversity of motion is necessary for catching fruit flies that have perfected their own quick-escape strategies. Equally important, hummingbirds' aerial gymnastics are crucial for them to be able to feed on flowers swaying unpredictably in the wind.

Fledglings in rehab commence practicing sophisticated flight maneuvers their first or second day in the starter cage. Beginners start by flying slowly back and forth between plastic-coated wire perches mounted eight inches apart. Within a few days of taking flight, most execute their first slow and deliberate 360-degree turn midway between perches. Their combined look of concentration and delight at pulling off this astonishing feat is enough to make anybody cry. Oddly, when beginning fledglings hear me applauding their success, they seem motivated to repeat the miracle. Some fly back and forth over and over, deliberately completing one rotation after another until I stop encouraging them.

After being moved to a larger, two-by-three-foot flight cage a week later, fledglings learn to execute successive midair spins while covering the two-and-a-half-foot distance from one perch to the other. At this point, many stop responding to my encouragement, as if their sublime magic is old news and they cannot be bothered to further impress me. But there are always a precious few who have connected emotionally and will continue to indulge me by repeating their aerial ballet back and forth across the cage until they get exhausted or I walk away.

By the time they graduate to the outdoor aviary a few weeks later, they have become expert spinners who can perform countless rotations in midair. For some inexplicable reason, young adults in the aviary like to place the tips of their bills on the flat bottom of a bolt that fastens the roof of the aviary to its metal peak and then rotate rapidly, like a top spinning in the air. Some are so adept at this maneuver they can continue rotating for over a minute. Others hang upside down on their perches while mining flowers I have gathered from around the neighborhood. Once their bodies are completely inverted, they let go of the perch and somersault in midair. Since I position the flowers so they can comfortably be eaten from the perch below, this exercise strikes me as entirely superfluous. I have no idea why young hummingbirds engage in such elaborate gymnastics, other than to sharpen their skills and amuse themselves with their newly discovered acrobatic talents.

Although most hummingbirds weigh less than a nickel, the speed and agility afforded them by their extraordinary wings give them admirable fearlessness in the wild. Because of their small size and unrivaled quickness, Southern California hummingbirds have few natural predators once they get out of the nest. While fledglings and young adults are not so bold, I sometimes see mature males harassing hawks and other predatory birds that dare enter their high-speed airspace.

When it comes to intimidation tactics, what hummingbirds lack in size, they make up for in attitude. Recent research indicates that hummingbirds have descended from fierce, six-hundred-pound carnivorous theropods that roamed the planet 220 million years ago. Over the ensuing fifty million years, these dinosaurs began shrinking rapidly, until they evolved into the first birds around 160 million years ago. So despite having radically downsized from their prehistoric origins, hummingbirds seem to have retained their giant ferocity and continue to act as if they still rule the earth.

Several years ago, a raptor rehabber riding her horse along the Southern California foothills described seeing a red-tailed hawk being chased by a crow that was being tailed by a mockingbird, and, to her astonishment, a determined hummingbird brought up the rear like a border collie herding the whole bunch out of his territory. Hummingbirds' inclination to take on creatures one hundred times their size is the key to their survival. Without their oversize aggression, these mini-flyweights would not stand a chance of defending their airspace against larger birds in the wild.

More than once from my patio in West Hollywood I have seen two or three hummingbirds banding together to assail a Cooper's hawk that sits on the power lines above the garage waiting for mourning doves to fly down for birdseed. While the hawk tolerates the harassment for a while, the hummingbirds' persistent irritation, like blowflies buzzing around your head, invariably drives the raptor away in search of peace.

Watching Pepper spin around on the bottom of her cage that night, I think of all the fantastic feats she has already accomplished during her short time in the wild. Before she landed in my garage, this broken teen could hover, spin, fly backward, do a straight vertical, spiral hundreds of feet into the air, and buzz short distances between blossoms in the park at twenty miles per hour. And now, only a few months out of the nest, she ends up here, grounded and powerless. Young hummingbirds like Pepper who have lost everything at such an early age hit me hard, even after all of the tragedies I have seen in rehab. Their memory of flight and overpowering desire to float freely again drive every fiber of their being and make me want desperately to help. Finally, Pepper stops thrashing around. Out of breath and panting, she stares up at me in terror at the recognition of her helpless condition. And I am determined to do everything I can to give her back her wings.

CHAPTER 15

Hang On in There Baby

ALMOST EVERY WAITER, dentist, hairstylist, and real estate agent in Los Angeles harbors some desire of landing an acting, screenwriting, film-directing, or other high-profile industry gig. There are a million hopeful stories out there in the naked city. And like many aspiring stars and wannabes whose dreams are cut short by the unforgiving nature of reality, a lot of Hollywood hummingbirds end up in rehab when things don't go as planned. Because of the dizzying number of rescues Southern California facilities take in, the rehab process has by necessity become increasingly streamlined after years of fine-tuning by committed gurus like Helen and Jean. As a result, apart from injured adults, nearly every hummingbird that enters rehab goes through the same educational process.

Ninety percent of rescued hummingbirds arrive young enough to go straight into a nest in the ICU, which serves as a nursery for nestlings and pre-fledglings. At this point, resident birds have no responsibilities. They are placed in a nest in an 85-degree incubator with dozens of helpless victims just like themselves. Babies at this stage range from day-old hatchlings to grounded fledglings who have lost contact with their mothers. Since babies in the ICU eat constantly, the consequences are predictable. In nature, nestlings rise up and shoot waste several inches over the side of the nest with the high-pressure stream of bathtub fish squirts. In the ICU, which is lined with paper towels, everything hits the back glass and runs to the bottom like raw eggs being thrown against a wall. So the ICU has to be cleaned several times a day. This is not an entirely unpleasant task in and of itself. Setting the plastic salsa cups overflowing with multicolored babies of all ages and species on the counter while polishing the glass walls inside the ICU can be a surreal and entertaining experience. It's the fifty other thankless, lonely tasks that slowly grind down the long-distance rehabber.

At least once a week, I end up at the hardware store stocking up on the raft of supplies developing hummingbirds require during their six- to eight-week stints in rehab. Accessories include electrical wire and dowel rods for perches; nails and staples to reattach caging; syringes; plastic feeders; springs to anchor feeders; plastic-coated wires for suspending sugar feeders; various sizes of measuring spoons, cups, and mixing containers; plastic salsa cups for nests and bathtubs; river rocks; paper towels, Kleenex, and Q-Tips; and, from the nursery around the corner, plants, plants, and more flowering plants.

Each day dozens of feeders have to be filled every three hours and washed at night. In addition to this labor-intensive task, formula has to be mixed, perches wiped down, plants trimmed and watered, bathtubs cleaned and filled, outdoor sugar feeders kept impeccably clean, and empty cages scrubbed and repaired as maturing birds move up through the ranks.

Rehabbers both eagerly anticipate and dread release days. The exhilaration of watching twenty sparkling hummingbirds spiral hundreds of feet into a brilliant blue sky on their first foray into the wild is unsurpassed. Young hummingbirds' delight upon experiencing their newfound freedom is spectacular, inspirational, and eternal. It takes my breath away, no matter how many times I see it. The rehabber's spirit soars alongside these celestial lights as they sail into the upper reaches, testing the limits of their newly discovered powers. These moments of unrivaled joy make all of the agony and hard work during their two months in rehab more than worth it.

But as with all things, there is duality. And as my shining angels spiral into the heavens, they leave a filthy aviary behind, which I spend the next hour scrubbing and hosing down in the blistering sun. Once the aviary is clean, I am faced with scouring twenty poop-encrusted cages as everybody else moves up a level to new challenges and accommodations. Each pair of fledglings in starter cages has to be transferred to a larger flight cage, where they are assigned two new cage mates. At the same time, experienced fledglings in large flight cages move into the aviary with anywhere from five to twenty young adults. Invariably, fights break out, as some birds decide it's easier to murder an irritating new cage mate than to live with him for the next two weeks. So a measure of reshuffling is always necessary. On top of all this, I juggle the tasks of monitoring injured birds like Gabriel and Pepper, who are housed separately, feeding the ICU bobble-heads every thirty minutes, and, most dauntingly, answering a cell phone that never stops ringing from April to August as a steady stream of emergency rescues continues to pour in through the front gate.

Because of the high volume of intakes, Southern California hummingbird rehabbers have invented an insider's nomenclature for quick reference when identifying the ages of young birds coming in. For the rehabber about to receive a new patient, knowing which crisis to expect facilitates preparation. At the same time, each designation carries its own special set of associations and emotions.

Naked babies refers to the newly hatched, from one to three days old. They are usually the casualties of a mother's abandonment or fatal injury and consequently arrive in their original nests. These thumbnail-size black beetles have just hatched from a white egg the size of a Jelly Belly and resemble baby dinosaurs. Their prehistoric features lend credence to the theory that ontogeny recapitulates phylogeny, meaning that the development of an individual organism reflects its species' evolutionary history. Featherless and blind, naked babies have lumpy, oversize heads and two lines of scraggly yellow hairs sprouting from their backs. They strike fear into even the most (especially the most) seasoned rehabbers. Just the sight of a naked baby in a photo elicits an instant and terrified response in hummingbird rehabbers. A naked baby is like a romance that ended badly; the mere mention of its name starts the heartache all over again. Because of their ridiculously tiny triangular bills and mouths, these mini-insectoids are almost impossible to feed without the aid of magnification. Even with it, they are still almost impossible to feed. I use high-powered telescopic surgical loupes sent to me by my sister, an orthopedic surgeon who had them custom made for microsurgery. Being able to see naked babies more clearly does not save the day, however, because unless their mother has fed them at least once or twice, they refuse food and usually die within a few days of arriving. But before they pass away, they murder their rescuers first, as we stress over them day and night in a futile effort to get their microscopic engines running.

Naked babies don't eat much their first few days out of the egg, and they cannot generate their own body heat. Even in a 95-degree ICU, most feel as cold as ice. The survival rate for naked babies deprived of their mothers is so dismal that state-run rehab centers won't even let them through the door. Nobody knows why naked babies never fed by their mother seldom make it. Some rehabbers speculate that the chicks receive enzymes from the mother that are crucial for digestion. As with some human babies born prematurely, when naked babies die, we record the reason for their demise as "failure to thrive." Naked babies that rally and miraculously come to life have to be fed every thirty minutes, beginning at five thirty a.m. and continuing until eight p.m. — or from dawn until dark — every day for three weeks. Helping those precious few survive and make it to adulthood and release is one of the most rewarding achievements a rehabber will ever experience.

Nestlings at the next stage of development, affectionately termed *dinofuzz*, are four to seven days old and featherless except for stringy, soft down that resembles the light tufts recently discovered on some dinosaur fossils. Dinofuzz arrivals are nearly always the victims of tree and bush trimming, so they too come with their original nests. Initially, dinofuzz babies can be resistant and difficult to feed, but if they hang in there through the first night in rehab, their survival is pretty much a sure thing. Once they get on their frenzied eating schedule, dinofuzz babies morph almost overnight into *bobble-heads*, a designation that requires no explanation.

Bobble-heads grow so rapidly you can see their progress from one day to the next. Although their eyes are still mostly closed except for tiny slits, bobble-heads pop up in their nests every time they hear me touch the ICU, and then they swing their heads wildly in the air, like flags flying in the wind, signaling their bottomless desire for food. The greatest challenge with bobble-heads lies in timing their gyrations with enough accuracy to pop an angiocath into each tiny gaping mouth as it swings by. In nature, the mother drives her long bill with rapid-fire precision into each baby's throat, disgorging a slurry of nectar and insects into the crop. Mimicking this behavior, a rehabber carefully aims the long-tipped angio toward the right side of the chick's gaping mouth and shoots formula into the crop to avoid causing the chick to aspirate the sugar water into its lungs, a fatal error amateur finders sometimes make. The rehabber's first experience executing the delicate feeding procedure with a fast-moving bobble-head remains unforgettable. Bobble-heads have to be fed every thirty minutes, but they are content to eat anytime.

After a few days of exponential growth, bobble-heads enter the *pinfeathered* stage, which lasts from ten to fifteen days of age. At this point, the chicks' mostly opened eyes mechanically follow everything the rehabber does. Pinfeathered babies are covered with long filaments running in slender rows down their heads and backs that make them appear snow-white. These quills begin to pop open on their backs, and within a few days they burst into technicolor feathers. When the filaments first begin to unfold, they look like long boat oars with paddle-shaped feathers sprouting on the ends. Nestlings at this stage scratch their heads and necks furiously with their sharp little toenails to help unsheathe their emerging plumage.

This unfolding advances chicks to the *feather-duster* stage, in which fluffy and multicolored new feathers erupt all over their bodies, making them arguably the cutest things on the planet. Feather-duster nestlings, who have stronger necks and can see me coming the second I enter the room, display more dignity than bobble-heads and are easy to feed. If they have been in rehab for a while, they perceive me as their incredibly gigantic mother and respond to my presence by requesting food with resounding *peeps* and gaping mouths every time I approach the ICU. They eat every thirty minutes.

After three weeks, once their feathers have unfurled completely, pre-fledglings begin to resemble adult hummingbirds, although their bills and tails are considerably shorter. A feathered nestling has a line of bare pink skin running down the sternum that often is mistaken by finders for an injury. The breastbone and belly are the last places young hummingbirds' feathers come in, since these parts of the body are tucked into a warm and well-insulated nest. At this stage, nestlings show an increasing restlessness that leads them to become highly mobile in the ICU, crawling like toddlers between nests, piling on top of one another, and sitting on the younger babies, who are subsequently immobilized. Feathered nestlings also spend a lot of time perched on the sides of their plastic-salsa-cup nests rapidly spinning their wings. The future is calling. Then suddenly, between twenty-four and twenty-eight days old, they magically airlift out of the nest just after breakfast and begin buzzing around like bumblebees inside the ICU.

Once they get airborne, fledglings are moved into a starter cage. Starter cages are one-foot-tall, eighteen-inch-long wood-framed structures enclosed by wire mesh. Two sets of dowel perches are positioned at each end of the cage, at two inches and eight inches from the bottom. Tiered perches allow those fledglings who have trouble achieving vertical flight, as many do, to start flying low. Two 12 cc plastic syringes painted with attention-grabbing red nail polish are anchored at both ends of the cage above the perches for easy access. Most fledglings learn to self-feed after a day or two of being directed to a syringe every thirty minutes by their patient rehabber. About 10 percent refuse to feed themselves, preferring to badger their caretaker with loud and nonstop crying. After two or three days, virtually all starter-cage fledglings know how to self-feed, though some stubbornly continue to demand personalized food service.

Upon entering a starter cage, each fledgling is assigned one or two cage mates that he may or may not be fond of in the future. Criteria for selecting cage mates include similarities in age, size, mental development, and levels of aggression. In general, there is little contention between fledglings at this level, as everyone is focused on acquiring basic skills such as perching, flying forward and in reverse, spinning in midair, and self-feeding. The youngest fledglings usually like one another a great deal, poke each other gently in the chest with their bills when sitting side by side on their perches, and snuggle close together when sleeping at night. But even at this tender age, a few antisocial firebrands refuse to coexist with other birds and prefer to throttle their cage mates ruthlessly. Such offenders usually can be cured of their aggressive tendencies by being paired with either an entirely nonconfrontational introvert who lets them assert their egomaniacal need for dominance or a self-possessed and more experienced veteran who won't put up with it.

The rare hummingbird that cannot be socialized is caged separately through his short stay in rehab. Once he has mastered basic skills, I happily grant him his independence. Of the several hundred hummingbirds that have come through my rehab facility over the years, I have encountered only half a dozen birds that fit the profile of the irredeemable social menace. And all have been, without exception, young males.

Once fledglings can sleep through at least seven consecutive nights in a starter cage without falling off their high perches, they are promoted to a large flight cage. A certain number of birds get held up at this point because they slip off their perches in the middle of the night and are crying on the bottom of the cage when I come out to feed them at dawn. Some birds enter rehab with one or two claws torn off by finders who unknowingly placed them on cotton towels with loops in the fabric. Hummingbirds' claws get hooked on the loops and tear out when people lift the young birds off the towel. Like having your toenails pulled out, this experience is terrifically painful for the bird. Missing claws also make perching through the night a greater challenge. Eventually these fledglings learn to compensate for their disability, but some take up to two weeks to get strong enough to remain on a perch for ten-hour stretches. Toenails that have been torn out never grow back and can reduce a hummingbird's chances of survival in the wild, so rehabbers are forever alerting finders to this threat.

The transition to a large flight cage presents new challenges and affords greater opportunities. Large flight cages stand two feet tall and three feet long, are enclosed with chicken wire so the maturing birds can easily see out, and have a single set of high perches mounted at each end. By the time fledglings reach this level, at five to six weeks of age, they can fly forward and backward without effort, rotate gracefully in midair, and hover for respectable lengths of time. Each bird remains with the same fledgling she started out with and joins one or two others vetted for compatibility and who possess equally adept aerial skills. Birds that falter at this point by straining to fly between perches, drifting to the bottom of the cage, or suffering excessive abuse from their cage mates return to a small flight cage with a younger bird for another week. Fledglings in large flight cages have a roomy plastic-cup bathtub filled with river rocks, a potted flowering plant from which to mine nectar, and fresh flowers when I have time to raid local gardens.

During the months that I don't have to teach classes in the morning, I gather fresh flowers for the fledglings in large flight cages and young adults in the aviary. All the residents of my neighborhood know what I'm up to when they see me coming, and they take the time to direct me to their latest blossoms. Neighbors have been inspired by the abundance of hummingbirds released in the area. A young man who lives two doors down from us spends all day photographing hummingbirds at his feeder while he conducts marketing research over the phone. The couple next door to him keep ten feeders running year-round to accommodate the grow- ing number of sugar addicts frequenting the vicinity. My neigh- bors across the street describe how they sit for hours and watch young birds playing in the fountain in their courtyard every morn- ing. And a new couple who just moved in next door to them began planting hummingbird-friendly flowers and bushes the minute they got wind of our rehab center.

When Frank and I first moved into West Hollywood, twenty years ago, it took me three months to attract one hummingbird to my feeder. Now, with the explosion in the local population that has resulted from over five hundred releases and their progeny, new sugar feeders immediately draw dozens of interested birds. With their growing ubiquity since the dawn of rehab in the vicinity, hummingbirds have become the pride of West Hollywood neigh- borhoods, so much so that the National Wildlife Federation has designated a local park and hotel as sanctuaries.

Because they spend so much of their time buzzing back and forth and hovering between perches, birds in large flight cages eat like teenage boys. In the case of a cage housing four Allen's fledg- lings, I fill two 12 cc syringes with formula every three hours, or five times a day. Cages containing three or four birds of a larger species, such as Anna's, may consume twice that.

The first day with new cage mates can be edgy, but after some reassignments, social relations in the large flight cages tend to run smoothly for a few weeks, until an inescapable boredom and im- patience overcomes the growing young adults. At this juncture, rapidly maturing residents are busy honing advanced skills in preparation for the simulated wild of the outdoor aviary. Spending two weeks in a large flight cage is critical for older fledglings' physical growth, developing flight skills, and psychological maturity.

With the exception of a few forces of nature like Chucky, young birds that look strong and self-assured in their large flight cage appear slow and terrified the first day they move up to the aviary. The minute they encounter unknown birds in a strange and large environment, all of their weaknesses and insecurities come out. Older and more experienced birds, even the smallest females, can easily dominate new arrivals in the aviary, who fumble around apprehensively and avoid confrontation by heading for cover like freshmen on their first day in high school.

Once in the aviary, young adults learn all of the advanced skills necessary to survive in the wild. An eight-foot-high, ten-by-ten-foot walk-in octagon with a security door, the aviary has galvanized wire siding, dowel perches mounted all around, and a long plastic-coated perching wire extending across the diameter. Several large cylindrical feeders are positioned five feet high around the octagon and secured to the aviary bars by metal springs for quick release. A raised stone birdbath containing plastic bathtubs filled with river rocks stands in the corner. Rotten bananas in a shallow container under a potted six-foot-tall ficus tree draw thousands of fruit flies every day. Aviary cohorts range from four or five birds in the slower months of late winter to twenty or more by peak season in early July.

As evidenced by Chucky and his four cage mates, social tension is more likely to erupt into physical altercation when aviary numbers are small. Although it seems counterintuitive—and here, as Lao Tzu reminds me, the truth often seems paradoxical—single-digit cohorts suffer more dangerous bullying than larger groups. Because of a phenomenon known as critical mass, the more birds residing in the aviary, the harder it is for one or two to dominate, so larger groups experience less violent aggression. Naturally, exceptions to this rule can arise, as I would soon learn.

During their first few nights sleeping outside in the aviary, young hummingbirds crowd closely together on an electrical-wire perch twisted into a six-inch-diameter circle and extended from the center of the roof. After all of their fighting and self-important posturing during the daylight hours, insecure young birds huddle tightly together for warmth and security against the cold and danger of the night. Just as hummingbird adults in the wild obey the law of the jungle and transition from Hobbesian warfare to sharing their sugar feeders on cold, rainy nights, young adults in the aviary seem to recognize that in the face of darkness and the unknown, they are in it together.

After a few evenings of forming a circle for protection, the budding adults move, one by one, from the wire perch into the ficus tree to sleep. Some continue to sleep side by side in the tree every night until their release. The soon-to-be lone wolves perch together on a branch, resting against one another in what will be their final days of close companionship.

When I enter the aviary on nights with a full moon, the birds, scattered in pairs throughout the ficus tree, glow like Christmas tree ornaments in the bright moonlight, just as they had in my dream two years earlier, before I owned an aviary or had seen hummingbirds sleeping in the dark. When I look at them from behind, the hummingbirds' green, oval-shaped backs appear identical both in form and color to the leaves on the tree, making them perfectly camouflaged as they sleep. How do they know this? I gaze at their transcendent beauty in quiet admiration, wondering at all the mysteries they possess that I will never understand. And I take comfort in my recognition of the boundless and unknown world that they inhabit, free from the limited, logical restrictions by which human life is so often enslaved.

After two months of eating, sleeping, growing, and learning the habits of a wild hummingbird within the safe confines of their manmade fortifications, rehabilitated young adults have mastered the skills necessary to make it on their own. And this confidence prompts maturing birds to turn their attention to the outside world and all of the exciting possibilities it holds for them.

With the birds' entry into adulthood, iridescent patches of magenta on the Anna's, tangerine on the Allen's, scarlet on the rufous, and purple on the black-chinned begin appearing on the males' throats. While they are completing their higher education, birds in rehab fill up their fast-paced days catching fruit flies, drinking quarts of formula, mining colorful bouquets of local flowers, splashing around in their bathtubs, chasing each other in blurred circles, and eyeing the wild birds on the other side of the bars with a mix of fear and fascination. Gradually, the bold recruits begin mirroring their wild counterparts by confidently parading their skills close to the bars that separate them from life on the outside. Observing my free spirits from inside the aviary, I detect the fire in their eyes that reveals their yearning to take on a larger life.

Finally, on a clear and cloudless day, I open the doors, granting my reclaimed treasures the freedom to fly home to the natural world from which they came. And as they drift out through the doors with cautious enthusiasm and make their transition back to the urban jungle into which they were born, they go with the unspoken assurance that I will be there to catch them if they fall.

CHAPTER 16

And the Healing Has Begun

IN THE FOUR WEEKS between Gabriel's and Pepper's dangerous encounters with the opposite sex, twenty young hummingbirds have come into rescue. By the time Pepper appears, in early May, I have taken in sixty birds; eight have been released, forty are still moving through the rehab pipeline, and twelve, despite my best efforts, could not be saved. The twenty that have come in since Gabriel's soggy arrival include a fledgling whose tail feathers were accidentally pulled out when he attempted to escape the grasp of a young jogger who picked him up in a park, a juvenile who'd been trapped and flying laps inside a Studio City apartment hallway, a nestling heard peeping under a car's windshield wiper when the finder got home from work, two nests of twins cut by gardeners preparing for house painting, a nest of wind-chime hatchlings abandoned by their mother during a powerful Santa Ana windstorm, and two unscathed nestlings brought home by cats, one by an Abyssinian whose owner was quite proud of his pet's gentle handling, and the other by an aged and toothless cat who, according to his doting guardian, had rescued grounded chicks in the past. The remainder of intakes consists of young birds discovered on canyon trails, city sidewalks, high-rise stairwells, and the classic Southern California scenario: floating in swimming pools.

When it comes to their approach toward hummingbirds, cats fall solidly into two camps. The first and most typical are the natural-born killers: cats that catch, maim, and dismember birds with savage abandon. The second, not as common but surprisingly frequent, are the search-and-rescue cats that locate young birds grounded by inclement weather and then gently transport them back to their owners. About half of the cat-caught hummingbirds that make it to rescue die overnight because the bacteria in a cat's saliva infects a bird's bloodstream like poison. If a cat-caught hummingbird's skin has not been punctured and he makes it through the first night of rehab, he's on the road to recovery. Interestingly, most dog-"found" birds ("found" because only an exceptional dog can catch a healthy hummingbird) that come into rescue survive and are successfully rehabbed because humans have, over tens of thousands of years, bred and trained our canine companions to retrieve with a soft mouth.

The morning after Hayley drops off Pepper, I set the tragic beauty outside in the sun for light and encouragement. Sitting quietly on her low perch, Pepper has a slender, delicate profile, with the Anna's characteristic shimmering green back, smooth silver chest feathers, and exotic black eyeliner like ancient Egyptian royalty. When I kneel in front of her cage to examine her in the sunlight, the source of her disability reveals itself. Across the right side of her breast is a thin, one-inch gash where the feathers have been sheared off as if with a razor. This cut is where Pepper came into contact with the metal edge of the chafing dish.

Hummingbirds have large pectoral muscles that power their wing strokes. Soft-tissue injuries can impair flight, and in nature, when wings do not rotate fully, it's a quick end. Remarkably, rehabbers have nearly a 100 percent success rate saving birds with this type of wound. But because the damage sustained by hummingbirds with chest injuries is often serious, the healing process takes time. Fortunately for Pepper, the nesting season runs another three months, so time is something I have plenty of.

The first hummingbird that came in with a chest wound similar to Pepper's puzzled me because he could fly forward between low perches in a starter cage but could not get any lift. The newly fledged Anna's, who arrived unconscious and in torpor, had been found under a jungle gym by a three-year-old boy named Brad. By the time Brad and his dad arrived with the bird, on a brisk afternoon in late March, the young father was certain his son's remarkable discovery was dead.

"I'm afraid we're too late." He grimaced after handing the silver-and-green fledgling over to me wrapped in a child's T-shirt as the not-quite-yardstick-tall Brad disappeared behind his father's legs in silent terror.

Cradling the inert bird lightly in my hand, I could feel an almost imperceptible vibration. "No, he's still alive," I assured him as bashful Brad peeked one wide blue eye out hopefully. "What do you think happened to him?"

"I'm not sure"— Brad's father shook his head —"but there were a lot of noisy crows in the yard a couple of hours before my son found him this morning."

"Ah, being at the bottom of the food chain is one of those unfortunate realities for young hummingbirds."

"Can you save him?" he asked anxiously.

"Yeah, I think I can," I said before glancing down at Brad, who immediately retreated back into his nook like a frightened mouse.

"Is it okay if we stay a few minutes?" His father looked at me uncertainly.

"I'm pretty sure I can save him," I said cautiously as I locked eyes with the father, "but I can't be certain, if that's okay."

"Yeah, we'll chance it." He nodded uneasily.

"All right," I agreed as I went to work warming and force-feeding the bird. After fifteen minutes of small talk with the father and intensive rehab with the bird, the young fledgling emerged from torpor, opened his eyes, and began looking around with the usual stunned expression hummingbirds get when they awake surrounded by giants.

"Thank you, Terry." Brad's father gasped as if he had finally come up for air after holding his breath too long underwater. "You don't know how much this means. It was a *very* big deal." He cocked his head toward the hidden cherub peering out again with one enormous blue eye.

"Do we have a name for this little bird?" I asked quietly.

The father turned his head and looked down; after a pause, the blond hair shook back and forth slowly.

"Well, he's a handsome young boy," I observed, examining the dark stippling running down the fledgling's throat. "So we'll call him Brad." I smiled, prompting the tousled blond head to disappear silently into its safety zone.

By the next morning Brad could perch, self-feed, and spin one wing perfectly. But he had a deep gash on the right side of his chest, and his right wing proved stubbornly slow to heal. For two weeks Brad sat on his low perch watching me go about feeding and tending to the forty hummingbirds buzzing in the cages around him. Frustrated with his lack of progress, I developed a kind of remedial flight training in which I positioned Brad on a slender twig two inches from the high perch in his cage then lowered my hand slowly so he would rotate his wings and fly to it. Brad responded to this physical therapy with delight, dancing excitedly on his low perch whenever he saw me approaching his cage with the stick. The second I placed him on the high perch and held the stick an inch in front of him, Brad would step gingerly onto the twig and begin fluttering his wings as I raised and lowered my hand inside the cage. After a few repetitions I would hesitate just long enough for Brad to fly-hop across the gap between the twig and the perch, thus giving him the sensation of being airborne. Like adults with soft-tissue injuries, young Brad could travel only a few inches from the twig to the high perch when I first began lowering him on the stick. But each day, I widened the gap a little farther, and he achieved more lift and greater distance; after several days, without realizing it, Brad was flying again. A week later Brad moved up to a large flight cage with a pair of Anna's twins whose mother had been killed in an automobile accident.

Similar to adults with head and back injuries, damaged fledglings like Brad recover with the dogged determination of returning war veterans. Slowly and deliberately they learn to fly all over again. Most sit passively for a week or two before attempting to do anything. Then they begin the long healing process by sliding off a low perch and bouncing back and forth across the bottom of the cage. For hummingbirds, intermediate forward flight is the easiest, while hovering represents the most demanding maneuver. Once injured fledglings and adults can fly forward between low perches, they begin working their way up. And gradually, as a result of the flight therapy I invented for Brad, birds with pectoral injuries regain vertical lift, learn to pirouette in midair, and, always last, relearn that most complex and strenuous of aerial skills, hovering.

Helping seriously injured adults recover their flight capacity is even more poignant than watching nestlings fledge. Keenly aware of what they have lost, adult hummingbirds put their absolute trust in me and seem to understand that I am bringing them back from an otherwise certain death. Sometimes I notice them watching me intently as I fill feeders in the cages around them, waiting for their turn as if looking forward to flight-training exercises they cannot perform without me. When I open the side door to their cages, they begin bouncing and fluttering on their perches in eager anticipation. And day by painstaking day, they recoup everything that was so suddenly stripped away from them.

By the time Brad made it into the aviary, five weeks after his arrival, he was the perfect hummingbird. Except for one thing: he refused to leave when I released the birds from the aviary two weeks later. When I opened the doors on a glorious morning in May, as the other young adults ventured out, first cautiously, then ecstatically, into the wild, Brad looked out the side door with trepidation, flew about three feet past the threshold, hovered for a few seconds, heard crows in the distance, turned, and bolted back inside to safety. When I entered the aviary and tried to lure him out with a sugar feeder, he perched in the back of the cage as far from the doors as he could get and stared at me with wide dark eyes. A few hours later, after scrubbing the aviary while Brad watched uneasily from his high perch, I finally closed the doors and brought in a new cohort. Two weeks later, when a dozen young adults bolted to freedom, Brad went through the same routine.

"Okay, Brad," I relented after an hour of unsuccessfully attempting to persuade him out the second time. "It's up to you to go when you're ready."

While Brad was involved in his to-be-free-or-not-to-be vacillation, another curious character emerged from the rescue ranks. A week after Brad's arrival, an animal hospital in Sierra Madre sent me a broad-tailed fledgling who had sustained a slight head injury after slamming into the window of a school bus. After a few tipsy days in a head-injury cage half the size of a starter cage, the young male began flying normally, so I ran him through the customary stages of rehab. But once he got into the aviary, he also refused to leave on schedule and stayed through two cycles. The day my emboldened broad-tailed finally took the plunge into the wild, he cut an impressive figure as an unusually large, powerful hummingbird. But a few hours after his release, I came out to find the distraught young adult hanging on the outside of the aviary screaming to get back in as if he had been terrorized by some unimaginable monster. When I put my hand over him, he didn't flinch, so I closed my fingers around his back, gently slid him off the bars, and returned him to the aviary with the new cohort. At the time, I had no idea what could have terrified my broad-tailed powerhouse so thoroughly his first day out. But I sensed something bigger and scarier than Brad's croaky corvids had made him fear for his life after that initial launch. And the next morning, the suspect appeared.

At six thirty, after feeding the crowd of nestlings in the ICU, filling aviary feeders, and setting cages out on the patio, I trudged back upstairs to lie down for thirty minutes. By late spring, my internal clock is so finely tuned to thirty-minute intervals that I no longer require a watch. Awaking at seven, I glanced out the upstairs window and then did a double take. A Cooper's hawk was skulking around on the lower roof of the aviary's security cage inspecting the fifteen young adults inside. Earlier that week, I had seen this young raptor hanging around the roof of the neighbor's garage where I throw birdseed to the doves and finches in the morning. He had been arriving at dawn every morning with his mother, who was teaching him to hunt. One day I watched her herding a squirrel in circles around the roof with her wide wings while he sat absorbing the lesson from his perch on the power lines above. Now he was checking out my hummingbirds as if he had dropped in at the local sushi bar for a quick snack. I slid the upstairs window open and shouted at him to get lost, at which point he rotated his head and glared at me defiantly with steely yellow eyes as if to say, *And what are you intending to do about it?*

"Oh, it's like that, huh? Okay, then," I mumbled as I raced down the stairs. When I came charging out the door he was still perched on the security cage, but my presence interrupted his menu perusing and he turned to look at me questioningly. I approached him at a steady pace, and I was surprised he held his ground even when I got within a few yards of the aviary. Only when I was close enough to grab his spindly yellow legs did he swoosh off with a few powerful pumps of his mighty wings. Recalling a story Jean had told me about how a hungry hawk had once pulled an adult hummingbird through the bars of her flight cage, I hurried into the aviary to do a head count. When I got inside, the aviary was a dead zone, with every bird sitting stone-still on the back perch with glazed eyes. Even my appearance, which normally sent the excitable young adults buzzing around in happy circles, failed to nudge them from their frozen poses. I counted fourteen, and my heart sank when I couldn't find the broad-tailed among them. Only after searching the aviary in a heart-pounding panic did I finally locate him, buried deeply inside the lower branches of the ficus tree with an expression of absolute terror. I had identified his demon.

After his second brush with the devil, the broad-tailed remained in the aviary for another two weeks, contentedly chasing fruit flies and mining fresh lantana. Then one balmy morning in early June, he appeared unusually restive, posturing assertively at the aviary bars as if he couldn't wait to get out in the mix. The minute I opened the aviary door, he catapulted fifty feet over the house, air-braked in midflight, executed two rapid-fire spirals, rotated while scanning the horizon, hovered a few seconds to look back at me, then shot off in a blur.

The young broad-tailed's hawk, who was a hundred times his size, had provided a crash course on the menacing perils of the wild. But after taking a little more time to consider the unmatched genius of his flight skills, my intrepid warrior had faced the enemy and gone out in a blaze of speed and spirit. That same day, Brad ventured six feet out the door and pirouetted once, then decided he wasn't ready for the wild world and shot back inside to safety.

As with all birds who refuse to leave the aviary or unexpectedly return to rehab, as soon as I secured the doors and filled the cage with a dozen new young adults, Brad relaxed and went back to catching fruit flies and mining freshly cut plantain lilies and honeysuckle. Brad stayed through four cohorts, always going through the same approach-avoidance routine at the aviary door on release days. But finally, one sunny, crow-free day near the end of June, Brad the brave led the charge out the door, taking fifteen newly minted hummingbirds with him. Aside from this bold and unprecedented decision to confront his fears, Brad revealed another secret I never would have known if he had not stayed so long. During Brad's three-month stint in rehab, his dark throat feathers, instead of transforming into the iridescent magenta of a male Anna's gorget, paled to a light shade of silver. And it was then that I gleaned another possible explanation for his shyness: Brad was a girl.

"Her throat feathers were so dark when she came in. I've never been more certain a bird was a male. How is that possible?" I asked Jean after recounting Brad's remarkable story.

"Don't ask me," Jean said before offering her usual humble twist on the Socratic paradox. "The longer I do hummingbirds, the less I know about them."

The first time Jean offered this self-effacing observation in response to one of my questions, I suspected her of being disingenuous, because if ten thousand hours committed to learning something makes someone an expert, Jean was ten times an authority on hummingbirds. But with each passing year, her humble words rang truer.

My experience with Brad marked a paradigm shift in my approach to hummingbird rehabilitation. Before Brad, I had treated all birds alike, insisting they leave the aviary on release days. By the time I let them out, rehabilitated young adults were at least six weeks beyond the age fledglings in the wild were when they gained their independence. And six weeks for a hummingbird was the equivalent of a year for a human, so I didn't want the young adults to get too comfortable and fail to launch. But after Brad's game-changing revolution, I no longer held birds to a uniform release schedule. Instead, I allowed them to choose freedom on their own terms. As long as they did not become aggressive and cause trouble, I let anyone who resisted release stay on with the new cohort. And to my astonishment, at least one or two birds in every group chose to remain in the aviary for an extra two, and sometimes up to six, weeks.

After a while, I became so tuned to their body language that I could predict with nearly 100 percent accuracy which birds would stay another round. With young adults preparing for release, I can discern by their flight patterns and the look in their eyes when they are ready to go. Eager birds buzz close to the aviary bars, bouncing back and forth in midair with the rhythm of highly conditioned boxers, as if they can't wait to get out and prove themselves. Some gain so much self-confidence before they depart that they pick fights with earlier releases that hover just outside the aviary, taunting them through the bars.

Birds that opt to stay longer, however, display an odd reticence toward all that is wild, avoid hovering near the bars, and retreat to the back corner behind the ficus tree whenever internal or outside combat erupts. And despite my fears, their extended time in captivity in no way compromises their ability to thrive in the wild. On the contrary, those that choose additional rehab invariably appear stronger and more adept their second or third time around. Even more important, several of these holdovers ultimately become valuable mentor birds who seem to take pride in modeling advanced skills for the fresh recruits.

Brad's memory of her youthful trauma and its enduring impact on her adult behavior left a deep impression on me. But the motivations of another hummingbird who came in the same week proved equally compelling. At six o'clock on a Sunday morning, three days after Brad had arrived, I got a frantic call from Sonja in Beverly Hills; an adult female Anna's had gotten trapped in the skylight of an outdoor covered porch the evening before, and she had found it lying unconscious on the brick entryway that morning. The second that Sonja rushed the prone bird into my garage I began administering my usual life-restoring routine. After an hour of treatment, the bird regained consciousness enough to be placed in a starter cage outside in the sun. When I came back outside ten minutes later, the frantic female was banging erratically against the sides of the cage. Assuming she had sustained some type of head trauma, I rushed her into the garage and tried to restrain her so she would not injure her wings. But she proved inconsolable and continued slamming herself against the sides of the cage before collapsing to the bottom in exhaustion.

I had never seen such agitation in an urban hummingbird, especially one that, according to Sonja, had been eating from a backyard sugar feeder for several months. Over the years, I had seen a few birds go off like this, but they were always fierce-eyed males brought in from the sparsely populated mountains northeast of Los Angeles who had likely never encountered a human being.

This female's level of anxiety was unprecedented for a bird who had arrived unconscious. Adult hummingbirds that come in weak and battered usually relax into their five-star lodgings and seem relieved to have a day to regroup while dining in the warm sunlight at all-you-can-eat feeders. And it's my policy to keep them overnight, since a lot of birds that appear recovered during the day lapse into torpor their first night in rehab when complications from their injuries set in.

Watching the hysterical female slam herself against the mesh siding of the cage, I was terrified she might break a wing or drop dead from a heart attack. Since Sonja's house was just a ten-minute drive away, I called her at seven thirty and said I was bringing the distressed hummingbird home. Once in the car, the captive bird began flying in tight circles and banging her head madly against the top of the cage, prompting me to drift through more than one red light on the deserted Sunday-morning streets. The second I arrived at Sonja's house, I stepped out of the car and unlocked the eye hooks securing the cage's top. Before I could swing the top completely open, the bird shot out like a missile and headed straight into the branches of a fifty-foot tree a hundred yards away. Five seconds later she darted back out, then returned to the same spot a few minutes later. When Sonja retrieved a pair of binoculars from the house, I scanned the dense brush in the canyon until the lenses finally alighted on the stressed-out mother who was perched on a dangling branch in a towering eucalyptus tree hastily stuffing food into two screaming nestlings.

CHAPTER 17

What I Like About You

AS WITH A HANDFUL of college students among the thousands I've taught over the past twenty years, a few hummingbirds, like Brad, have proven unforgettable. Discovering unusual characters is one of the most rewarding aspects of rescuing hummingbirds, or any wildlife. Just when rehabbers think they have seen the full range of possibilities, an exceptional personality arrives to remind us, as Jean loves to point out, how little we understand about them after all.

One female black-chinned, named Iris by the classics professor who rescued her in the hills above Santa Barbara, changed everything I thought I knew about hummingbirds. Iris was unable to fly after being bumped out of her nest by a moving van and plunging twelve feet to a concrete driveway below. Once inside the ICU, the three-week-old Iris abandoned her Kleenex nest and took up residence sitting on a pair of ten-day-old Anna's in their original nest. Every time I came out to the garage to feed the bobble-heads, Iris would be resting calmly in the nest with a little head poking out from under each side of her chest. Occasionally, she would reach down with her bill and groom the babies or reposition them with maternal tenderness.

When she fledged, I put Iris into a starter cage with a painfully shy Allen's that had been kept too long by a woman who came across her in the backyard and thought it would be fun to let her kids raise a hummingbird. She called me a few days after bringing the nestling into the house, when it was too late to reunite it with its mother, and wanted to know what to feed her. The woman did not say it directly at the time, but whenever someone inquires about long-term dietary needs, it's a red flag, signaling he or she intends to keep the bird. So I explained to her that harboring a hummingbird is not only illegal but cruel and inhumane and that the bird would suffer and starve to death on sugar water. This information usually does it for most callers and they surrender their precious discoveries. Nobody wants to spend a week watching a hummingbird die, especially when he or she is the one killing it. But even with this strong caveat, some people can't see past themselves.

"Well, my daughter is nine and she's very intelligent for her age. So I think she can handle it," the woman pushed back smugly.

"It's not about intelligence," I said, trying to reason with her. "She has no idea what she's doing and she's not equipped to deal with this situation for ten different reasons. Hummingbirds need to be in the hands of licensed rehabilitators with years of experience."

"Well, my daughter makes her own decisions, so it's up to her."

This kind of laissez-faire parenting always pushes me over the edge. Some parents think they are doing their kids a favor by handing their own jobs over to them. While studying educational psychology in graduate school, I read volumes of research on different parenting styles, and laissez-faire was always singled out as the most disastrous method, even worse than a strict authoritarian approach, of which I'm no fan either. But given a choice between the two and their respective prospects for future dysfunction, it's no contest. I tried to imagine what it must be like in a permissive home like hers when the kid comes skipping into the kitchen and shouts, *Hey, Mom, I'm going to smoke meth and watch some hard porn on the Internet this afternoon.*

Oh, sure, honey, here's a pipe and the password. Do you need anything else?

Or how about *If I can get my hands on the right detonating device, I can blow up city hall tomorrow.*

Oh, wow, now that sounds like a challenge.

Nobody was steering the ship here. But a young hummingbird's life was at stake, so I had to try.

"It's not up to her," I shot back. "First of all, keeping a hummingbird without a permit is a violation of federal law," I reiterated. "And second, this is an adult decision, and"—news flash—"you are the adult. It's up to you to provide parental guidance, just as you would"—and here I meant "should"—"with any decision a child is not capable of making on her own, given her lack of maturity and limited understanding of the world."

"Well, my daughter will cry if she has to give up this bird."

"She's gonna cry a lot more when she has to watch it die." I hardened my tone. "Use this as an opportunity to teach her the proper care and respect for wildlife, and explain to her that someday, when she's ready, she can get into rehab"—*After going through her own*, I think—"if she chooses."

The hands-off-to-a-fault parent finally said she would call me back. A week later, when the nestling stopped eating and it all got too real, she broke down and called. Barely breathing, the fully feathered Allen's female was lying on her side, too weak to eat, the morning the mother and her three kids arrived with her in a flimsy birdcage crammed with flowers, handwritten love poems, dolls, and children's jewelry. The cramped cage was so cluttered with junk the bird couldn't have moved if she had wanted to. Not that she had enough strength to do anything after being starved on sugar water for a week.

Cases like this are among the hardest we encounter in rehab. I can see the desperation in the birds' eyes when they arrive. And when a parent allows, even encourages, her children to subject young hummingbirds to such agonizing pain and deprivation, it gets my blood boiling, because there is no excuse. It's the one thing that infuriates every rehabber. Without exception, birds kept too long by members of the public come in underweight and malnourished and are brought to us when they are shutting down. Then we get to watch them die.

"I warned you about this a week ago and now here we are. I don't know where to start with you." I shook my head in disgust as I struggled to cap my anger after her three kids wandered outside. But when I glanced up, she was staring back at me, frightened and stricken.

"No ... I ... see now," she whispered haltingly as her eyes darted back and forth between the plump, fluffy nestlings in the ICU and her dying bird encrusted with dried sugar water.

"Okay, fair enough. But make sure they get it too." I cocked my head toward the children outside. "Educating kids is an important part of what we do."

"I will." She bowed her head slightly as tears streamed down her expressionless face.

After I spent the first harrowing night force-feeding the famished bird every three hours, followed by a week of giving her intensive protein and vitamin infusions, she achieved enough lift to move into a starter cage. But the apprehensive fledgling refused to eat unless I reached in and held the syringe while gently coaxing her bill into it. Rescued hummingbirds that have been traumatized by sugar water early in life often harbor deep anxiety about eating from any human apparatus, turning away in terror from plastic syringes that resemble the eyedroppers people fed them with. Like most nestlings that recall the pain of starvation, this young female constantly sought reassurance while learning to self-feed during her first few weeks in rehab. Noticing her cage mate's need for extra attention, Iris adopted a similar disposition and also refused to eat unless I touched her syringe first. Although well aware of the location and purpose of the syringe, which she had learned to use early on in the ICU, Iris would sit on the perch beside her timorous cage mate and cry until I relented.

"You know how to do this," I chided Iris every time she made me go through the motions. At times I would resolve to force her hand. But it did not matter how long I ignored her. She wouldn't give in. After an hour, Iris would begin to fluff up her feathers and close her eyes, threatening to lapse into torpor as she continued peeping softly. Tough love wasn't going to work. She won every standoff with me.

Iris turned out to be a born teacher, and I became her first student. In the end, she finished rehab brilliantly. After graduating to the aviary, Iris refused release for over a month. Instead of heading out to the wild when the doors stood wide open, Iris put her strong nurturing instincts to work, becoming one of those rare mentor hummingbirds for the next two groups of new arrivals. With each fresh cohort, Iris taught aviary etiquette by example, modeling how to eat from new feeders, catch fruit flies, hide in the ficus tree at night, and stand up to bullies. She was especially solicitous of the smallest and most frightened underdogs in each group. Whenever she noticed a fearful bird hanging back, she alighted on the perch beside him, tapped his chest lightly with her bill, then encouraged him to join the fray by dropping down and snapping up a fruit fly.

On one occasion, early in the morning, when hummingbirds like to bathe, Iris brushed a young aviary recruit lightly on the back with her feet as she flew over before heading for the bathtubs. This is what mother hummingbirds do when prompting older nestlings to fledge. Hovering over them, the mother taps her babies with her bill or runs in place on their backs to get them up and out of the nest. When it came to nurturing the young, Iris ran far ahead of the curve.

Throughout her stay in the aviary, Iris exuded admirable confidence and self-possession. She never got in anybody's way and nobody messed with her, not even the bossiest young males. Iris had a calming influence that taught me some things about hummingbirds, and about people, too. Her need for special care early on did not mean she was weak or inferior. On the contrary, Iris displayed the most striking example of empathy I have ever seen in a hummingbird. Like several other psychologically complex birds that would come through my facility, this little future saint just needed an extra dose of compassion during her formative youth. And once granted this consideration, Iris turned the tables by nurturing timid rescues in need of the same support.

I liked everything about Iris. The morning she finally shot out the aviary door with her third cohort and original cage mate, who had stayed on with her, marked the first time I shed tears over a hummingbird from an emotion other than grief. But in her uncommon sensitivity, Iris seemed to glean that even rehabbers occasionally need emotional rescue, and the day after her release I came out to the aviary to find her perched in the bougainvillea above the redwood fence on the patio. Thrilled to see her, I greeted Iris warmly and she responded by buzzing around the sugar feeders before dancing off over the house. Iris came back to the same spot every morning until early September, at which point, being a black-chinned, the forces of nature beckoned her to Mexico for the winter. I never saw Iris again after her departure, but a young male named Blacktop who went through rehab later that summer would convince me of my rescued black-chinneds' abilities to succeed in fulfilling their long-distance destinies.

As the goddess of the rainbow in Homer's *The Iliad*, Iris flies on the wind in a flash of speed and light. Linking the sky and earth, she facilitates communication between mortals and the divine. Brought to me as a young fledgling in the summer of 2007, Iris could not have been given a more appropriate name. Her very existence forced me to discard false assumptions I had held throughout my life about the nature of birds and their possibilities. After my enlightening summer with Brad, Iris, the terrified broad-tailed, and the frantic nesting mother, I came to recognize that hummingbirds' complex and varied nuances would always outrun my imagination.

Over the years, a dozen rescues have upended all of my preconceptions about the psychological and emotional capacities of hummingbirds. And like them, Pepper would reveal deeper secrets about the hearts and minds of these remarkable creatures than I ever could have imagined.

CHAPTER 18

Hurt So Bad

BY MID-MAY, despite engaging in the regularly scheduled flight-therapy sessions I created for Brad a year earlier, Pepper hops from the twig in my hand to her perch but still cannot fly. Like Brad, Pepper dance-steps enthusiastically on her perch when she sees me approaching with the twig. And she is proving to be a tireless rehab candidate, spinning her good wing and hopping to the perch over and over until I have to take a break. Because of Pepper's superior stamina, I exercise her at least four times a day. I can see the iron resolve in her eyes as she struggles to flap her right wing fast enough to fly to the perch. And although I have noticed only incremental progress in the wing's rotation over the past two weeks, Pepper's indomitable spirit seems to promise success.

Between exercise sessions, Pepper sits on her low perch and sucks down formula. Her voracious appetite has made her positively rotund compared to the slender physique she entered rehab with. As I am raising and lowering her on the twig one morning I begin to wonder if her chubby body might inhibit her flight recovery. Then again, I laughingly remind myself, hummingbirds can burn off half their weight in a few days under challenging cir-cumstances, and Pepper's expanding waistline is the least of my worries.

While Pepper's recovery seems like a long run, Gabriel's is start-ing to feel like a marathon. After six weeks in rehab, Gabriel con-tinues to rest on his low perch without trying to fly or do much of anything. He just sits bolt upright all day, watching me tend to the rescues whose ranks are mushrooming around him. At times Ga-briel marches from side to side on his perch, the only movement he can manage. I have never kept an injured adult as long as Gabriel, and doubts are starting to creep in. But he remains healthy and strong. He just can't fly. Judging from his unusually straight, rigid posture, I suspect Gabriel suffered a serious back injury as a result of his collision with the Beverly Hills limousine. Recalling my own experience with a back attack, I know exactly how he feels.

A dozen years earlier, I sustained a back injury that took nearly a year to heal. It happened several months after I had earned a black belt from the grandmaster of *shotokan* karate, a sixty-five-year-old Japanese ninth-*dan* black belt with a serious smile and the classroom affect of a war-hardened drill sergeant. I had been studying under Sensei Nishiyama for many seasons before the mishap, advancing from white to black belt during several years of rigorous training.

A student-soldier in World War II Japan, Sensei was strictly old-school, and his training sessions proved fast-paced, strenuous, macho, and rough. He embodied the traditional "get in there and take your punishment, never lick your wounds in public, always be prepared to fight or die" approach to martial arts. I had stumbled on Sensei's hardcore workouts while driving aimlessly around the city a week after dropping out of law school, and through them I finally discovered the true meaning of discipline. Sensei's intense and combative classes often meant getting large swaths of skin bruised and abraded and having every aching muscle begging for relief as screams of "More speed! Strong spirit!" and a litany of indecipherable Japanese commands — which I intuitively translated as "Work harder, you lazy slobs!"— echoed in my ears. At the end of each training session, two hours of physical and psychological abuse, an international contingent of drained and nearly immobilized black belts drenched in sweat would scurry into a lineup, kneel, bow, breathlessly gasp, "Thank you, Sensei," and then head to the locker room to collapse on a hard wooden bench.

Sensei had subjected me to a sufficiently heavy dose of this friendly torture during the six months leading up to my promotion to *shodan,* or first-level black belt, that I was in prime fighting condition. At the same time, however, my lower back was already causing me considerable pain from nightly drills that included hundreds of repetitious punches and kicks executed while racing up and down the dojo floor at top speed. Standing in the classroom at UCLA for five hours a day before submitting to Sensei's tough love every night did not help ease the pain.

Only a handful of courageous women had dared venture into Sensei's testosterone-driven school of hard-hitters who excelled at this particular form of socially acceptable aggression. As one of the thinnest, lightest, and frequently most terrified members of the dojo, I often found myself on the receiving end of punches and kicks calculated to incapacitate an opponent with one blow. Still, Sensei praised my unusual foot speed, which I displayed each time I broke rank to flee the iron grip of another human time bomb. The advanced black belts at the dojo loved me because I moved quickly and could be thrown easily. Five days a week for six years, the boys and I had been sparring together on equal ground, with me skidding and rolling across the hardwood floor while they provided the momentum to perform these elaborate maneuvers.

On that fateful afternoon in which my back finally succumbed to the pressure, I had gotten paired with a highly primed fifth-*dan* black belt who had just won the national title and was punching his way to international fame. I had been sparring with the newly crowned champion since the day I began training. That particular afternoon, while I was playing the role of the attacker and he was practicing defense training, I punched him in the mouth and bloodied his lip. It was a freak accident. I couldn't have done it if I had tried. Not only did he have four inches and fifty pounds on me, but his skills were so advanced and his timing so sharp, I had never gotten close enough to graze him. And because *shotokan* black belts are trained to inflict serious damage on their opponents with a single attack, practitioners avoid contact at all costs. But when hyperconditioned and overzealous athletes spend years practicing techniques intended to destroy another human being as swiftly as possible, accidents are bound to happen. So, despite efforts to curb serious injuries, everyone absorbs a painful blow occasionally.

In the case of my encounter with the budding fight champion of the world, it happened so fast I didn't even know I had done it until I saw him wipe a trickle of blood off his chin with the back of his hand and suck in his bottom lip. Shocked and contrite, I immediately stepped back and apologized. When roles are reversed, a man's heartfelt apology to a woman he has accidentally punched in the face is always a welcome relief. But when a woman apologizes to a man for bloodying his lip, I would soon learn, it only adds insult to injury. After all, he was the national champion headed for international renown, and no chick was going to smack him in the mouth and get away with it. And then I made my greatest mistake of all. I tried to appease him by going soft on the next punch, foolishly believing he would accept my pullback as a further concession. He did *sasoi*, inviting me to attack, and I obliged with a telegraphed and conciliatory punch. Only when he executed a break balance that flipped me backward over his knee and flat onto the hardwood floor with such resounding force that twenty black belts froze in midpunch and gaped in our direction did I realize my error. After a brief moment of room-spinning confusion, I bounced back to my feet, but already I could tell something wasn't right. The only thing I could feel in my left leg was a hot, tingling sensation. I had to look down to see if my left foot was still attached, because I couldn't feel it at all.

Within seconds, Sensei, who had witnessed the whole exchange, stopped the class, strolled over with a commanding presence, and proceeded to take my vindictive opponent apart. Accusing him of unfairly brutalizing a lower-ranked and smaller competitor, Sensei delivered a verbal finishing blow deadlier than the most masterful karate technique. In a rare display of emotion, Sensei mocked my attacker for giving in to his desire for revenge and insisted that, rather than being angry with me, he should be mad at himself for letting a *shodan* (and a girl, no less, though Sensei didn't say this directly) punch him in the first place. The chastened champ obediently shrank into a posture of humble respect and chagrin. But it was all too late for me. A strange tension had begun tightening its grip around my spine like a vise, making it increasingly difficult to remain upright. I bowed out and limped gingerly to the locker room as everyone looked on in horror. Because whenever you hear that someone has suffered a broken bone, smashed nose, pulverized spine, or tooth extraction in an advanced traditional karate class, you never ask for whom the bell tolls. It's only a matter of time.

After the numb drive home, during which I operated the brake,

The dazzling iridescent crown and gorget on this mature male Anna's hold a magnetic attraction for females during the breeding season and give us a sense of how humming-birds appear to one another. *Brian E. Small*

Nestlings like these twin Anna's on a wind chime, brought to rehab after their mother was killed by an outdoor ceiling fan, spend six to eight weeks in rehab before being released into the wild. *Terry Masear*

This young female Anna's shows how hummingbirds' unique capacity to invert the leading edge of their wings during flight generates lift on the upstroke.
Sara Michele

A female Allen's fledgling, brought to rescue after being carried into the house by the family cat, explores local succulent blossoms during her stay in rehab.
Sara Michele

This close-up of an adult male Allen's reveals how the gorget shifts from gold to a brilliant tangerine depending on the angle of the sunlight in relation to the viewer.
Rocky Stickel

A male rufous nestling dropped off in rehab after being slightly injured during a heavy rainstorm. *Sara Michele*

The same rufous, six weeks later, perched in the aviary awaiting release into the wild. *Sara Michele*

An adult male black-chinned sports a velvety black gorget and purple neck band. A migratory species, the black-chinned is recognized among rehabbers for its exceptional intelligence. *Brian E. Small*

Male and female black-chinned fledglings get acquainted while they practice perching during their first day in the starter cage. *Terry Masear*

Costa's nestlings saved from an ant invasion by a finder who consulted Los Angeles Hummingbird Rescue. Some hummingbird species prefer to nest on manmade structures, like this light pole, which offer protection from predatory birds.
Steve Diggins

This adult male Costa's sports a stunning violet crown and gorget. Costa's adapt easily to the presence of humans and are quick to take advantage of fountains and sugar feeders put out for them by hummingbird lovers in the desert. *Brian E. Small*

The adult male broad-tailed has a brilliant rose-red gorget. Although typically found in western mountains, broad-tailed hummingbirds have begun appearing in Los Angeles rehab facilities in recent years. *Brian E. Small*

A calliope with the characteristic burgundy striping on the adult male's gorget. At three inches long, the calliope is the smallest breeding bird in the United States. *Brian E. Small*

Allen's twins whose nest was destroyed by a Santa Ana windstorm and repaired by a caller after consulting with Los Angeles Hummingbird Rescue. *Bella Hummingbird*

See more photos of hummingbirds who have been rehabilitated and released at losangeleshummingbirdrescue.org.

accelerator, and clutch on my five-speed Datsun almost entirely with my right foot, I collapsed onto the bed. And with this surrender, I entered a world unlike any I had ever known before: the endless arctic night of lumbar-vertebral-disc injury, wherein I would learn the true meaning of physical suffering in its uncut version. Despite a long night of trying, I could find no position on the bed that allowed me to sleep or breathe without excruciating pain. Sitting up was torture; lying down was worse. By the next morning, I was so incapacitated that I could crawl only short distances, from the bed to the refrigerator and back, and was incapable of reaching down far enough to put on my socks. Ice packs and a heating pad became my closest companions.

Since this crisis occurred near the end of the two-week break between UCLA's spring and summer sessions, I had no choice but to take that summer off from teaching. Because I could do nothing else, I read armfuls of books Frank carted home from the Beverly Hills library for me. Three months and a five-pound bag of assorted painkillers later, I gradually rose up from the ashes to spit in the eye of mortality, though not before the whole episode had reduced me to a physical and emotional two-year-old. And for months after I regained bipedal locomotion, the most insignificant twist or bend could still render me incapable of lifting a newspaper off the front porch.

But as Lao Tzu happily points out, *One gains by losing.* And when I finally crept back to the dojo several months later, my repentant assailant treated me with the utmost care and respect for the rest of our acquaintance, which I accepted as a small victory. And in the end I felt I owed him a debt of gratitude, since, during my summer of pain, I began writing my first book, which I finished a few years later and which is still being used in English classes at UCLA today.

Recalling my spinal collapse as I watch Gabriel step lightly back and forth on his perch that hazy morning in mid-May, I feel his pain. My wounded warrior moves carefully along the wire from side to side when I approach him. But he remains bolt upright just as I had when I first learned to walk again. People assume that back pain makes the sufferer walk twisted and bent like a ninety-year-old. But a serious lumbar injury causes its victim to stand, walk, and sit as if a steel rod is extending down the spine, with virtually no range of motion.

"I know, Gabriel," I empathize as he shuffles along the plastic-coated perch with his tiny feet in a feeble effort to get some exercise. "I've been there."

Throughout his first month in rehab, Gabriel had maintained a dull and impassive look in his eyes as he sat on his low perch staring into nothingness. Concerned about his psychological health, I began placing a large flight cage containing an unusually active pair of rufous twins adjacent to him every day. The striking pair of teenagers, rescued by Ricki Lake after their mother perished in a windstorm, had arrived as dinofuzz two weeks before Gabriel came in. Both chicks, a female and a male, sport dark-rust feathers on their tails and flanks and already fly faster than most birds upon release. Since Gabriel began watching the two perpetual-motion machines jet back and forth between perches as they tussle in midair and splash exuberantly on river rocks in their tub, his expression has shifted from one of defeat and resignation to interest in the youthful activity carrying on around him. And this sudden dawning of hope has translated into light physical activity, making me cautiously optimistic about his recovery.

Every time I look at Gabriel, I marvel at how he got here. I still can't believe he is the nestling I rescued from that punishing rainstorm four years earlier. His mere presence tugs at a raft of thoughts and emotions I cannot bear to address. Every time I suspect that, in his return, he may represent some kind of messenger, as so many of my finders have imagined their hummingbirds embody, I have to remind myself not to read too much into it. Because when I regard him with the sober eye of a battle-scarred rehabber, the same old nagging doubts rush in to undermine my idealism: *What if he doesn't make it? How are you going to handle that? And how impossible would it be to try to reconcile any belief in his special significance with such a dismal outcome?*

While pondering these haunting questions in relation to Gabriel after going to bed late one night a few weeks earlier, I suddenly realized that I could not afford to focus on results with him. And this recognition led me to the most important lesson I would learn from rehabbing my boomerang bird. For the first time since I began rescuing hummingbirds, I was being forced to act from instinct rather than reason, an insight I would learn Lao Tzu supports in his assertion, *The sage is guided by what he feels and not by what he sees.* In my efforts to mend Gabriel, all I could do was ensure that I was using the proper means to achieve the desired end. Past that, the future was irrelevant. Embrace the uncertainty and move forward in good faith. Because, as I would one day come to understand, Gabriel was, is, and always would be beyond any rational explanation.

The mystery surrounding Gabriel is enhanced by the white spot on his crown that Jean pointed out when I first saw him as a fledgling four years ago. Some reptiles have what is called a third eye on top of their heads. Although it's not really an eye, the coloration on the skin resembles one, and researchers believe this spot is connected to the pineal gland, which is sensitive to changes in light and heat. Like reptiles and birds, humans also have a pineal gland. In ancient times, people believed the pineal gland, or third eye, held mystical powers and facilitated insight into the spiritual realm. In the seventeenth century, the French philosopher René Descartes posited that the pineal gland was the location of the human soul. Recent research indicates this gland is responsible for the production of melatonin in humans and is connected to circadian rhythms. Avian studies suggest that it may account for birds' capacity to detect magnetic fields and therefore functions as the center of navigation during migratory flights. As I gaze at Gabriel's white spot shining in the sunlight breaking through the clouds, my mind reels at all the magical possibilities his third eye conjures up, if not in reality, at least in my colorful imagination.

While contemplating the significance of Gabriel's third eye, I glance over at Pepper, who is perched quietly in the cage next to him and following my every move. As I approach her to offer the thrilling adventure of flight, my phone rings. The caller tells me he has two baby hummingbirds in a nest and wants to bring them to me right away. When I try to pin him down on the specifics of the nestlings' age and circumstances, he balks and insists on delivering them immediately.

"Where did they come from?"

"I'm not sure," he answers hesitantly.

"How old are they?"

"I don't really know."

"Well, it's best to try and get them back to their mother if that's possible."

"I don't think so."

I continue to press him about returning the nest to its original location, but he keeps asking for my address, and finally I relent.

While waiting for him to arrive, I give Gabriel a handful of red columbine and exercise Pepper before carrying them into the garage to clean their cages and fill feeders. A young male Anna's brought in at sunrise after being found grounded under a pine tree during a windstorm the night before has been floundering around on the bottom of his cage since being dropped off. I spent most of the morning bathing and examining him with my surgical glasses and discovered that nine flight feathers on his right wing were missing. Beyond that, the young bird appears robust and struggles desperately to fly. After stressing over him for five hours, I'm falling into a funk and have been avoiding a decision that is almost certainly headed toward a sad conclusion.

After filling feeders and changing the paper towels in the bottom of Gabriel's and Pepper's cages, I hear a car pull into the driveway and head out to the front gate to meet the caller with the twins. When he slides slowly from the passenger's seat and shuffles toward the gate, I feel foolish and embarrassed about grilling him with so many questions over the phone. He is at least ninety years old, carries a walking cane, and appears nearly blind. A young woman talking on her smartphone waves to me from the driver's seat as I usher the old man through the gate. As we pass the aviary, his face lights up in astonishment. He tilts his head toward the aviary and stands listening with an expression of childlike wonder.

"This way," I coax softly as we start moving again and he shuffles along with me toward the garage. Once inside, I open the Earl Grey tea box he hands me and find a nest with two dinofuzz babies wiggling around inside. Because the chicks are in such perfect condition, my first reaction is that he has cut the nest in the mistaken assumption that the mother had abandoned it. But then I wonder how he could have been watching the nest in the first place.

"Where did you find these?" I ask in confusion.

"My cat," he answers matter-of-factly.

"Your cat?"

"Yes." He nods resolutely. "He brought the nest into the house, through his door."

I look down at the perfectly intact nest and the undisturbed nestlings huddling together. "Really? Just like this?"

"Uh-huh," he asserts proudly, pointing to the nest with a wrinkled and trembling hand. "He brought it into my bed this morning and set it on the pillow by my head."

I stare at the nest in speechless awe.

"After that windstorm, you know," he adds.

"That's right," I agree. "There was a lot of wind last night."

"Yes." The old man smiles. "And my cat loves to go out early in the morning and look around after a storm."

"But—" I hesitate for a second. "Sorry to ask, but how did you know they were hummingbirds?"

"Oh, my housekeeper." He gestures toward the car in the driveway. "She's from Costa Rica and she knows birds. So she asked her son, he's six, to look up hummingbird rescue on her phone and he found you in less than a minute."

We stand together in the garage in silence as I marvel at the confluence of events and the unlikely cast of characters that brought these lucky twins to my door. A midnight windstorm, a curious and compassionate cat, a sleeping blind man, a Costa Rican bird enthusiast, and a six-year-old tech whiz.

"They seem healthy," he volunteers as I place their nest in a plastic cup in the ICU.

"Yes, they do," I agree, wondering how he could possibly know such a thing.

"What's wrong with that one?" he inquires, pointing in the direction of the young male Anna's who is flailing awkwardly around the bottom of his cage in a frustrated attempt to fly.

"Oh, he has a lot of wing feathers missing," I answer despondently. "He's a tough case because it takes so long for them to grow back that the bird usually breaks off the ones on the other wing in the meantime."

The old man closes his eyes, cocks his head in the direction of the Anna's cage, and listens intently for several seconds before shaking his head. "Not missing," he finally concludes. "Still there, I think."

"Well, I examined him for a long time this morning," I begin confidently, "and I couldn't —"

He raises a quivering hand in the air before I can finish.

"Check again." He knits his brow. "I think they're still there."

"Okay." I shrug, unconvinced.

"That one will be fine too." He points in the direction of Pepper resting silently on her perch. "Just needs more time," he avows as he shuffles out the garage door. I glance at Pepper, who is sitting motionlessly in the corner of her cage and has not so much as flinched since we came in. I follow the old man out the door and across the patio, but he pauses by the aviary again.

"Like a helicopter," he shouts before wandering toward the gate.

After escorting him out, I stop by the aviary on my way back to the garage and close my eyes. I never realized what a racket hummingbirds' wings make. The buzz from the eighteen young adults flying around inside is so deafening, I can hardly hear the ambient traffic and construction noise emanating from the urban machinery churning ceaselessly around us.

When I get back to the garage, the young male is still spinning and tumbling across the bottom of the starter cage in a futile effort to get airborne. I reach in and lift the panting bird out. I put my surgical loupes on again, gently pull the right wing away from his body, and examine it. As before, except for the longest outer feather, all the primary feathers seem to be missing. I run my thumb and index finger down both sides of the feather a couple of times. After a few swipes, my finger comes across a hard bump about halfway down. I turn the bird over in my hand, examine the feather closely under magnification, and discover a nearly invisible lump of dried tree sap glued to the underside of his wing. After setting him back in the cage, I hurry into the house, warm a tablespoon of canola oil in a plastic cup in the microwave, and bring it back out to the garage. When I rub the oil down the feather several times, the lump suddenly breaks and dissolves, releasing nine primary feathers that magically pop out into a perfect hummingbird wing. I wash the oil off with warm soapy water and rinse the squirming bird thoroughly in a tub before placing him on the bottom of the cage outside in the sun. Ten minutes later, the nimble young adult is gliding smoothly back and forth between high perches as if nothing happened.

Astonished by his surreal transformation, I move the vigorous male into a large flight cage with the intent of running him through the advanced stages of rehab. But it quickly becomes clear he has already been out on his own, and the capable young adult shows growing impatience with this rescue business. I toss a rotten banana peel crawling with fruit flies into the bottom of his cage and head into the house, where a trio of jealous cats is, as always, waiting for me.

Our three cats sit in a lineup inside their caged, outdoor walkway every morning watching me tend to the hummingbirds on the patio. Occasionally they plunge into loud, fur-flying wrestling matches to call attention to themselves. The second I step through the back door, they race one another to the kitchen, darting between my feet and tripping me all the way down the hallway. They engage in this ritual twenty times a day, which is good exercise for them and has improved my balance considerably.

Observing the tree-sap bird from inside the house, I can see him buzzing gracefully back and forth between perches but I don't believe he is catching any fruit flies. Until I head back outside. As I approach the cage, he flies the length of it and I see his bill twist slightly for a split second before he alights on a perch. When I glance at the banana peel, there isn't a fruit fly in sight. I gaze in admiration at the practiced hunter and he stares back at me with annoyance, as if to ask, *Are you happy now?* Five minutes later, I open the top of the cage and let him go. As I watch him disappear over the Pacific Design Center in a blur, the irony of his rescue is not lost on me. After inspecting this seemingly doomed young flier for half a day with all of my youthful faculties and my high-powered microsurgery glasses, it took an ancient blind man less than ten seconds to show me the way.

CHAPTER 19

I'll Be There for You

BY THE FIRST OF JUNE, Pepper is able to fly short distances between perches in her starter cage. At various points during my ongoing trips around the patio to fill feeders, I stop and invite Pepper onto the twig, then raise and lower her in the cage until she spins her powerful wings and flies to the high perch. She can execute intermediate forward flight with ease now and strains with focused intensity each day to achieve vertical lift. Judging from her steady progress over the past two weeks, I no longer doubt that Pepper will recover as thoroughly as the blind man foresaw.

Gabriel, however, still spends most of his time sitting on a low perch watching the rehabbed birds around him come and go, though lately he has started to tumble across the bottom of the cage by half spinning his wings. Gabriel's wings are synchronized and flap with moderate speed, but he still cannot get full rotation, which is typical for a back injury. Nevertheless, like young birds learning to fly, he responds to my words of encouragement by exerting greater effort. Each time Gabriel finishes buzzing across the paper towels on the bottom of his cage, he hops onto the far perch

and looks at me questioningly. I want to reassure him that everything is going to work out, but Gabriel has been with me far longer
than any adult hummingbird I have taken in, and my confidence in
his recovery swings between excited optimism and grim despair.
Since his arrival, several injured adults have come in and failed to
make it for one reason or another. But unlike the badly damaged
birds that fall on their backs as their condition deteriorates and
have to be relinquished, Gabriel maintains an unusually straight
posture and never falters. And because of who Gabriel is and what
he represents, I cannot bear to give up on him.

Since Pepper's appearance a month ago, thirty additional hummingbirds have come into my rehab facility, totaling eighty-five for
the year. Of the thirty-five adults who have been released, many have
stuck around to take advantage of the seven one-quart sugar feeders dangling around the patio's perimeter. The health and success of
these early releases provides the encouragement I need to face the
exploding number of babies that will flood into rehab during the approaching peak of the nesting season, as the most demanding month,
with its onslaught of lost and distraught fledglings, looms large.

By the first week in June, I'm feeling the strain when I get up
every morning at five but still remain fundamentally strong and
convinced I can endure the next three months without being overtaken by the escalating demands of nonstop phone calls and the
daunting workload they deposit at my house. With the spring
quarter at UCLA wrapping up, I am about to make the transition
from juggling rehab and teaching to plunging full-time into saving
hummingbirds for the summer. Although the season is half over,
like running a marathon, early strides in the race come quicker and
easier than the numb slog toward the end.

With the transition from spring to summer, tree-trimming victims are beginning to come in at a faster rate. Over the past month,

in addition to three cut nests that for various reasons could not be reattached, I have received two dog-found nestlings, a nest of twins taken off a porch chandelier by real estate agents, a nest cut from ivy by exterminators, pinfeathered twins whose mother hit a window and died after being frightened from her nest by kids blowing noisemakers at a birthday party, and several grounded and slightly injured fledglings, three of which came from city animal shelters.

As the weather turns hot and dry in June, mites arrive, and every bird that comes through the door has to be isolated and dusted with a special insecticide. Female hummingbirds pick up mites from the flowers they eat and then transfer the roving insects to their babies during feeding. In warm summer weather, mites proliferate on feathered nestlings and suck their blood. Some chicks are so covered with mites in the photos sent to me that I can barely see their bills. In nature, these birds stand no chance of surviving, though most are healthy and beautiful once we get them cleaned up, dusted, and hydrated. When people call about mite-infested nests, I coach them on how to dust the nest and babies with diatomaceous earth — a term nobody can pronounce — if they have a swimming pool and cornstarch if they do not. These home remedies work on all but the worst infestations, which we direct to rehab as an alternative to the nestlings' certain death.

Mites, which represent nature in its rawest, most unforgiving form, create their share of distress in callers. The first week in June, Kristin calls and describes how two nestlings in the schefflera just outside the door on her front porch are being devoured by mites. She hasn't slept all night and is desperate to get the chicks into rehab. Before Kristin can finish explaining the problem, she begins sobbing so hard she can't speak. She puts her husband, Kyle, on the phone, and he apologizes for his wife's implosion.

"So what's the backstory here?" I prompt.

"The backstory is we had a hummingbird nest in the same tree last summer and the babies got mites. My wife was pregnant at the time and we were so preoccupied we didn't do anything to help, so the mites got worse. Then one day ants attacked the nest and the next morning when we got up, both babies were dead, and my wife had a miscarriage later that afternoon."

"So you're expecting again."

"Correct. And, well, you can imagine."

"Of course," I say sympathetically before asking Kyle to send me a photo of the nest. A minute later I get a photo of two feather-duster Allen's with squinty eyes and upturned bills who are covered with mites. I call Kyle back immediately.

"It's pretty bad, so we have to act fast," I tell him. "So here's what I think we should do. Take a wet Q-Tip and wipe the mites off the chicks' bills. Then — do you have any diatomaceous earth?"

"Any what?"

"Diatomaceous earth. It's that gray powder you put in swimming-pool filters."

"Ah." He brightens with sudden recognition. "No, but my neighbor down the street is a pool guy."

"Perfect. So get some from him and, using a Q-Tip, dust the nest and the babies with the diatomaceous earth. Put it on pretty thick, being careful not to get it in their eyes. And make sure you dust heavily under their wings, on their bellies, and especially all around the inside of the nest."

"Okay," Kyle says haltingly, as if he's writing everything down. "But won't this make the mother abandon the babies?"

"No, you're doing her a favor, and hummingbirds know it."

"That's amazing. They're so smart," he exclaims.

"You have no idea," I agree. "Now, when the chicks get weakened by mites, the ants move in because they smell death, so get some Vaseline and coat the vertical section of the trunk supporting the branch the nest is on. Put the Vaseline all the way around and as thick as you can. That way the ants can't get to the branch the nest is on and the chicks won't get Vaseline on their feet when they fledge. Do this right away, okay?"

"I'm all over it." Kyle embraces his assignment before hanging up.

Three days later Kyle sends me a photo of two bright-eyed Allen's and calls to report his victory over the parasite invasion.

"The mites are gone and there are no ants on the tree. The babies look great and Kristin has totally mellowed out. I don't know how to thank you, Terry," he says in a tone steeped in gratitude.

"Well, just in reference to the baby, my name is gender-neutral," I joke.

"I'm gonna think about that." He laughs.

"No, you couldn't do it to him, or her. You need something trendy like Kai or Quinn if your kid's gonna make it in preschool in LA."

"Well," he responds playfully, "we are planning to adopt a dog too."

"There you go. And it will always be a story, because who would give their dog a name like that?"

"Exactly," he laughingly agrees.

The first week in June, I take in a dozen fledglings and a concussed young adult who flew through the open window of the finder's car, hit the inside of her windshield, and dropped onto the dashboard while she was sitting at a stoplight in Beverly Hills. The following week, on June 9, I get seven young birds in one day. By five p.m., the ICU is jammed with hummingbird victims of all ages and species, more than fifty fledglings are advancing through cages on my patio, and I have answered thirty phone calls, including a request for an interview from a *Los Angeles Times* reporter.

Around five o'clock, as I am racing around, madly filling feeders, my cell phone rings again. When I answer, a well-spoken gentleman informs me he has rescued a fledgling from his tennis court and has her in his house in Holmby Hills. Anticipating a vigorous debate, I sink into my chair on the patio. I know when I get a call from one of the guard-gated streets in the Platinum Triangle — Holmby Hills, Bel Air, Beverly Hills — that persuading anyone to make an effort is going to be a challenge. Callers from the Beverly Hills flats south of Sunset are not so resistant. These struggling millionaires will usually work with me. It's the bottomlessly deep pockets of Holmby Hills that drive me over the priceless canyon edge. Never mind that I am working day and night, taking thousands of calls, and caring for hundreds of rescued hummingbirds all for the love of wildlife and without getting a penny for it. High-net-worth residents calling from the upper echelons expect quick service, and a lot of it.

"Can you bring her to me?" I gently coax the articulate gentleman.

"No, I can't, really," he replies. "I have to prepare dinner."

"Prepare dinner?"

"Yes," he replies in a British accent. "I'm the butler."

"The butler," I repeat in the same accent.

"Yes, and I can't go off right now because I have to prepare dinner."

"Well. That's funny, because I was just doing the same thing myself," I remark as I grab a carrot that is the only food I will see until sometime after nine and that's if I'm lucky. But I know this is not my world and I cannot possibly convey that a young hummingbird's life is of greater importance than one of thousands of dinners that will be served during the next who-knows-how-many years in the butler's precious world.

"Is there anyone else on the staff who can bring her? It's only ten minutes away," I cajole.

"I'm afraid not," he answers unapologetically. "The chefs, servers, and everyone else are busy preparing for a rather large dinner party as well."

I wonder how many bustling minions "everyone else" entails, but I'm too spent to ask or argue, and I know that if I don't give in and go, the hummingbird will likely take a back seat to the splendid festivities occurring at Gatsby's house that evening.

"Okay." I surrender. "I'll come and get her. What's your address?" I ask with exaggerated patience, trying not to let my annoyance about his lack of effort break the deal. Before leaving the house, I feed the ocean of gaping mouths in the ICU and fill every feeder on the patio, and fifteen minutes later, after announcing "Hummingbird rescue" to the intercom at the end of a leafy, tree-lined driveway, I'm admitted through the automated wrought-iron gates.

"I love your car," the butler gushes, running his hand seductively over the flank of my silver Audi TT as I get out. I bought the car seven years ago, and although it still looks immaculate and drives even better, the lavish amenities of my immediate surroundings, which include an army of house staff, an opulent mansion, and fleets of luxury European cars parked in the driveway, make my modest little sports car appear singularly unimpressive.

"Yes, it so cute," a young au pair agrees as the housekeeper looks on from the doorway before ushering me into a cherry-paneled library slightly larger than my house. As I step inside the high-beamed library boasting floor-to-ceiling windows along the south wall, I notice a flawless Anna's fledgling perched on the edge of a pair of designer sunglasses that are balanced atop a life-size marble bust of Venus de Milo on the desk.

"She's perfect," I observe as I gather the fledgling up and place her into the portable cage I use to retrieve birds from shelters.

"We named her Ava." The butler tilts his head pensively as he sets a lead-crystal champagne glass filled with bubbly gold liquid on the desk in front of me. "In honor of her exotic beauty. And a former acquaintance." He smirks as the au pair and the house-keeper laugh knowingly.

"Fitting." I nod as I eye the glass curiously.

"That's for you, not the hummingbird," the butler announces as everyone laughs again.

Glancing around the ornate room, I have no idea how I wandered into this gilded world where such magnificent lives are being carried on less than five miles from my humble little stucco cottage in West Hollywood. After drinking a glass of the finest champagne I have ever tasted in my not-untraveled life, I discover as we stroll down a wide hallway lined with personal photos of everyone who has ever been anyone in Hollywood that the estate belongs to a famous producer whose name, the butler says with a wink before sending me out the front door with a crisp one-hundred-dollar bill tucked into the top of the birdcage, is best unmentioned in any future exchanges.

"Paparazzi; you understand." He narrows his eyes.

"Uh-huh. I have the same problem." I wink as everyone jovially waves goodbye from the veranda.

The following afternoon I get a call at five o'clock again, this time from the shelter in West Los Angeles reporting that a man just phoned about an injured hummingbird in Hollywood and wants someone to come and pick it up.

"I'm too busy to be doing pickups all of the time," I protest with impatience.

"Well, he says he has a hummingbird but no car and no money to take the bus," the animal-control officer from the shelter informs me.

"Did you get his number?"

"No, he barely speaks English. All I could catch was that he has a hummingbird and will be waiting on the corner of Sunset and Western."

"So he's sitting there waiting for me now?" I ask incredulously.

"That's what he said."

After taking over a hundred calls already this week, I'm exhausted and furious about the shelter's presumption. Everyone knows how impossible it is for overworked rehabbers to do pickups from individuals on top of retrieving rescues from shelters. But city shelters are understaffed and overwhelmed too. And when I look at the dazzling collection of hummingbirds buzzing in the cages around me, I can't quit thinking about this poor fledgling that will slowly starve to death from sugar water if I don't show up. So I recruit Frank to feed the ICU babies, get in my car, and go.

It's a scorching, smoggy day, and rush-hour traffic is deadly all the way. When I arrive at the designated corner nearly an hour later after what is normally a twenty-minute drive, a throng of weary commuters is lingering at the bus stop. I turn onto a side street and park but see no one among the crowd who might be in possession of a hummingbird. I step out of the car and begin wandering idly around the congested street corner when a harried, middle-aged man approaches me carrying a cardboard moving box big enough to hold a washing machine.

"Did you call about a hummingbird?" I ask.

"¿Como?"

"*¿Tiene una chuparrosa?*"

"*¿Chuparrosa?*" He looks at me in confusion.

"*¿Tiene un pajáro?*"

"*¡Sí!*" he replies excitedly. "*Ella no puede volar,*" he announces as he opens the giant box.

I peer cautiously inside and see a petrified adult mourning dove crouched in the corner of the box.

"She is a harm-ed bird," he says slowly in broken English.

As an ESL instructor who spent three years teaching pronunciation, I immediately grasp the lost-in-translation gaffe that brought us both to this busy Hollywood street corner on this sweltering afternoon. English verbs have three possible pronunciations for past-tense endings: the *t*-sound ending, as in *looked;* the *d* sound, as in *moved;* and the *ed* syllable, as in *wanted.* Even though the *ed* syllable is the least commonly used in everyday English, beginning English-as-a-second-language speakers use the *ed* pronunciation (what ESL instructors fondly refer to as Mr. Ed) for all past-tense verbs. So when my Latino rescuer called the shelter and reported he had a harm-ed bird, the American on the other end of the line heard *hummingbird* and called me right away.

"*Gracias.*" I laugh in resignation as he squeezes my hand while thanking me effusively in Spanish.

Shaking my head, I jam the box into my hatchback and make the slow crawl back to my house. As soon as I get home, I climb a ladder onto my neighbor's roof, where I feed wild birds every morning, and open the box. The dove shoots out and flies into a towering elm tree in an adjacent yard. Ninety minutes of driving. To rescue a bird that needed no help.

I hurry into the garage and open the sliding glass door to the ICU as twenty bills pop open and begin peeping. While I am going down the assembly line, the phone rings.

"Terry?" a voice asks nervously.

"Yes."

Mindy has come across an adult male hummingbird sprawled on the sidewalk in Hancock Park and asks me what she should do. In the spring and early summer, people often stumble upon grounded adults that have just been engaged in a breeding episode and are taking a few minutes to regroup after their exhausting encounter. In this particular instance, Mindy wants to know whether the bird will attack her if she picks him up. I have to contain my laughter when I get questions like this and I remind myself that growing up in the city, for all of its cultural advantages, has its limitations too.

"Well, hummingbirds can be pretty brutal if you come in under four grams. But in this case, you weigh about twelve thousand times more than he does, so I think you're safe to pick him up."

Five seconds later I hear her shriek before coming back on the phone. "He just flew off!"

"See? You saved him."

"Yeah, I did." She laughs. "It was effortless."

Later that week, I get a call from an anxious young woman worried about a hummingbird walking around her front yard. Unlike other birds, hummingbirds are physically incapable of walking and spend their entire lives either perched or flying.

"He's been walking around and crying for hours. I don't know what to do."

As difficult as it is for me to imagine, no small number of callers mistake other kinds of birds for hummingbirds. Some Angelenos are so thoroughly urban they don't even know what a hummingbird looks like. Misguided calls to hummingbird rescue include a number of impossible scenarios, such as a hummingbird walking down the sidewalk, two hummingbirds "attacking us every time we step out our front door" (always nesting mockingbirds, bless their fearless souls), a nest with four hummingbird babies (usually black phoebes), and "a huge hummingbird sitting on a nest in our tree" (also usually a black phoebe, or sometimes a bushtit).

Since I answer my phone at odd hours, I have also gotten calls about baby raccoons, squirrels, rabbits, all types of birds (ravens, crows, hawks, owls, swifts, doves, ducks, gulls, pigeons, finches), and, late one night when nobody else could be reached, a bobcat cub, which I was dying to take but responsibly referred on. When Jean first started doing rescue, a nervous young man who spoke little English called her about a snake he found in his garage. Assuming it was some type of garden snake and too busy to draw out the details, Jean told the caller to bring the reptile to her house. An hour later, two guys arrived at her door with a fifty-pound boa constrictor, which, after some hesitation, Jean accepted.

Fortunately, Los Angeles is home to a dedicated contingent of compassionate souls who rescue every form of wildlife under the Southern California sun and moon. Opossum rescuers are the most zealous of the bunch. Their passion for their chosen species runs so deep that they pull over when they see a dead opossum on the highway and race through traffic to check the pouch of North America's only marsupial for babies.

"What color is it?" I ask the caller with the perambulating bird.

"Kind of a light grayish brown," she answers vaguely.

I give her the number of a rehabber who rescues songbirds and go back to filling empty feeders. I love mockingbirds, but I cannot rehab them because they imprint, or bond, or whatever you choose to call it. Young ravens and crows are worse. In their quest for attention and affection, they are akin to domestic dogs. And when you placate young wild animals with a tender human touch, it changes them forever. So rehabbers have to reject the overtures of creatures who attempt to bond, to ensure they retain their wild nature. Some people are good at this. I am not. I have too much of what John Keats called *negative capability* as well as a close corollary, empathy. When birds arrive at my door lost, broken, and terrified, the distinctions between us fall away, and they are no longer wild animals separate from my humanity. Instead, I am right there with them, sharing their troubles, fear, and pain. I see myself in them and want to protect, love, and reassure them.

Apparently, I am not alone in this impulse. Recent studies indicate that people exhibit more compassion toward injured young animals than toward suffering adult humans, because empathy increases with the perception of a creature's helplessness. And while young hummingbirds do helpless as convincingly as anything, all babies have evolved to activate the nurturing instinct. I could probably rehab red-tailed hawks, because they don't hesitate to drive a talon into your face if you get too close. But there are so many wild animals I cannot rehabilitate. I couldn't do baby bears or foxes. I would have them sleeping in the bed, listening to poetry, and eating homemade treats at the kitchen table. On top of fighting against the brutality of nature and human interference, I would be at war with myself all the time. And in the wildlife-saving business, there is no room for that level of internal conflict. It requires too much psychic energy, which is a rehabber's most precious resource.

That's one reason I chose hummingbirds. They don't want to get too close. They never imprint or bond. And once you let them go, they don't come back. Or so I had always been told.

CHAPTER 20

Under Pressure

WHEN YOU ARE JUGGLING sixty hummingbirds in rescue, you walk a lot. I walk to the ICU in the garage forty times a day, to the aviary every thirty minutes, in and out of the garage a hundred times carrying cages, up and down the patio for twenty minutes every hour, and in circles around the kitchen when I cannot remember what I am looking for — a phenomenon known to rehabbers as Kitchenheimer's disease. Nearly every day of the summer brings in new birds with special needs. A trip to the kitchen can involve retrieving freeze-dried fruit flies for undernourished chicks kept too long on sugar water, nystatin for adult birds with fungal infections contracted from dirty sugar feeders, canola oil for all forms of sticky substances inhibiting flight, and extra sugar for injured adults who object to the comparatively bland flavor of formula.

In the normal course of events I have an extremely sharp memory. Too sharp, in fact, as there are a lot of things I would prefer to forget and cannot. But at the height of hummingbird season, as the circuits get overloaded, the soft machine struggles to keep track of the endless details of individual birds, the demanding feeding schedule, the supplies that are always running short, the parade of finders appearing at my doorstep, and the daily barrage of phone calls, voicemails, and text messages coming in every five minutes. So gradually, over the course of the summer, as each damaged hummingbird's troubles become mine, I shift into survival mode.

Since March I have been getting up before dawn every morning so I can mix formula, fill syringes and feeders, change bathtub water, and put twenty cages outside before sunrise. Hummingbirds in the wild arrive at the sugar feeders at first light, so we mimic their habits to acclimate young birds to the same natural rhythm. Counting up the sixty-five birds on the patio and in the crowded ICU the second week in June, I can't imagine taking in another hummingbird. But the fledgling season is gaining momentum and the wave is cresting.

At six o'clock one morning, as I am removing sugar feeders I hang in the aviary before dark every night so the young adults can learn how to use them before their release, I notice a hummingbird sitting quietly on the end of a dowel perch that extends about six inches outside the aviary. I approach slowly until I am within a few feet of the slender, cigar-shaped black-chinned perched on the dowel watching me carefully.

"Blacktop?" I ask in astonishment. As I inch closer, he doesn't flinch. "I can't believe it."

Blacktop came into rehab the summer before after being knocked out of his nest by a city gravel truck and tumbling into wet asphalt. When I got him, the immobilized nestling had dried asphalt caked all over his feathers and was nearly dead. For the next three days, every morning and afternoon I washed him with warm canola oil and then bathed him in soap and water. After his brilliant recovery, Blacktop became unusually interactive, like the brown-sugar twins. Perhaps Blacktop understood that I had saved his life, because he remained exceedingly friendly throughout rehab. Once inside the aviary, Blacktop became a lean hunting machine who could snap up fruit flies with effortless accuracy. But Blacktop never hunted randomly like the other young hummingbirds still in training. Instead, he displayed an intense focus and laserlike sense of purpose in his quest for protein. Blacktop's preference for fruit flies was so overpowering that he would perch on the side of the Tupperware tray containing the rotten bananas for hours every day and nab newly hatched insects before they could get fully airborne.

After his release in late July, Blacktop perched on the dowel jutting out the side of the aviary every morning at dawn and waited for me to pick up the Tupperware container inside. And every morning when I shook the container, the new recruits in the aviary would make their clumsy attempts to catch the lively prey. Because of the young birds' amateur skills, most of the fruit flies escaped out the aviary bars, at which point Blacktop would snap them up with mechanical precision. By September, when it was time for him to migrate, Blacktop was the most corpulent black-chinned I had ever seen. Then one day in early September, when I came out to put feeders in the aviary, he was gone, and I had not seen him since.

"Is this for real?" I wonder aloud, certain I am imagining his return. But the black-chinned continues gazing at me calmly as if waiting for something. "Oh, of course. Like old times." I enter the aviary through the security doors, pick up the Tupperware container, and shake it in the air. Several young adults drop from their perches and start chasing fruit flies as they swarm toward the aviary bars. And the second the unsuspecting escapees make their exit, Blacktop lifts off his perch and begins snapping them up with practiced ease and efficiency.

"So how was Mexico?" I ask Blacktop as I exit the aviary. But he is too busy preening his wing feathers to engage in small talk. "You sure turned into a handsome devil," I observe as I approach more closely to examine his purple throat and bleached white neck ring. At which point Blacktop rises off his perch, makes the soft *chup-chup* sound characteristic of a black-chinned in flight, hovers directly in front of my face a few seconds, then vanishes over the tall ficus tree in the driveway. After reconnecting with Blacktop, who came back to his dowel perch every morning that week before heading for the hills, I never again questioned the power of a hummingbird's memory.

On June 12, I release fifteen young adults from the aviary and exhale at the substantial reduction in my numbers. But that afternoon while I am cleaning perches and scrubbing cages, five new rescues come in, with all of the attendant stress and emotionally charged conversation their arrivals imply. My phone rings without relief all day and late into the night. I move all of the caged birds up a level and get to bed sometime around eleven thirty. In a rare mid-June reprieve, only two injured birds arrive the next day.

At five o'clock the following morning, curious about how far rehabbers walk each day during peak season, I strap on a pedometer while I'm mixing hummingbird formula in the kitchen. Before noon, I take in three female nestlings — an Allen's, an Anna's, and a black-chinned — that, thanks to one obstacle or another, cannot be returned to the wild any time soon. That same morning I get twenty calls about nest crises, downed fledglings, and an Allen's male chasing a female inside the caller's expansive living room in Bel Air. By mid-June, female hummingbirds are no longer interested in breeding because their babies won't fledge until late July, when food sources become scarce as flowers disappear. But in their quest to disseminate their genes, some motivated males disregard the laws of nature and continue pursuing unreceptive females despite the indifference and hostility they invariably encounter.

At two p.m. my friend Ashley, the wildlife specialist from the Pasadena Humane Society, shows up at my door with five young birds — two Allen's, an Anna's, a black-chinned, and a fuzzy male rufous half the size of my little finger and too adorable for description. Most of the new arrivals go into the ICU, but two are feeder-trained and fly straight from my hand into starter cages. Between noon and three o'clock, another ten calls have come in. At three thirty I get a call from the Santa Monica animal shelter informing me they have a healthy fledgling that needs to be picked up. Since it is rush hour and I try not to be away from the house longer than thirty minutes during the day, I ask the officer to feed her sugar water for the next four hours until I can get there. After getting the new arrivals situated and on track, and as I am eating lunch at four o'clock, Jean calls and asks how things are going, even though she knows all too well.

"I've had thirty calls already today. I'm ready to blow my brains out."

"Well, here's some ammunition," she says, and then she gives me the number of an exasperating caller who insists she has an abandoned nest, although all indicators point to the contrary. "She's called me at least five times and I can't get anything done. Can you just have her send you a photo of the nest?" Jean pleads. "I've been arguing with her all day."

"Okay." I sigh. "And thanks, Jean. It's reassuring to know I can depend on you for that extra push just as I'm hitting the wall."

While rushing to finish my now-cold microwave quesadilla, I call Jean's latest headache and ask her to send me a photo. Just as Jean surmised, the plump Allen's twins in the photo look perfect. After reassuring the caller, who is also exhausted by now, I head out to the garage. I have fifteen nestlings in the ICU, most of

which are fully feathered this time of year. As I am feeding the ravenous crew, I notice a mite on the bill of a young Allen's I have had
for over a week. When I lift the plastic cup nest he and his twin are
resting in, an army of mites swarms out onto the paper towels in
the bottom of the ICU. Keeping the ICU chicks mite-free is a high
priority, since if one nestling has mites, they all do. I know the
mites did not come from Ashley's Pasadena rescues, which always
arrive clean. It's a point of pride for her. And I isolated a pair of
new arrivals that came in caked with mites this morning, placing
them in a clear plastic small-animal box with a tight lid after dusting them thoroughly. But when I pick up the box, the unfastened
lid slides off, and hundreds of mites are crawling all over the outside, on my hands, and, as I look more closely with magnification,
on every bird in the ICU.

Pushed past my emotional limit by this setback, hot tears
stream down my face even as I frantically brush mites off everything in sight. When I pull myself together a minute later, because
even my meltdowns have to be brief this time of year, I take everything out of the ICU, replace every nest, dust each bird with insecticide, and wipe down every inch of the interior with a sterile cloth.
After an hour of damage control, the ICU and its colorful residents
appear mite-free. As I am scrubbing the wooden shelf the ICU sits
on, because even it has mites, I get a call from José, who has a
fledgling that rode on the windshield wiper of his truck while he
was barreling down the freeway at seventy miles per hour during
his ninety-minute commute from Riverside to Los Angeles.

"I was driving into the sun and had to turn the windshield
washer on and I could hear a squeak every time the wipers moved,
so I figured there was something wrong with them," José reports.
"But when I got home and lifted the wiper to check it, he was hanging onto the bottom edge, crying."

"So he was actually going back and forth on the wiper blade while you were driving?"

"Yeah," José replies in amazement. "I could see a dark bump on the wiper blade, but I thought it was a leaf or something." Anxious about his hummingbird's traumatic experience, José insists on delivering him from East Los Angeles immediately, even though it is rush hour and he won't make it to my house before seven.

Rehabbers always encourage finders to bring birds during off-hours, when the trip does not take so long. This strategy has the dual purpose of sparing the hummingbird from going hungry for hours while riding in the car and preventing the rehabber from being tied up while waiting for a finder to arrive. Even though I'm home, I'm still held up, and there are a lot of things I cannot do when I'm expecting someone to walk in with a distressed bird any minute. Waiting for people to show up with birds is the main reason I abandon all efforts to cook during the breeding season. Receiving a bird takes at least ten minutes, and—after I talk to the finder, get his contact information, clean up the new arrival, check for damage, and get her fed and situated in the ICU or a starter cage with the appropriate nest and syringes—most intakes require an hour. And without fail, every time I cautiously pull a few pans out of the cupboard and turn on the stove, the phone rings.

Shortly after talking to José, I get a call from a woman in Brentwood who had cut a nest with a pair of two-week-old chicks in it from a rosebush in her yard earlier that day and then carelessly set the babies on a covered porch on the other side of the house for a couple of hours. I explain to her that she needs to return the nest to its original location immediately and watch for the mother for half an hour. Thirty minutes later she calls and informs me the mother has not come back to feed the babies. I ask her to send me a photo but she insists there is no point and refuses to cooperate.

When I ask her to bring me the nest she claims she is too busy and that I need to come and pick them up. I have fifteen screaming nestlings in the ICU and a baby on the way, so I explain to her why I can't leave home. The conversation deteriorates so quickly that I lose my temper for the first time this year. After the caller hangs up on me, I sink onto the patio beside the starter cages in the late-afternoon sun and call Jean for one of our famous therapy calls because that's what we do and, well, she owes me one. The second Jean answers I start the debriefing.

"When I explain to her why I can't come and pick up the nestlings she says, 'I thought this is what you do, save hummingbirds.'"

"Oh, please," Jean scoffs.

"Exactly, like she's not trying to push any buttons. So I point out that I save thousands of hummingbirds every year, which is precisely why I can't take an hour to drive out to her house. I tell her I have sixty birds in rehab right now and another one on the way and all of the other volunteers are working day and night. So then she gets ugly and says, 'Well, I suppose you'd come out if I paid you.'"

"Ugh," Jean groans in disgust. "Don't you hate it when some people do that? They think everything is about money."

"It's so pathetic. So I tell her this isn't about money, which really pisses her off because clearly everything is for her. So she says, 'Well, I guess we'll just have to let nature take its course, then.'"

"What nature?" Jean exclaims incredulously. "She cut the nest!"

"That's what I said. 'This is not nature. You created this problem by cutting the nest and now it's your responsibility to correct that. These are living creatures that are going to die if you don't do something.' And in this irritating, blasé tone she's like, 'Yeah, well, I have a lot of other things to do today.'"

"Oh, shit. Like her hair, probably."

"That's what I figured. So I give her three options for where she can take the nest, and she's like, 'Those are all a long way to drive.'"

"What a piece of work."

"So I ask her if she will feed the chicks sugar water until tonight, when I can come and get them, but no, she's too busy, can't be bothered. So finally I ask her if she feels tired and she says, 'What do you mean?' And I point out that it must take a lot of energy to remain that indifferent. But then she has to get in the last word about how I obviously don't care that much about hummingbirds or I'd come and get them. By then I'm pushed so far past my limit all I can say is 'Find something to love.'"

"Besides herself."

"Exactly. So then of course she hangs up."

"How can anybody be that self-centered? It's criminal."

"No shit. I'll bet if it were some new eclectic cuisine hotspot that was the latest 'it' place on the west side, she wouldn't hesitate to hop in her Escalade and drive way more than an hour to drop two hundred bucks so she could stuff her face."

"Wouldn't think a thing about it," Jean adds.

"Her apathy was so bottomless. She was like a caricature of the idle princess, with such misplaced priorities. And the whole time I'm on the phone with her I want to explain how she needs to take time off from her busy nail-polishing, hairstyling, boutique-browsing schedule to attend to these fragile lives that she so thoroughly screwed up and that are so much more real than anything on her salon-hopping agenda. I mean, get over yourself."

"For starters. And grow a conscience."

"Right? Better to be broke and compassionate than rich and heartless. It's time to turn the page."

"Long time ago."

"But then I think, what's the point?"

"No, there's no use." Jean sighs disparagingly. "It's all about her."

I hang up, but my phone rings before I can set it down. A free-spirited young finder named Sophie is calling from the Hollywood Hills to report a grounded fledgling with a damaged wing.

Still wound up from my conversation with the rich and aimless, I begin cautiously, "I have a couple of places you can take him if you don't mind driving—"

"Oh, I'll drive him anywhere," she says, cutting me off enthusiastically. "I just love him and he has so much personality. I'd do anything to save him."

God bless you, Sophie, I think, and I give her directions to my house and hang up. This bright light not only saved a helpless hummingbird but also restored my trembling faith in humanity.

At 8:15, after taking in Sophie's fledgling and José's surprisingly unscathed male Anna's who braved the freeway from Riverside, I put the caged birds in the garage for the night, feed the ICU nestlings one last time, and wash sixty feeders before slumping into a chair in the kitchen and checking my pedometer. I have walked eight miles today.

"That's some serious legwork," I say to our cat Gyppy, who hops off the kitchen table and begins rolling around on my lap, oblivious to the hard-hitting day that is not yet behind me. Marathon walking is the reason for the physical exhaustion hummingbird rescuers begin straining under by the middle of the summer. Despite my rigorous karate conditioning, I am struggling to put one foot in front of the other. And Jean, who is seventy-two years old, is a force of nature.

In a phone conversation at the end of my first grueling summer of rehab, I praised Jean for sailing through six months of stress and fatigue that I, twenty-four years her junior, nearly buckled under on more than one occasion. "Let's face it, Jean," I told her, "you're Wonder Woman."

"Yeah, I wonder why I'm doing all this," she responded dryly.

As demanding as the physical component of rescue is, it pales in comparison to the emotional toll callers and birds exact on the lifesaver's weary psyche. In reflecting on my contentious conversation with the indifferent nest cutter in Brentwood, I realize that Lao Tzu, who advises against arguing and fighting, would not be proud. Because people like her are exactly what he has been trying to warn me about and prepare me for. *No fight. No blame,* Lao Tzu counsels. Or as my karate sensei likes to say, "The best fight is no fight." But in my frayed mental and emotional condition, I had failed utterly and given in to my anger. There may not have been anything I could do to save the two young hummingbirds, which is enough to kill me, because in dedicating my existence to this project every summer, I have so much invested. But in letting the coldhearted caller get to me, I allowed her to drag me down to her miserable level, and I ended up the loser. I resolve to spend more time consulting Lao Tzu as soon as I get enough sleep to focus my eyes on the written word.

Sitting at the kitchen table that night, I begin scrolling through the fifty received calls on my cell phone when I come across the Santa Monica animal shelter. Under the pressures of the day, I had forgotten about the fledgling there whose life depends on me. I check the time on my phone. It's eight thirty, and the shelter closes at nine. Without a minute to spare, I rush out to the garage, grab a small cage, fill a syringe with formula, give a baffled Frank, who is exercising in the back room, a kiss goodbye, and find myself in the car speeding west on Olympic Boulevard less than five minutes later. I arrive at the shelter just as it is closing and pick up a young female Anna's who is encrusted with dried sugar water and whose chest feathers have been stripped off. When sugar water is spilled on a hummingbird, it desiccates the feathers, causing them to peel off in clumps. Because we get a lot of young birds with bare chests during the summer, we are constantly alerting callers to this danger. But fledglings dropped off at animal shelters usually have been through it all.

Despite her sorry condition, the sturdily built Anna's is fundamentally sound and has sustained no damage that a warm bath and six weeks in rehab won't cure. But she is cold and starting to lapse into torpor, so the second I get back to the car, I administer my magical breathing remedy and within five minutes have her gulping formula from a handheld syringe. After she has eaten nearly all of the formula I brought along, I get out of the car and go around to the passenger's side. As I am buckling her cage into the passenger's seat, two middle-aged men in expensive dark suits approach my car with a medium-size moving box.

"Excuse us," they interrupt from behind me. "Do you know what time they close?" the one holding the box asks as he cocks his head toward the shelter door.

"At nine," I reply, turning. "Why?"

"Nobody answered the door when we rang the bell." He shrugs.

"Yeah, they're closed now, but they'll be open tomorrow morning at eight."

The two men look at each other blankly. "Well, we need to give them this box."

"What's in it?" I ask warily.

The guy holding the box opens the top and a mass of fuzz rushes into the corner. In the darkness, I can't make out any distinct form.

"What is it?"

"Ducks," they answer in unison.

"Ducks?"

"Yeah, nine baby ducks," the one cradling the box explains. "They were following their mother through a busy intersection on Montana and a car almost hit them. When the car braked and honked its horn, the mother flew off and the babies started running around in circles in the middle of the intersection. So we jumped out and grabbed them because cars were squealing their tires all over the place trying to avoid hitting them."

I listen to the story in stunned silence. And I thought my windshield-wiper bird from Riverside had had a hard day.

"Do you have any idea what we can do with them?" he asks as they both look at me innocently.

"No, I just do hummingbirds." I try to deflect his overture.

"Well, we have to be at the airport in an hour," he says, looking at his watch. "Could you take them for us?" he entreats as his companion pulls out his wallet and begins stuffing ten- and twenty-dollar bills into my blue-jean jacket. "Please?" They both look at me with exaggerated pleading in their eyes. "It would be such a relief," he says while his friend continues extracting crisp bills from his wallet and tossing them onto the hummingbird cage inside my car.

"Okay, okay." I laugh as I close the car door and take the box in my arms. "Your language is persuasive. And the ducks and hummingbirds thank you for your generosity."

"And we thank you." They both bow in deference with their palms together in the Thai gesture of gratitude as they back away. "You're a beautiful person."

"Who knows nothing about ducks," I mumble to myself as I watch them speed off in their Mercedes coupe. And suddenly, looking at the nine little brown-and-yellow fluff balls crouching in the corner of the box, I am overcome by layers of fear that course through me with terrifying urgency. I have never taken care of a duck in my life. What do they eat? How do I feed them? How warm do they need to be? What about their mother? She must be going crazy looking for them. Will they make it through the night without her? Should I try to put them back so she can find them? But where? And what if they start dying? What will I do? What have I done?

After putting the box in my hatchback, I hop into the car and glance around anxiously. Sitting in the dimly lit parking lot with the heater blasting, I look at the young hummingbird buckled into the passenger's seat and derive tremendous comfort from her presence. As messed up as she seems, I know exactly what to do. I can save a hummingbird while I am half asleep and with my eyes closed, and I often have. But I'm in the dark with baby ducks. I call Jean immediately, rattle off my fears, mention some possible alternatives, and beg for guidance.

"No, you can't put them back out on Montana," Jean says as if she's talking to an idiot.

"Of course not," I agree, coming to my senses.

"They'll be pressed duck in under a minute if you do."

"What should I do, then?"

"Let me call you back."

Jean makes a few calls and finally reaches a colleague who at one time or another has rescued just about every wild creature you can find in Southern California and who calls and deftly advises me on what to feed them. When I stop at a local market on my way home to pick up duck-appropriate food for the fuzzy bunch, "Rescue Me" by Fontella Bass is playing over the store's PA system, reminding me of all the nights I have spent shuttling helpless birds around the city. When I get home, Frank and I coax the insufferably cute ducklings, which all scurry from one corner of the box to the other in a tightly knit group like cartoon characters, into eating enough to get through the night.

By ten thirty I have the sugarcoated shelter bird bathed and blow-dried, and the ducklings have settled into a furry mound for the night. In the dim light I inspect the long line of nestlings in the ICU, who are sleeping in tangled piles like a class of preschoolers stranded at the airport. I look more closely, examining the chicks for parasites. Mites have an odd effect on the human mind. For hours after you have gotten the creepy crawlers off your skin, they live on in your brain like phantom limbs. And despite the nestlings' clean and relaxed appearance, I begin to hallucinate that I see mites on the birds and feel them crawling all over my hands and arms. I don my surgical loupes and examine the nestlings' bills and then myself. Not a mite in sight. I let out the longest exhale of the year, turn off the light, and head for bed, where Frank is sleeping soundly through what to me is starting to feel like war. At eleven thirty, just as I am slumping into bed so drained I can barely move, my phone rings.

"Terry?" a hesitant female voice asks.

"Yes, this is Terry," I repeat for the fortieth time that day in what is starting to sound like some haunting Nietzschean mantra.

"Sorry to call so late . . ."

"It's okay," I lie as I tiptoe downstairs with the phone. "What's up?"

"I have a ruby-throated hummingbird that was trapped in my garage all day and finally fell to the floor. He's still alive but I don't know what to do with him."

"He's not a ruby-throated," I correct her. "He's probably an Anna's. But I can help you with him," I assure her, and then I walk her through our overnight-care routine for trapped or unconscious adults.

"Well, I've been giving him sugar water for a while now but he still isn't trying to fly."

"It could be because it's so late and he's going to sleep. How long have you been feeding him?"

"A couple of hours. He seemed fine at first but now I'm really worried because his feathers are getting all puffy."

"That means he's going into torpor."

"I'm so scared he's going to die. What should I do?" she pleads helplessly.

"Okay, look, I'm not asleep yet, so why don't you bring him to me and I'll take over so you won't have to stress about him all night or deal with it in the morning."

"Um, well I'd like to bring him, but it's kind of a long drive."

"How long?" I ask with trepidation, trying to avoid another contentious phone encounter.

"I'm not sure exactly."

"Well, why don't you tell me where you are and I can tell you how far the drive is."

"I'm in Ohio," she answers flatly.

"Ohio. That's a long drive," I concede. "And you're right. He is a ruby-throated."

As I'm heading back to bed after advising my long-distance caller, I hear the wind kicking up outside and immediately feel a sense of impending doom that leads me to reflect on the alternate reality hummingbird rescue has dropped me into. My awareness of the myriad dangers in the hummingbird world has ruined so many things that once were pleasures in my earlier, uninformed life. Like the way I used to love listening to the rain while lying in bed at night, and even more, the wind. I once relished falling asleep to the rhythm of raindrops pattering on the skylight overhead or the sound of the wind gusting through the jacaranda branches outside the bedroom window. But now whenever a downpour starts or a windstorm blasts into the city, I lie awake and worry about young hummingbirds. I think of all the nests hanging in the balance out there that might, with a heavy rain or a strong wind, be swept away and destroyed in seconds.

Pondering the differences between rehabbers and normal people brings to mind the weighty demands wildlife rescue places on its human foot soldiers. A lot of callers who stumble upon lost and injured hummingbirds assume anybody can rehabilitate them. It looks so easy when they bring one bird into rescue. But nothing could be further from the truth. To rehabilitate a single hummingbird, and do it conscientiously enough to ensure his survival in the wild, is anything but simple. And when I consider the mental, physical, and emotional toll rehab exacts on its human volunteers — the arduous days, six months of nail-biting stress, crushing workload between April and August — on top of the focus, patience, tenacity, self-sacrifice, organization, and people skills required, I realize that precious few people have the resources to pull it off.

Just do what needs to be done, Lao Tzu advises. And there's the challenge, Lao Tzu. Now that I know, I do. Over the years, dedicated rehabbers have taught by example that the best don't quit, cut and run, or hand their problems off to others when the going gets tough. The best press on through illness, injury, and personal trauma, remaining steadfast and resolute despite the chaos erupting around them. They go down with the ship. That's commitment. That's character. And that's the devoted band of rehabbers who persevere through the levels of pain that bear down on them with the weight of the world every spring and summer. And as I stagger up the stairs sometime around midnight, too tired to sleep, and then sink into bed, I'm proud to be one of them.

I report to Jean's front door with the ducklings early the next morning, and she arranges to deliver them to the Wetlands Wildlife and Care Center in Huntington Beach, where they will be rehabbed and banded before being released into a protected natural habitat nearby. As I hand the drowsy ducklings over to her, with the hopping beat of "Rescue Me" still pounding in my head from the night before, I describe to Jean how songs I hear on the radio frequently get stuck on extended play in my brain as a result of my late-night adventures. "We should have a list of rehab's greatest hits."

"Yeah," Jean agrees wryly. "Guaranteed to make you cry."

"And keep you up all night."

Despite the undue stress the ducklings created for me during their twelve hours in my possession, they proved instructive. In the heat of the summer battle, I am beginning to lose patience with finders who are unraveling over hummingbird problems for which the solutions seem absurdly obvious. But my anxious night with the ducklings reminds me how easily the tables can turn and how quickly I can be thrown out of my comfort zone when confronted with wildlife whose needs are entirely unknown to me. I vow to remember that heart-pounding moment when I found myself running scared with the ducks the next time I get a hysterical call about a hummingbird.

And my pledge of forbearance comes just in time. Because despite the extreme stress I have been straining under the past few weeks, the worst is yet to come.

CHAPTER 21

Somewhere Over the Rainbow

EARLY ONE MORNING about a week later I have a dream that I am standing on an outdoor porch when a giant, eight-foot hummingbird suddenly air-brakes and hovers directly in front of me. His unexpected appearance, imposing size, and brazen approach are frightening, like encountering a hungry Tyrannosaurus rex. But he isn't trying to kill me. At least I don't feel he is trying to kill me. Though maybe he is. Either way, I'm scared to death. After several seconds with this oversize hummingbird hovering so close to me that the air from his wing beats blows my curly hair straight like I'm in a wind tunnel, he inches in and taps the center of my forehead with his needle-like bill before flying backward and retreating into the sky. Then another giant hummingbird appears and does the same thing. And pretty soon there are dozens of enormous hummingbirds coming at me. And although they exhibit no aggression or ill intentions, they all seem to want, to need, something from me. But instead of being relieved, I am more terrified than ever. I awake in a heart-pounding panic at five o'clock, just in time to get to work.

I get up feeling tense and exhausted. When I check my phone, I see it's June 21. Summer has officially arrived. And Jean's prediction three years ago that the day would come when the number 21 wouldn't feel so lucky has proven correct. I scroll through my missed calls and see that I have three, one of which is a voicemail from Jean asking me to call her when I get a chance. After filling stacks of feeders and getting forty caged birds situated outside for the day, I take in a pair of twins discovered crying at dawn after spending the night in a dumpster in Century City, and a hybrid fledgling that appears to be an Allen's crossed with an Anna's. Hybrids are rare, but I get a few every year, and their unusual combination of size and color prove endlessly fascinating. This particular hybrid, which came from the UCLA botanical gardens, sports the earthy-rust tail feathers of the Allen's but has the long, heavier body and grayish-green back of an Anna's. Because the bird looks so unlike anything I have ever seen, I cannot determine if it is a male or female. Time will tell.

At ten a.m. I call Jean and before she can say anything, I recount my giant-hummingbird nightmare. Thinking she will be impressed — after my rotating blue-spruce dream and its twenty-one swirling and magical birds three years earlier — at how my perception of hummingbirds has evolved, or devolved, as she so presciently warned, I describe the swarms of gigantic hummingbirds, their distraught appeals for help, and my absolute terror in the face of their demands. Jean listens in silence and then considers the symbolism for a few seconds.

"Actually, that's not so far-fetched," she muses matter-of-factly. "Now get a pen, because I need you to call a guy about a nest in Beverly Hills."

"That's it? You're blowing me off?"

"I can't talk right now. I'll call you in an hour." She gives me the number and abruptly hangs up.

I should have gleaned from my ominous dream that I was heading into a rough day. By now I should know that my nightmares aren't just late-night entertainment. At eleven I give Pepper her regularly scheduled flight-training exercises. With the exception of Pepper and Gabriel, each bird in my facility has at least one cage mate. Despite their hostility toward one another in the wild, most hummingbirds welcome the presence of a familiar face in rehab, so every day I place Pepper's and Gabriel's starter cages side by side, and they have been eyeing each other for over a month now. I have constructed a multitiered perching structure in Pepper's cage so she can focus on gaining lift when I am not available for flight-training exercises. And Pepper has risen to the challenge, buzzing up and down the perches with dogged persistence. A few weeks ago she would drift to the bottom of the cage and be unable to get back up to her four-inch-high perch without my help. Now when I notice her on the bottom and approach to offer assistance, she flies to the low perch, then rapidly scales the tiers to the top before I can get there. Gabriel watches her closely, and, as with the rambunctious rufous twins earlier in the summer, her activity encourages him. Every time she pops up and down her stairs, he buzzes across the bottom of his cage and then alights on a low perch and looks back over his shoulder at her hopefully. Sometimes their interaction is so poignant I want to sit and watch them all day. And if it were not for the seventy hungry hummingbirds blossoming around us, I just might.

The minute I finish administering Pepper's advanced physical therapy session, my phone starts ringing and doesn't stop. Before noon, I get a fledgling found on a Burbank movie set that is suffering from a blocked crop after being fed mashed strawberries.

Soon after that, I receive a young adult who sustained a head injury when he slammed into the front window of Jamba Juice, followed by a fledgling with a badly damaged and infected eye, an adult who got stuck on flypaper while trying to escape a cat and who is missing all of his tail feathers, and a nest of mite-covered twins cut by tree trimmers who left the chicks in the back of a pickup truck for five hours before calling me.

It's one of those hot, suffocating days when the city air weighs thick and heavy on its residents and the sun beats down with desert ferocity. At one o'clock, I have to move all of the caged birds into the shade close to the house and mount a fan outside the aviary to circulate the stifling air. After I get everyone cooled down and step into the aviary to change the feeders that always leak badly whenever the sun gets too hot, I find a bird named Rosie lying on the concrete floor breathing hard.

Rosie is an adult female Anna's who arrived after crashing into a glass-walled office building in Beverly Hills a month ago. The sensitive young man who picked her up off the sidewalk named her for the unusually bright red spot on her throat. After Rosie's dizzy arrival, I kept her on a nest in the ICU for a few days until she began flying. Because of serious damage to her right hip, Rosie was incapable of perching. So I isolated her in a cage with especially wide perches, where she struggled to achieve enough stability to rest for a few seconds before flying back and forth in the cage for hours at a time. At first, whenever Rosie reached a dangerous level of exhaustion, I placed her in a small head-injury cage, but her desire to fly was so overpowering she would throw herself against the sides of the cage in an effort to break free. Afraid she might sever her wing feathers in a small cage and unable to restrain her any other way, I resorted to wrapping Rosie in a tissue and holding her in my hand for five minutes every two hours so she could rest. Sitting in the

garage, cradling the flaming jewel in my palm, I believed that anything was possible and eventually she would prevail, even as I felt
her heart beating wildly as if she were racing against some imaginary clock.

After four weeks of incremental progress, Rosie was able to
stay perched for short periods, so I put her in the aviary with a
fresh cohort. Each night I retrieved her from the aviary and placed
her on the bottom of a dark cage so she could sleep, returning her
to the aviary at dawn. Being an experienced adult, Rosie was by far
the strongest flier in the aviary and able to hold her own, making
larger males who sought to intimidate her back down. But after
two days, her flight ability began to decline. While removing feeders just after sunset the night before, I found her lying on her side
on the cement. Assuming she had tried to fly off her perch in the
dark and gotten disoriented, I put her in a cage for the night and
returned her to the aviary that morning. Now I reach down and
pick her up off the ground, but instead of kicking and fighting to
break free the way she usually does, Rosie goes limp in my hand. I
rush her to the ICU, place her in a natural nest, and feed her some
formula. A menacing sense of dread threatens to shatter my fragile
emotional state as I am feeding the feathered nestlings in the ICU,
but I suppress it when the phone rings.

When I check my list of missed calls, I notice that I have accidentally turned the ringer off and have four new voicemails. I push the
call-back button on the first message without listening to the voicemail, which is always a mistake because some people phone me just
to chat about hummingbirds, as if I have nothing else to do.

Rehabbers' nerves are so jagged by the end of June that we
begin pressing long-winded callers to get straight to the point.
But some conversations dwell on the hypothetical to an absurd degree. On this unusually stressful afternoon, a caller named Marty

answers every question I ask with a baffling non sequitur. After going on at length about his feeders and his love of hummingbirds, Marty begins explaining that he has a problem, but after three minutes of his failing to come to the point, I finally interrupt.

"So are you calling about one hummingbird in particular or . . ."

"Well, I've had so many around this year, I fill my feeders every day and I can hardly keep up."

"But other than that, is there a problem?"

"Well, you know, sometimes they don't hang around that much and then *bam,* all of a sudden there's hundreds of them buzzing all over the place, like when it rains."

"So do you have a bird that's sick or injured?"

"Well, yeah, I've had birds like that before that can't fly or something. I've been feeding them for ten years, so everything has happened. It's just so fun to watch them but I can't go away for more than a day because they empty their feeders really fast so I don't know what I'm going to do if I have to go somewhere or—"

"I'm confused," I interrupt, wondering if my communication skills have fallen off a cliff. "Do you have a problem with a specific hummingbird?"

"Well, a lot of things can go wrong with these guys so I was wondering what to do if, first, a mother builds a nest where we have to trim the trees; second, I find an injured bird in my yard; or, third, a sick bird starts hanging around the feeders."

"Marty," I say with exaggerated patience, "it's like John Maynard Keynes said about economics: We only have today, so let's wait until we have a specific crisis to address and then we can panic. So do you have a hummingbird with a specific crisis we need to panic about right now?"

"Well, no, not really. Not right now. But I'll sure call you if I do."

"Terrific. Thank you."

The second and third voicemails are about nests infested with mites, and the fourth is from a bright and articulate college student in the South Bay who has a fledgling, leaves me his number, and asks if I can have Jean call him when she gets a chance. This call signals that the other shoe has finally dropped. When Jean is no longer returning her calls, it's because she's so swamped she can't. I call him back, instruct him on how to care for the bird for a day, and promise to call Jean. The second I set my phone down, it starts ringing, and calls flood in without a break all afternoon.

By five o'clock the weather has cooled off enough to put the cages back out in the late-afternoon sun. After filling fifty feeders I head into the garage to feed the ICU nestlings for the twenty-fifth time that day. As I open the sliding glass door, I notice Rosie splayed on her stomach next to her nest. I reach in to pick her up, but she's already gone. I lift her out of the ICU, feed the fifteen nestlings, sink down into the chair I always sat in when I held her, and weep. While I am busy crying my pain out, the Santa Monica shelter calls with a fledgling. I assure the officer I will be there before they close at nine.

Fifteen minutes later, as I'm trying to pull myself together and cradling Rosie's still-warm body in my hand, a call comes in from a monk at the Vedanta Society who is afraid they have an abandoned nest outside the monastery in Hollywood. I give him the usual instructions on how to sit and watch for the mother for thirty minutes without taking his eyes off the nest.

"It requires a lot of patience, but I assume that's something you've been working on," I say encouragingly.

"Oh, yes," he agrees with exaggerated seriousness. "That's definitely a quality we emphasize here."

Thirty minutes later he calls to report the mother is still missing. From his description of the chicks' behavior, however, I am almost certain she is still there. So I ask him to recruit another monk to sit and watch. After an hour of back-and-forth calls, a third monk finally catches a glimpse of the mother flying off the nest.

"Everybody has been so worried," the original monk says in a voice steeped in relief. "I don't know how to thank you for your time."

"Well, after the day I've had, it would be helpful if you could put in a good word for me with your boss. And I think you know who I mean."

"Yes, I do"—he laughs cheerfully—"and I will!"

I carry Rosie out to the agapanthus beds growing by the redwood fence alongside the aviary and dig a shallow grave. Hummingbirds' bones are so light, they decompose within a few days, leaving behind no trace of their short time on earth. While lining her grave with bougainvillea blossoms the same vivid magenta as her iridescent spot, I contemplate Rosie's experience. As children we are taught that if we fight long and hard enough for something, we ultimately will prevail. In the great tradition of Vince Lombardi's "Winners never quit and quitters never win," and popular culture's celebration of iconic underdogs like Seabiscuit and Rocky, we grow up believing that perseverance and determination will overcome the greatest odds. I have never seen a hummingbird fight as tenaciously as Rosie, hour after hour, day after day, to make it back. But Rosie's demise drives home a sobering recognition: sometimes we fight like hell and lose. And this is the point at which we featherless bipeds turn to religion and the belief that there must be something beyond the immediate battle. Something within the struggle that takes us to a higher plane until, in the end, it is the struggle itself that carries meaning.

"Time to rest now, Rosie," I whisper tearfully as I cover her life-less body with damp, rich soil that smells like something just be-ginning. And with her glowing red circle reflecting the last rays of the setting sun, Rosie departs over the proverbial rainbow to a more peaceful realm.

I get the caged birds put away for the night and wash an arm-load of plastic syringes, then I feed the drowsy nestlings once more and head to the Santa Monica shelter. I arrive just as they are clos-ing and pick up the most jaw-droppingly gorgeous black-chinned female I have ever seen. Black-chinneds are the latest-breeding species in Southern California, so the appearance of black-chinned fledglings in rescue signals the beginning of the end. Hummingbird rehabbers love young black-chinneds not only for their exquisite beauty and superior intelligence but for the end of the nesting sea-son their arrival represents. And I could not have asked for a more outstanding example of the species. The fledgling has a bleached white breast, a regal demeanor, and an otherworldly elegance, as if she dropped straight from some pure celestial realm into my lap. If this magnificent beauty had not fallen, she likely never would have been seen by human eyes or appeared as a reminder of the splen-dor flying around out there that we don't even know about.

That was quick, I say to myself before thanking the Vedanta monk for his appeal that brought about this instant show of appre-ciation. The shelter attendant locks the door behind me as I leave. While I'm buckling the angelic hummingbird into the passenger's seat, an athletic, middle-aged man in a navy blue designer running suit approaches me.

"Excuse me." He clears his throat hesitantly. "Sorry to bother you, but do you know what time they close?"

"They just closed," I say before noticing a small cardboard mail-ing box in his hand.

"Damn," he mutters, looking around the parking lot vaguely.

"Why? What do you have?" I ask with trepidation.

"Oh, a baby kitten," he replies, opening the box gingerly. "A homeless guy was trying to get rid of him outside the drugstore."

I peer into the box in the dim light and see the outline of a surprisingly large kitten, his umbilical cord still attached, lying on a dirty white washcloth.

"Wow, he was just born."

"Yeah, and I didn't want to leave him with that guy because, well, you know." He shrugs with world-weariness.

I bite my lip, because I know what's coming.

"Listen, I have to be —"

"At the airport," I finish his sentence.

"How did you know?" he asks with a stunned expression.

"Lucky guess."

"Well, do you think you could take him somewhere for me? I would really appreciate it," he says, pulling two twenty-dollar bills out of his wallet and giving them to me.

"Sure, I'll take him," I agree as he hands me the box.

"Thank you so much. You're terrific." He opens his arms wide in a gesture of a giant embrace while jogging backward to his car, and then he drives off.

When I get into my car, I open the box and examine the newborn kitten sleeping soundly inside. In an odd twist, his color scheme is identical to that of the female black-chinned, with a bright white chest and blackish-tan cape extending down his head and back. This time I don't have to call anyone for advice, because I know cats inside and out. I drive him straight home, feed him formula that he sucks down with a hearty appetite, call a young couple who do kitten rescue and whom I have run into a few times while walking my Abyssinian cat around the block, and arrive with the kitten at their door before ten. When I step into the kitchen, rescue cats of all ages and colors race up to greet me affectionately.

"He's huge for a newborn," Jonathon remarks as he lifts the substantial kitten from the box.

"And incredibly beautiful." Daniel frowns with mock seriousness.

"Thanks for taking him so late." I hand them the twenty-dollar bills. And then, posing a question I had been asked myself a dozen times that week, I say, "Can I call you?"

After dusting and tucking the exotic black-chinned into a nest in the ICU and feeding the two or three groggy nestlings who mechanically open their mouths more out of habit than hunger, I close the garage door and head into the house just as my phone rings. It's Jean.

"That's the longest hour I've ever lived through," I tease, recalling our conversation that morning.

"Sorry," she mutters, "I had eight people lined up in my kitchen with shoeboxes when you called. They were backed up out the front door. It was like the ER on the Fourth of July around here."

"And the Fourth isn't even until next week."

"Yeah, I can hardly wait," she says dryly.

"Listen, I have the number of a guy who wants you to call him. He's got a fledgling that he's been feeding sugar water all day, but he sounds pretty together, so I think you can wait and have him bring it tomorrow. But I told him I'd have you call him, so can I give you his phone number?" I ask as my call-waiting beeps.

"Yeah, just a minute." I hear Jean shuffling things around on a desk. "I can't find a piece of paper. Oh, wait, here, I'll just write it on a paper towel."

"Okay, it's—"

"Hold on, the towel has sugar water all over it . . ." She trails off. "Okay, go ahead."

"It's —"

"No, wait, the pen's not working," Jean mumbles. "Oh, here, I'll just write it with this."

"Three —"

"Wait, oh, I don't know, I don't have anything to write with. So maybe I can just . . ." She trails off again. "Hold on a minute."

Ten seconds later she comes back. "Okay, now, what did you want to tell me?" she asks innocently.

"Jean, have you had a few glasses tonight?"

"No," she answers matter-of-factly, "I'm drinking straight from the bottle."

I hang up with Jean just in time to field a call from Heather, who has a fledgling she just found sitting on the sidewalk outside her yoga studio in West Hollywood.

"I looove hummingbirds more than anything," Heather gushes in a perky, singsong voice. "She looks really great and is so lively. But people were walking right by her and she almost got stepped on. I want to save her so bad. What can I do?" she asks enthusiastically.

"You can bring her to me. I'm in West Hollywood too."

"Oh, that's awesome, Terry. Yeah, I'll bring her right away. But what are you going to do with her?"

"Well, tomorrow I'll put her in a cage with a drop-dead gorgeous young male Allen's I got this morning and she can go through rehab with him."

"Wow, that's so awesome. She's got a hot boyfriend already!" Heather squeals. "But do you think she'll make it?"

"I know she will. I never lose a healthy fledgling."

"Oh, how awesome, Terry!"

"And after I rehabilitate her, I'll set her free in a month or two."

"That is soooo awesome," Heather shrieks.

"And next year she'll build a nest and make more beautiful baby hummingbirds just like herself. How awesome is that?"

"Oh my God, Terry, I love it," she answers breathlessly. "I'll be right over."

Hanging up the phone, I glance at the clock. It's ten thirty and I feel as though I'm teetering on the brink. I desperately want someone to talk to who will understand what I am feeling right now. Someone I can express my doubts and fears to. But there is nobody. Because like me, all of the dedicated soldiers who wake up to the punishing demands of wildlife rehab at dawn every morning are plagued by the same feelings of isolation and despair this time of year. And like me, they are feeling the strain.

Since I have nothing else to do while waiting for Heather's awesome arrival, I pick up the *Tao Te Ching*. As I am perusing the pages, I wonder if Lao Tzu ever had a day so long and unforgiving that it felt like a hard week. Looking at the filled-to-capacity aviary looming quietly outside in the darkness, I feel my resolve slipping away as I'm overtaken by numbing fatigue and a gnawing uncertainty about what I'm doing. And of course, the master steps up at this point to offer sage counsel during my moment of doubt: *The bright path seems dim; going forward seems like retreat; the easy way seems hard.*

I set the book aside and close my eyes just as the doorbell rings. If all of these insights apply to saving hummingbirds, Lao Tzu, then I most assuredly am on the right track. And if my efforts can help lift another feathered wonder from the hard earth to the open sky, I will go those extra miles before I sleep.

CHAPTER 22

We're Almost There

THE LAST WEEK IN JUNE, ten birds come in, including three fledglings from the Pasadena Humane Society, each of which is perfect
in its own adorable way. By July 1, I have taken in one hundred and
forty-five hummingbirds and released seventy-seven robust young
adults into the wilds of Hollywood. Sixty-five lives rest in my still-
steady hands, awaiting future freedom. The Fourth of July, which
is always a tough weekend for rehabbers, is upon us. Thousands of
hummingbirds fledge the first week in July and, more important,
millions of Southern Californians are outside finding them while
picnicking, partying, and blowing themselves up with fireworks.

At the same time, overcrowded state-run facilities, most of
which take in other kinds of birds year-round, start closing their
doors and turning hummingbirds away as they exceed capacity.
Dozens of callers report being rejected by rescue centers in their
area and having to reach out across the hills, valleys, and snarled
freeways to Jean and me. And despite the longer commutes, most
Angelenos remain undeterred and rise to the occasion, agreeing to
drive their helpless treasures that extra hour, another thirty miles,

whatever they have to do. And in spite of our grinding fatigue, Jean, Linda — another true believer stationed in West Hills — and I hold the desperate line through this last hard weekend. We don't set a limit on intakes, and by this time of year we are always asking one another for an extra cage, a few more feeders, or another box of formula.

The closing of state-funded facilities is the reason I get a set of Anna's twins from the hills above Santa Clarita the first day in July. I meet Eric, who stumbled upon the pair outside a grocery store near Santa Clarita, in Gelson's parking lot in Van Nuys on a sticky July morning. Eric had discovered one fledgling trapped inside an outdoor newspaper dispenser and the other clinging to the side of a flower basket near the store's entrance. When Eric hands me a gerbil carrier with the twins inside, the fledglings look so big I assume they must be another kind of bird. But on closer inspection, I see they are indeed Anna's hummingbirds, though incredibly large, and not just for their age. I feed them some formula in the car before racing over the hill to Benedict Canyon and back home. When I get the twins inside the garage and open the carrier, they both fly out and perch on the edge of the ICU, crying loudly for their mother. As I reach for them, they fly off in terror and circle the garage ceiling in tight helicopter loops. I finally net them and put them in a starter cage — which is too small — before transferring them to a large flight cage and setting them outside with the other beginners.

But the Santa Clarita twins are nothing like the other fledglings stationed beside them on the patio. Remote, guarded, and innately suspicious, they buzz around in panicked circles whenever I approach their cage. Both take to their feeders after one brief lesson, which is a relief because they want nothing to do with me and flee to the back corner of the cage whenever I reach in to fill their syringes. Unlike the friendly city birds that have been coming through my door from the streets of Los Angeles all summer, these supersize twins are truly wild creatures, and their fundamental distrust of me reveals how thoroughly acclimated our feathered urban companions have become to humans over the generations.

The wild twins are also the largest fledglings I have ever taken in. Most Southern California Anna's hummingbirds weigh about four grams at maturity. Since hummingbirds consume their weight in nectar each day, two fledglings in a large flight cage eat around 70 ccs of formula during their fast-paced waking hours, which means I can get away with filling their two 12 cc syringes three times a day, or every five hours. The still-growing Santa Clarita brothers weigh in at a heavyweight five grams each, and they empty two 12 cc syringes every three hours, consuming 100 ccs of formula their first day in the flight cage. Their excellent health, imposing stature, and impressive wing power give them a dominating presence among the fifty-five fledglings and young adults caged on the patio. As the brawny brothers inhale formula from their syringes, I can almost see them expanding before my eyes.

Even more interesting to me, they are only the second set of male twins I have received since I started doing rehab. Hummingbird chicks normally hatch one or two days apart. When I first began rehabbing hummingbirds, I noticed that the older twin was nearly always a female. Since the older sibling has a greater chance of survival, I concluded this was nature's way of perpetuating the species, since it ensured that more females entered the breeding population. It also explained why we tend to get more male than female nestlings in rehab, as the older sister boots the younger brother out if the nest gets too tight for comfort.

After noticing this gender distinction in 2007, I began paying attention. Since then, of the fifty sets of twins I have received, 80 percent consist of an older female and younger male. The other

20 percent have two males or two females, with the majority of the anomalies being twin girls. I have seen only one hummingbird nest with three chicks (Allen's), and after I helped the caller add an extension to the nest, the two older females and younger male fledged successfully. The fact that nature has arrived at the conclusion that the oldest nestling has a greater chance of survival and therefore must be female in order to maximize the species' numbers into the future blows people away. And despite all of our technological advances in studying wildlife, this is the kind of startling discovery that only rehabbers receiving a cross section of nests straight from their natural environment can make.

On July 2, I get ten calls but no rescued birds. I take advantage of the calm before the Fourth of July firestorm to work with Pepper on her flight training. Pepper has graduated to a large flight cage that sits adjacent to Gabriel's starter cage on the patio. Gabriel can fly low and forward for short distances now. When he is not exercising, he watches Pepper buzz up and down the tiered perches in her cage with obsessive attention. I approach Pepper's cage with her twig, prompting her to dance expectantly on her highest perch. When I press the twig against her stomach, she hops onto it and spins her wings with startling speed. Encouraged by this sudden display of power, instead of lowering the twig slowly, I drop it to the bottom of the cage. The moment I let go Pepper releases her grip and flies to the far perch in a fraction of a second before lifting off and hovering in the center of the cage with ease. And in that brief and shining moment, her flight training is complete. Pepper doesn't need me anymore.

Watching her dart around inside the cage with fresh confidence, I feel a deep tenderness for Pepper, although I try to refrain from showing it. To make it in the wild, Pepper cannot trust humans too much. In reflecting on her two-month journey back to health, I recall the hundreds of times we worked together to regain the power of flight. And that last afternoon when she finally gets airborne and fulfills our dreams, I am reminded of a horse I rode as a child.

As a skinny, eleven-year-old farm girl, I learned to ride on a blind horse. Being so young and mostly on my own, I had trouble with the other farm horses, which were too strong, willful, and, at times, unruly. But the blind horse, a palomino named Princie with a perfect upside-down white pyramid on her forehead, exuded Zen calm. Princie, given to us by a local farmer after a failed treatment for a severe eye infection, came to us gentle and well trained. Several years later, I inherited her when my sister went off to college. Princie had her own private fenced pasture and barn at an abandoned farmhouse a half mile down the road from our farm. I visited her every afternoon. Whenever Princie heard me pedaling down the country road on my bicycle, she would turn her head alertly in my direction with ears perked in rapt expectation. Princie lived to go riding because she could run freely only when a human functioned as her eyes. After getting home from school I would put on her bridle, a moth-eaten wool blanket with a colorful Native American pattern, and a small western saddle that was so light I could hoist it onto her back myself and then take her out.

During our first few months together, Princie walked cautiously up and down the ditches and hay fields as we adjusted to each other's touch and motion. Plodding through the prairie grass in the late-afternoon sun, we bonded deeply. Since my sister had been training her for years, Princie was hypersensitive to the slightest tug on the reins prompting her to turn left, right, or walk downhill. When I lifted the reins slightly, she would raise her knees high in the air, as if prancing, to scale the steep incline of the ditch running alongside the old country road we frequented. Eventually Princie began trotting, then galloping, and finally she trusted me enough to run at full speed as I deftly guided her around obstacles and potential dangers. Running flat out with Princie brought a rare feeling of exuberance, as though we were some fantastical centaur floating across the prairie with her legs and my eyes. Sometimes, after surveying the approaching terrain in advance, I would close my eyes briefly to get a sense of her experience. And it was even more thrilling racing through darkness with the rhythmic pounding of hooves in our ears on our way toward some lighter being that transcends the sensory world. I never felt as free as when we were gliding along with the wind at our backs as one entity. And I sensed Princie felt the same way, as she ran faster and faster toward some imaginary destination that could be felt but not seen. Amazingly, during the four years we sprinted together across the fields and prairies, we never had an accident.

After Princie died of old age, I inherited a solidly built, dappled-gray quarter horse built for speed and with perfect vision. The first time I took her riding, I loosened the reins and let her run flat out back to the barn; halfway home she accidentally stepped in a gopher hole in the lawn alongside the driveway and tumbled head over heels, and I somersaulted over her ears before slamming flat on my back on the hard ground about ten feet in front of her. After pulling ourselves up to sitting positions and staring at each other in stunned silence for a few minutes, we got up and limped back to the barn. Back then, people didn't wear helmets or padding the way kids do today; I wore nothing but faded blue jeans, a T-shirt, and old Keds sneakers. Remarkably, except for a little blood from superficial abrasions, neither of us was injured, though I moved with robotic stiffness for a few days and she seemed content to be left alone grazing in her pasture for a month. After the accident, the dappled-gray mare, also named Pepper, became my horse in the same way Princie had been before her.

Some early indigenous cultures believed that if you share a powerful and affecting experience with an animal, your spirit becomes forever entwined with that creature. I feel I have connected deeply with hummingbirds many times, through hours of joy and sorrow. Pepper's inauspicious arrival in rescue and her gradual return to the exhilarating world of flight make me feel the pull of something higher. Just as I once functioned as Princie's eyes, I served as Pepper's wings during those long weeks of renewal. And now that she is back in the air, I wonder what part of her I have become and how she might fly me to freedom just as Princie had let me run.

CHAPTER 23

Cruel Summer

PREDICTABLY, THE FOURTH OF JULY marks a day of freedom for hummingbird fledglings throughout Southern California, and I receive eight young birds and fifty phone calls over the weekend. I also get my cell phone bill for June. In a typical off-season month I talk for less than 1,000 minutes. Today my service provider sends me a text informing me that I have used 8,000 minutes in June, exacts a painful overage charge, and encourages me to upgrade to a more suitable plan. But if I have to spend another month coaching frantic callers through 8,000 minutes of hummingbird crises, there is no doubt in my mind I will go mad, a victim of my extraordinary success in reaching the public. I pay the penalty and respectfully decline the offer for more talk time.

Although I have an aviary full of restless young adults raring to go, I have to wait until after the Fourth of July to grant my birds their independence because the noisy explosions of fireworks can alarm inexperienced hummingbirds when they are sleeping at night, prompting them to bolt off their perches into the darkness and injure themselves. So I tend to the young, read Lao Tzu, and wait patiently, because when life becomes too heated, the master points out, *Stillness and tranquility set things in order in the universe.*

On July 6 I release fifteen immaculate adults, seven of which came from city animal shelters. And in a rare display of collective confidence, every bird in the aviary shoots into the wide July sky with ease and does not come back. And now, for the first time since early May, more birds are going out than coming in. The end is in sight.

After the release and mandatory scrub-down, I move twenty fledglings into the aviary, including the burly Santa Clarita brothers who are racing ahead of schedule, the Anna's dumpster twins from Century City, the sugar baby from the shelter who came in with the ducks, the stunning black-chinned female who arrived with the kitten, the UCLA hybrid, and an Allen's female brought in six weeks ago after being fed sugar water far too long by a Los Angeles veterinarian.

I get a lot of calls from veterinarians in Southern California seeking advice about hummingbirds that clients have dropped off at their offices. Although a state regulation prohibits animal hospitals from keeping wildlife without a permit, it's a law without teeth and many veterinarians assume, erroneously, that they know how to care for hummingbirds. To their credit, most vets make the responsible decision to call rescue right away. But like the general public, a few vets become enthralled with the magical young birds and don't contact us until things are down to the wire. In this case the veterinarian kept the fledgling on sugar water for two weeks, leaving her so weak and undernourished that she fell on her side whenever she tried to fly. When the vet had her husband drop off the starving bird because she was too afraid to bring it in herself, I called him out.

"This bird is suffering horribly. Why didn't you call someone sooner?"

"Well, we c-couldn't find anybody," he stammered halfheart-edly.

Reflecting on the countless calls I get from teenagers whose parents can't speak English and recalling the six-year-old son of the blind man's housekeeper who found my number in under a minute, I shook my head. "I don't buy it. How long did it take you to find me once you started looking on the Internet?"

He stared at the floor uncomfortably.

"Tell your wife I can understand this kind of thing from people with no education or experience with animals, but in the case of a professional with her credentials and years of training"—I shook my head—"there's no excuse, so please don't do it again."

"I'll give her the message," he replied stonily, avoiding my eyes.

"Thank you for bringing her in," I said and shook his hand before he hurried out the door.

As with the female Allen's who became Iris's cage mate the year before, the vet's bird, whom I named Powder for the dried sugar residue on her feathers, began flying after a week of protein-in-fused formula. Despite damage to her flight feathers resulting from a lack of protein during crucial growth stages, the deter-mined fledgling has moved through rehab steadily and now, be-cause of her strong spirit, seems ready for the aviary.

After filling the aviary with twenty restless young adults and moving the fledglings in starter cages up a level, I observe Pep-per flying in quick circles around her large flight cage. As much as I hate to pull her away from Gabriel, who watches her with an obses-sive fixation, it's getting late in the summer and she appears more than ready to take the last step toward freedom.

"What do you think, Pepper?" I ask, lifting her cage as she zips effortlessly between perches. "Let's try it." I carry Pepper's cage into the aviary and open the top. Pepper flies out confidently and alights on a perch next to Powder. I am surprised to see the Santa Clarita brothers begin snapping up fruit flies as if they have been doing it all their lives. They display an adequate level of skill and proficiency their first day out, and again I marvel at these two forces of nature who seem to have sprung from some exceptional tribe of hummingbirds. The other birds in the aviary sit motionlessly on their perches, watching the twins in rapt silence. I think this is a good thing. But I am wrong.

Twenty minutes later, while washing cages, I hear a loud commotion in the aviary and hurry over to find the older Santa Clarita twin body-slamming every bird within range. Unlike the notorious Chucky, who selected his individual targets carefully, this take-no-prisoners shooter blasts through the aviary like an armed assassin, randomly knocking off four and five birds at a time while leaving collateral damage in his wake. The fierce aggression behind his assaults makes Chucky look like an international diplomat. Before I can get inside, I notice he has Pepper pinned to the bars and is pecking her head violently. I race inside, chase him off, slide Pepper off the bars, and let her go near a perch in the back of the aviary. Checking the ground for victims, I linger inside for a few minutes until things settle down. As is sometimes the case with new aviary cohorts, I hope the brazen bully simply needed to display his formidable prowess and will relax now that he has made it clear who's in charge. But the second I exit the aviary, before I can close the security door behind me, the Santa Clarita assassin hooks the male dumpster twin, a substantial Anna's who is not easily intimidated, and drags him to the ground.

"That's it." I rush back inside. "You're so out of here," I announce, herding the bloodthirsty killer into the security area and opening the door, prompting him to shoot fifty feet straight in the air before disappearing north into the hills.

I stand inside and monitor the visibly shaken aviary birds for a short time. After everyone calms down, I go back to washing cages. Within five minutes, the same ruckus breaks out. I sprint back to the aviary and see that the younger Santa Clarita twin has appointed himself the new bouncer and picked up where his abusive brother left off, hooking the other birds and slamming them to the ground with the ferocity of a professional wrestler.

"Damn it," I mutter under my breath as I race inside, corner the second outlaw in the security area, and kick him out. He too shoots into the sky before heading due north and back to the land of the larger-than-life hummingbirds. When I survey the aviary, I notice Pepper hanging on the bars again, this time crying hysterically. I hurry over and slide her off the bars before letting her go. But it's too late. Out of her mind with fear, she flies onto the bars, drops her head back, and wails like a banshee. I slide her off the bars and return her to a large flight cage.

It takes the petrified Pepper, who is panting laboriously, an hour to decompress enough to eat. I set her cage next to Gabriel's and leave her there for the rest of the day. The next morning, Pepper seems fully recovered from her giant ordeal and flies around her cage assertively. I take her back into the aviary and open the top. This time she doesn't waste any time before heading straight to the bars, dropping her head back, and screaming in terror. Again, after an hour back in her flight cage she relaxes. A few days later I try again, but each time I put Pepper in the aviary, she suffers the same panic attack. None of the other birds in the aviary has displayed aggression toward Pepper or one another. In fact, the remaining group proves so even-tempered that even the underpowered Powder can easily hold her own.

Observing Pepper lounging in her flight cage after her fourth emotional breakdown in the aviary, I suddenly see clearly what is causing her to freak out. She remembers being assaulted in the park as a teenager and is suffering from posttraumatic stress disorder. Pepper's first run-in with an adult male was so violent it proved nearly fatal. So getting attacked a second time by a male, particularly the vicious Santa Clarita twin, was her worst nightmare. Now Pepper associates the aviary trauma with her initial assault and the long road back from her injury. As I stare at Pepper in amazement and recall the famous Brad and her extended battle with dark memories of the crows, I start to wonder if hummingbirds ever forget anything. Pondering the options, I decide to hold Pepper back and try to reintroduce her to the aviary with the next cohort.

Later that afternoon, I get a call from a bird lover named Maggie asking about the sugar feeders hanging in her yard. As with false alarms over abandoned nests, sugar feeders sometimes become the source of family conflict too.

"My daughter says feeding hummingbirds sugar water is like giving them crack."

"Crack?" I repeat. "Like cocaine?"

"Yeah, she says it's like a drug for them and it destroys their brains. And that's why they fight so much around the feeders."

"Your daughter has a lively imagination."

"She's always been different."

"And how old is she?"

"Thirty-nine."

I laugh, having expected her to say fifteen. "Well, if she means they get addicted to it, she may be right. But sugar is a staple of their diet in the wild, so it's like a person getting addicted to rice or potatoes, I suppose."

"Well, I didn't think she was right because my hummingbirds don't act like crazed maniacs or anything."

"You must be doing something right, then, because a lot of hummingbirds do. The most important thing with feeders is to keep them clean, which can require extreme vigilance in a hot climate like Los Angeles. Hummingbirds get fungal infections from dirty feeders and it's the most horrible way for them to die, so you have to make sure you change the feeders before the sugar water goes bad. It's better not to hang feeders at all than to leave rotten ones out."

"How often should I change them, then?"

"A rule of thumb is every three days in the summer in LA because the sun and heat make them go bad fast. If the sugar water gets a milky haze, it means the feeder is slimy inside and the sugar water has gone sour. And if you see black spots on the glass that's fungus and then the feeder becomes a deathtrap."

"I never buy that sugar with the red dye in it. But should I?"

"Absolutely not. It's entirely unnecessary and may be harmful. White table sugar is the best option."

"How about in the winter when it gets cold?" Maggie quizzes me with bullet-point precision, as if she's interviewing me on a radio talk show. "Should I put more sugar in the water?"

"No, it's overkill. A four-parts-water, one-part-sugar mix approximates the twenty percent solution hummingbirds get from most flowers in the wild."

Maggie thanks me for the advice and reiterates that her daughter has been hounding her for years to take down the feeders before too many birds become full-blown sugar addicts.

"Worse things could happen to them," I assure her. I point out that feeders help hummingbirds and are contributing to expanding populations in parts of North America, so in fact the explosion of feeders in backyards across the country is a positive thing. "As long as people keep them clean."

I have this conversation every day during the summer. Angelenos love to compete to see who can get the most hummingbirds at their feeders. But attracting them to yards also invites a lot of work, and it's easy to get sloppy, which leads to suffering and death. Over the years, I have seen too many victims of human negligence. So I continue to be a broken record on this point: "Dirty feeders kill. If you don't have the time and energy to keep them clean, take them down."

Two weeks later, near the end of July, I release sixteen birds and move fourteen young adults into the aviary with the hybrid and Powder, both of whom have elected to stay on. The members of the fresh cohort, consisting mostly of large-brained black-chinneds, are poised and nonconfrontational, so I optimistically toss Pepper in with them. But again she heads straight for the bars. Although none of the birds in the aviary harasses or even pays her passing notice, Pepper clings to the bars and cries, so again I return her to a flight cage, where she calms down. Watching her fly smoothly between perches, I wonder if her close connection to Gabriel may be contributing to the problem, and I entertain the idea of holding her back until he is ready for the aviary. But Gabriel's progress remains glacial, and even though he occasionally manages to fly-hop up to a midlevel perch, I still am not convinced he is ever going to hover again. And without the ability to hover in the wild, a hummingbird is doomed.

It's nearly August and the summer deluge of fledglings has slowed to a trickle. I have been giving Pepper fresh flowers every day, so she is well versed in varieties of local vegetation. But she still hasn't caught a fruit fly and needs to spend a couple of weeks sleeping outside in a tree at night before her release. I wonder if she might be better off in an outdoor cage by herself for a few days. I don't have another aviary to put her into. But I know someone who does.

CHAPTER 24

Don't Leave Me This Way

THE LAST WEEK IN JULY, I take in just four fledglings. Two do not survive their first night in rehab. Late-summer fledglings suffer a multitude of hardships, including stiflingly hot weather, deadly mite infestations, a paucity of flowers, and an overall lack of nutrition. On July 30, I release the birds in the aviary, and again the hybrid and Powder choose to stay. The nine black-chinned beauties, however, who have to head for Mexico over the next several weeks, shoot high into the sky as if propelled by an external force. An hour later I put the smallest group since April, just six young adults, into the aviary. The ICU and the starter cages, except the one Gabriel occupies, sit empty in the garage. Aside from Pepper, an adult female black-chinned missing two primary feathers, an adult male rufous, a male Anna's blinded in one eye and named One-Eyed Jack, and another adult Anna's I call Iron Mike, my large flight cages are empty as well. Even more liberating, apart from a call every day or two, my cell phone has suddenly fallen silent.

Any hummingbirds remaining at my facility by mid-August have to be comfortably adjusted to life in the aviary so I can return to teaching at UCLA for the second summer session. I feel I have been away too long already and am eager to get back to the classroom. In addition to their formula feeders, birds in the aviary can drink from sugar feeders during the day and do not require such close monitoring. They also have an abundance of fruit flies to chase around and grow fat on.

On Friday I call Jean and describe Pepper's psychological hang-up. Jean offers to put her into a small, walk-in flight cage she uses for birds with physical and emotional disabilities. I agree to bring Pepper down on Saturday afternoon. As I begin power-washing the last cages to put away for the winter, my phone rings. Aaron, a real estate agent from Toluca Lake, is calling to report a hummingbird flying around the ceiling of a house he has listed for sale.

"I have a private showing in an hour and I'm afraid this distraction is going to blow the deal. I have no idea how to reach him," Aaron explains with agitation.

"How high is the ceiling?" I cut to the chase.

"It's high."

"How high?"

"Like, thirty feet, maybe more."

"Thirty feet!" I exclaim. "That's like a warehouse. Who would want a house with ceilings that high?"

"Well, a lot of celebrities live in this area."

"Ah, I see. So they need rooms with ceilings high enough to accommodate their towering egos."

"Yes." He laughs. "That's a good way of putting it."

"Okay, Aaron, this might be a lot simpler than it appears. Are there any bright red fabrics in the house?"

"Yeah, actually, there are. The owners have kind of garish taste and they have red velvet drapes in the den," he observes disapprovingly.

"That sounds like it has greater potential to be a deal-breaker than the trapped hummingbird."

"I couldn't agree more."

"So take the red drapes down and — I assume there are double doors in the living room?"

"Several."

"Open all the double doors, and drape the curtains over them."

"Really?"

"Red is an irresistible magnet for these guys. Try it. And call me if it works."

The minute I hang up, the phone rings again. Cliff has a fledgling grounded in his driveway that he has been assisting for three days.

"The avocado tree is too high to put him back in the nest," Cliff informs me. "His mother is still feeding him during the day and I take him into the garage at night. I wouldn't even be doing all this if it weren't for my kids."

"Well, it's good to know you're learning something from them," I encourage.

"Yeah, I grew up in the sticks in Wisconsin and we didn't interfere with nature."

"Yes, we did," I counter. "I grew up in the same sticks and we interfered in all kinds of ways with our farms, subdivisions, freeways, pollution, deforestation, water management, and hunting. But when it came to saving wildlife, people just didn't get involved in any positive way. If a wild animal needed help, everyone retreated into that lazy and convenient 'Let nature take its course' line. As if we haven't screwed everything up already."

Cliff is silent for a moment. "Yeah, I guess you're right," he finally concedes. "There was a lot of indifference. But my kids aren't like that at all. They've been so worried about this little bird and insist we can't just leave him out there. It's so important to them that we help him survive."

"It's heartening to know that they're taking the lead." I praise Cliff's effort before advising him on how to build a faux nest and secure it to a tree nearby, which will ensure the chick's safety at night. "That way you don't have to get up at dawn every morning to put him back out."

After dispatching Cliff, I get an excited voicemail from Aaron. "I can't believe it worked!" he exclaims. "The hummingbird flew down almost immediately to check out the red drapes, then buzzed straight out the door."

I get two or three emergency calls every year reporting hummingbirds trapped in fire stations. I tell the firefighters to move the trucks just outside the door. They always call me back in astonishment when it works.

At nine o'clock, after going through my usual routine of securing the caged birds inside the garage for the night and washing feeders, I head upstairs to get ready for bed. As I am taking a shower I notice a swelling mosquito bite on the right side of my waist that I had gotten the night before. When it comes to mosquitoes, I'm candy. Since my early youth, the little bloodsuckers have seized every opportunity to gnaw on me. As a kid on the farm, I used to suffer dozens of bites on hot summer nights. Frank can stroll through a tropical swamp half naked at dusk and not get a single bite. I take a bath in extra-strength Cutter and cover myself like a sheik and still get bites on every inch of exposed skin and even on some that is not. Being outside with the hummingbirds around the clock, I have gotten used to having a few irritating bites every night when I go to bed despite my daily ritual of dousing myself in insect repellent until I choke. But this bite is enormous, the size of a half-dollar and maddeningly itchy. As I am drying off after my shower, I show the bite to Frank.

"Eww! Are you sure that's from a mosquito?" he exclaims in horror, slathering a handful of hydrocortisone on the expanding welt.

"Yeah, I got it last night. But it wasn't this bad. It itches like mad." I grimace as he empties the tube.

"Come on," he says, leading me out of the bathroom. "Let's get you to bed and see how it looks tomorrow."

On Saturday morning I get a text from Cliff reporting that his young bird has successfully fledged. "Thank you for your insight and advice," he writes. "I feel a lot better getting involved in a positive way."

My encounter with Cliff triggers haunting images of the violence against wildlife I witnessed during my farm youth in Wisconsin that I wish I could erase. But along with those grim recollections, my involuntary detours into the past also remind me of the long road to enlightenment I have traversed in my thirty years since.

Talking to Cliff makes me remember a funny story Jean told me a few years ago about a woman who called to report a fledgling that had been struck by a car in Long Beach and was flapping around in the gutter just outside her house. The caller wanted to save the suffering bird but her husband insisted she let nature take its course. Jean promptly told the caller to ask her husband whether, should he ever get hit by a car and be left helpless and crawling in the gutter with a broken leg and no hope of saving himself, he would prefer that everyone driving by let nature take its course and leave him there to die. Twenty minutes later the caller showed up at Jean's door with the injured bird and her husband sitting stone-faced at the wheel in the driveway.

We hear this kind of anthropocentric smugness a lot in rehab. Some people insist that individual humans are more important than members of all other species and therefore they do not believe that injured wildlife, even something as wondrous and amazing as a hummingbird, should be rescued. The survival-of-the-fittest argument goes something like this: (1) animals live in nature; (2) nature is a big sorting mechanism that weeds out the weak, which are meant to die, while the strong go on to perpetuate the species; (3) saving the weak propagates a less robust species that ultimately will create the need for more rehab and so on; and, finally, (4) rescuing several hundred hummingbirds every year means nothing in the big scheme of things.

As a young graduate student in my early twenties with no clear career plan, I studied ancient Greek philosophy and spent three years teaching Aristotelian logic to hundreds of exceedingly illogical college undergraduates. Hence my answer to the natural-selection proponents in relation to hummingbird rescue is (1) there is nothing natural about Los Angeles; (2) young hummingbirds who end up in rehab after their nests get cut out of trees to clear the way for an unobstructed view of the city/hillside/ocean whatever are not constitutionally weaker than those born far from such urban threats and don't deserve to die; (3) some of the strongest, fastest, and most striking birds I have released started out at a disadvantage but nonetheless will produce offspring as physically impressive as any hummingbird on earth; and, finally, (4) next time you are lying in the hospital facing certain death without medical intervention, ask yourself (and this one requires brutal honesty) how important your life really is in the big scheme of things. If you have trouble with this last question, try imagining the minuscule planet we inhabit from across the universe, from a vantage point, say, a hundred million light-years away, keeping in mind the immense sweep of history and the billions of humans who have inhabited the earth before you. If, after this philosophical exercise, you are still convinced of your relative importance in the universe, seek help.

Fortunately, the outdated view that endorses, at best, ignoring creatures in nature and, at worst, exterminating them is heading for the dust heap and, in many young hearts and minds, being superseded by a more compassionate commitment to caring for the planet's rapidly dwindling wildlife populations. And I derive comfort from the fact that, in rescuers' quest to promote care and concern for our wild companions in nature, Lao Tzu backs up our efforts, reminding us, *The sage takes care of all things, and abandons nothing.*

Just after noon on Saturday, I get a call from Emma, a few blocks away in West Hollywood, about a hummingbird that has not moved off her backyard sugar feeder for two hours. I ask Emma to reach up and slide the bird off the feeder. When she does, the hummingbird collapses in her hand.

"Her colors are incredible," Emma marvels.

"Can you bring her to me?"

"I'll be right over." Emma arrives five minutes later, and I open the Godiva truffle box she hands me to find an adult female Allen's adorned in the bold green, orange, and white hues of the Irish flag.

"Wow, she is spectacular." I shake my head in amazement.

"She flew a little when I tried to put her in the box," Emma says. "But she just went down to the floor kind of on an angle."

After Emma leaves, I put the stunning female in a starter cage for observation. She can perch and spin her wings perfectly, and her dazzling feathers are flawless. Watching her fly a short distance and then sink to the bottom of the cage, I notice that she looks unusually rotund. But she does not appear fat and squishy all over like Pepper or the birds bulking up for migration. Instead, she seems abnormally bottom heavy and begins panting each time she drops to the bottom of the cage. I call my expert for guidance.

"Take her out of the cage, press lightly on her abdomen with the tip of your index finger, and tell me if you can feel something," Jean advises.

Holding the bird in my right hand, I press on her abdomen with my left index finger. "Yeah, there's a hard lump there, like a tumor or something," I tell Jean. "But Emma didn't feed her anything. I'm sure of it."

"No, it's nothing she ate," Jean corrects me. "She's egg-bound."

"Egg-bound?"

"Yeah, her egg is stuck. That's why she can't fly. I see it sometimes in early winter and late summer."

Having never heard of such a phenomenon, I ask Jean how many other unexpected surprises await me in the enigmatic world of hummingbirds.

"There's a lot more going on than we'll ever understand," she assures me.

"Well, I have no idea how to treat this," I begin nervously, recalling our conversation two years earlier about the fledgling who left a permanent mark on my heart. "I'm bringing Pepper down in a few hours. Can I bring this one too?"

"Yeah, it's better if you do," Jean agrees, to my infinite relief. "I had two kids. I have some idea what to do."

Late Saturday afternoon, I load Pepper and the egg-bound bird into my car and head for Jean's house. In discussing Pepper's paranoia, we decide that on Sunday morning, Jean will isolate her in a small outdoor flight cage adjacent to an aviary full of birds awaiting release. That way Pepper can see the other hummingbirds but won't feel physically threatened by them. After four or five days of this exposure therapy, I'll pick her up and bring her home so she can go through my aviary with Gabriel and the last group of adults. I drop the two birds off at six o'clock. Jean has just four older nestlings in her ICU and a few fledglings in starter cages. When I remark that I've never seen so few hummingbirds at her house, the expression of relief she shoots at me defies description.

"Call me if it pops out." I motion toward the egg-bound beauty, say goodbye to Pepper, and hurry out the door. Driving home that evening, I am excited and relieved that after three months, Pepper will finally have an opportunity to make the transition to a full-time outdoor life that takes her another step back to the wild. And although I already miss her, I believe I am doing the best thing possible to promote her recovery.

I have never been so wrong about a hummingbird.

CHAPTER 25

Sunday Morning Coming Down

WHEN I GET UP AT DAWN to put my last five caged birds outside and fill the aviary feeders, I have a voicemail from Jean asking me to call her right away. Her tense tone alerts me to danger, and although I have braced myself for bad news, I still hold on to hope that the gorgeous egg-bound female survived the night. As soon as I come back into the house and feed three impossibly whiny cats, I call her. Jean answers on the second ring, which is a first.

"Something tells me this isn't going to be the happiest news," I begin cautiously.

"No, I'm afraid not."

"Well, she didn't look too good yesterday and I guess she was suffering," I reflect philosophically.

"No, Terry, it's not the egg-bound bird. It's the other one."

"What?" My breathing stops dead as if I've had the wind knocked out of me. "You mean Pepper?"

"She wouldn't eat last night and when I got up this morning she was on the bottom of the cage."

"No, Jeannie . . . not . . . not Pepper," I protest, putting a clenched fist to my mouth as I begin pacing around the kitchen in a sudden cold sweat. "There was nothing wrong with her, she . . ." I struggle to catch my breath as hot tears burn my eyes. Jean remains silent for what seems like an eternity. "Well . . . is she . . . what is she?"

"She's in torpor," Jean replies ominously. "I can't bring her out."

A dozen thoughts race into my mind in that instant, but one elbows its way to the head of the line. "I'm coming down," I announce as if a higher authority has made the decision for me and issued immediate marching orders.

I expect Jean to argue, the way she always does, with rational explanation and reality-based consolation. But instead she just says, "Okay, I'll see you," then abruptly hangs up.

I don't know how I get dressed and into the car in less than five minutes. All I remember is racing down a deserted six-lane freeway as if my life depended on it. Halfway there, I am overtaken by a brain-splitting headache as rivers of sweat stream down my temples and drip onto my powder-blue polo shirt. It's a balmy morning, maybe 70 degrees already at six o'clock, portending a sweltering afternoon. But inside the car, it already feels like a hundred even with the air conditioner roaring on high. By the time I turn off the 110 freeway onto Pacific Coast Highway, I can hear my heart hammering in my head and I am soaked in sweat, even though, when I put my hand on my forehead for reassurance, my skin feels cold and clammy to the touch. As much as I try to calm myself with deep breathing, as I pull into the driveway, my agitation escalates. When I rush to Jean's doorstep, I have a flashback of her expressionless greeting the first time I arrived at her front door drenched to the skin with young Gabriel in tow, four years earlier. But this time when she opens the door, Jean can't mask her shock.

"My God, Terry, you look like shit."

"Thanks." I tilt my head in acknowledgment. "But rest assured, no matter how bad I look, I feel a lot worse."

"Are you okay?" Jean stares at me with such frightened concern as I hurry inside that I begin to panic even more.

"I don't know." I sink into a chair at her kitchen table as I struggle to catch my breath. "I don't feel too good. I'm so parched. Can I have some water?"

Jean pours me a tall glass from a plastic container in her refrigerator, which I drink in a second, and I nod when she offers to pour another.

"Do you have any aspirin?" I ask before gulping down the second glass.

Jean opens a cupboard over the sink lined with a dozen brands of aspirin, anti-inflammatory drugs, and other unidentifiable pharmaceuticals.

"Wow." I admire the collection. "You come prepared."

"You're looking at twenty years of hummingbird rescue," she mutters dryly.

As I swallow two aspirin I wonder how such a mild treatment can possibly address the skull-splitting headache that makes me feel like dropping to the kitchen floor.

"Where's Pepper?" I ask anxiously.

Jean directs me to one of her ICUs sitting on a table against the wall. Four fully feathered nestlings are huddled in two nests on one side, and at the far end is Pepper, perched on the edge of a plastic-salsa-cup nest with her eyes closed, bill in the air, and feathers puffed up.

"Oh, Pepper," I sigh sadly. I slide the glass door open, reach in, and close my hand around her cold body, and my heart starts to pound faster. "I have to get her home." I look at Jean urgently.

"Terry," Jean begins cautiously, "I'm not sure you should be driving—"

"Jeannie." I raise a palm toward her. "Just . . . don't."

"Okay." She quickly relents. "Take this." Jean hands me a head-injury cage.

"Good." I set Pepper and her nest on the bottom of the cage and head for the door. "Oh, wait." I turn suddenly. "What about the other one?"

"Oh, she's fine." Jean gestures toward the animated female Allen's zipping back and forth in a starter cage on the table. "While I was massaging her last night, she dropped it right into my hand," Jean announces, proudly holding up what looks like a white Jelly Belly between her thumb and index finger. "She's been flying around since I got up."

"I'll take her too, then. Just in case she has a nest." I move to pick up the cage but freeze in midstride from a sudden stiffness in my arms and legs.

"Here, let me." Jean lifts the cage by the handle and follows my slow exit out the door and to the car. "Be careful, Terry." She looks at me sympathetically as I slide into the driver's seat. "I don't want to have to give up rescuing hummers because you're not around to help me anymore."

"Don't worry. You're not going to get out of this nightmare that easily," I assure her, then I pull out of the driveway and speed home.

Once on the freeway, I think back again about dropping Gabriel off, four years ago. Rather than seeming like four years, though, my journey feels more like twenty after all I have been through with hummingbirds. I recall the early mornings and late nights, the endless barrage of phone calls and anxious finders arriving at my door, the long commutes on the freeways, and the hundreds of otherwise-doomed hummingbirds flying around the city now. I can't believe how far I have come from that emotionally paralyzed rookie weeping on the garage floor to this summer spent rescuing hundreds of hummingbirds and their people all over town. And now Pepper, with yet another lesson on how little I understand.

Pepper's lapse into torpor after being left with Jean also makes me ponder the difference between wild and domestic animals. I can't help but regard domestic pets, like our cats, as extensions of ourselves. Their charming and endearing qualities are a result of our influence, just as their failures somehow reflect our shortcomings. This is what people mean when they describe themselves as pet parents. Like human parents, we have maternal and paternal relationships with our cats and dogs and are to some extent accountable for their deeds. But I have none of this sense of responsibility with wild animals. A wild animal is mean or sweet, aggressive or friendly, because that's the way he was born. With hummingbirds in rehab, as with all creatures in nature, I have nothing to do with their violent behavior or bad temperament. I have not failed them. That's just how they are. And I can dismiss them as natural and wild.

The problem with Pepper is that by being so affectionate and interactive, she has pulled me in, made me responsible, and, therefore, accountable. Pepper never acted *wild* in the detached sense of the word. She was always right there with me, watching and relating. Her connection to me wasn't something entirely in her, nor was it outside of her and only in my mind. It was a bond that arose between us, through our interactions. And as much as I have tried to conceal my affection for her, I always loved her, and she sensed that. So when I left her at Jean's house, Pepper did not understand that I was trying to do the best thing for her or that I would ever come back. She just felt abandoned, and as hard as it is for me to believe, because she is a hummingbird, she was suffering from a broken heart. And now I'm feeling the same pain. After three months of my working with her every day, giving her flight lessons and encouraging her determined progress, Pepper has taken on exaggerated importance for me, and I can't bear the thought of losing her. In my overwrought condition, I even convince myself that if Pepper dies, the entire summer will be a monumental failure.

Partly because it is early Sunday morning and mostly because of my subconscious decision to avoid consulting my speedometer, I make it home from Jean's house in half the time I usually do. Before the car's engine stops completely, I'm out the door and rushing through the gate with the two cages. Halfway across the patio, I set the Allen's cage on a cast-iron table and open the top, and in a second she disappears over the house. When I get into the garage, I turn on the ICU, put Pepper inside, sit down on a chair, and begin stroking her head and repeating her name softly. I don't know what else to do. After several minutes, she opens her bill slightly in response to my supplication. I fill an angio, touch her head, and inject some formula into her mouth. And to my immeasurable relief, she swallows, slow and hard. We sit together quietly as I continue rubbing her head and prompting her with food. Pepper remains in a state of suspended animation with her eyes closed, although she eats a little more each time I touch her bill with the angio. Finally, after an hour consoling Pepper, when the spinning in my head begins to make me feel dangerously dizzy, I stagger toward the house. As I am crossing the patio, my phone rings and I answer it automatically without realizing that I have neither the focus nor the energy to explain anything about hummingbirds to anybody right now.

Ariel from Pacific Palisades apologizes for bothering me about what she refers to as a silly question and then describes how a hummingbird nest in her yard with a chick inside has been carried off by crows. "The mother keeps circling around, looking for the nest, and now she's been sitting in that same spot for three hours. I know there's nothing I can do but it makes me so sad, Terry, and I was just wondering, do you think hummingbirds can get broken hearts?"

"Well, if you had asked me that yesterday," I answer Ariel in a weary tone, "I would have said no. But today, yes, I am certain that they can."

Inside the house, I find Frank in his office working on the computer. When he glances up at me before doing a double take, he can't hide his dismay.

"What's going on?" Frank asks with grave concern. "You look horrible."

"I'm getting that a lot today," I respond faintly, wiping sweat off my face and arms with a hand towel I grabbed from the adjacent bathroom. I head to the swivel chair in the corner, collapse onto the seat with a shaky weakness, and find I can't get back up.

Frank rushes over and escorts me to the bedroom at the end of the hall, covers me with a heavy cotton blanket, and delivers tall glasses of orange and cranberry juice. While he's in the kitchen retrieving more liquids, three cats appear and begin walking all over my inert body, purring and looking me closely in the face with wide, frightened eyes. As they sink down, one after another, on the blanket beside me, I glance around the bedroom in the bright morning sunlight.

It's a small, cozy room I have always preferred to the larger suite upstairs when I come down with a cold or the flu. The half-size bedroom has wood venetian blinds covering a tall window behind the bed's headboard that invites abundant natural light, a seven-foot-high glass-covered Italian bookcase in the corner jammed with poetry anthologies and literary classics, louvered wood doors on a large walk-in closet off to one side, and a beamed pine ceiling that gives the room a snug, cabinlike feel. It's the secluded hide-away where Frank and I do the *Los Angeles Times* crossword puzzle together while drinking coffee and hot chocolate on brisk Sunday mornings in the winter as the cats burrow into the plush blankets wrapped around us. A private sanctuary we can crawl into with books on a hazy autumn afternoon, getting up only to shuffle into the kitchen ten steps away. Of all the places in the world I could be right now, this warmly familiar room is by far my first choice. After a few minutes, Frank arrives with a thermometer, which quickly alerts us that I am running a temperature of 103.2.

"That's pretty high, isn't it?" I knit my brow.

"It ain't good," Frank concedes, squinting at the thermometer. "Do you wanna go to Cedars?" he presses, referring to the sprawling Cedars-Sinai Medical Center a block away.

"No, not yet." I shake my head before offering him blurry instructions on how to fill the hummingbird feeders in the aviary and care for Pepper in the ICU. I always keep a container of mixed formula in the refrigerator for emergencies, and Frank has assumed these duties in the past when my back was against the wall, so there are no surprises. I look at my phone and realize that despite the heated and whirling events of the day, it's only nine o'clock. "I just need to rest for an hour or so," I say to reassure Frank as he stares at me apprehensively.

To combat my brain-scrambling headache, Frank brings me a potent painkiller and disappears on his assignment as I spiral into a deep sleep. As I am drifting off, I experience that universal sensation of falling and then I have restless, disjointed dreams about people crying and hummingbirds dying. My dreams are not about the ones I have saved but about those I have failed. Every now and then, I surface into a breathless, semiconscious state before being pulled under again. When I finally awake and check my phone, it's one in the afternoon and every joint in my body is throbbing. The headache has been replaced by a dull mental lethargy, and the sweating attacks supplanted by a heavy immobility. Frank hears me rustling around on the bed and hurries in.

"Are you okay?" he asks with an expression of anxious concern that I have seen in his eyes only once or twice in twenty years, at times when life was really unraveling.

"I think so." I struggle to pull myself upright as he sits down beside me on the bed with palpable relief.

"Are the birds okay?"

"Yeah, they're all fine." He nods. "Except for that one in the ICU."

"Why?" My heart tightens in my chest. "What's wrong?" I glance up at him in alarm.

"Well, I've been trying to feed her every thirty minutes," he says, frowning, "but she just keeps flying around the ICU and I can't keep her on the nest."

I fall back onto the pillows, close my eyes, and breathe again.

CHAPTER 26

There's No Me Without You

FRANK'S NEWS OF PEPPER'S surprise comeback elicits a sudden burst of energy that gives me the strength to hurry out to the garage, return her to a flight cage, and set her outside with the rest of the late-summer stragglers. Although I am too punchy to grasp the full impact of Pepper's revival, her return brings a profound inner peace to my troubled mind. After filling the feeders in a daze, I stagger back to bed. Huddling under the blanket with a resurging headache and chills, I contemplate the advantages of torpor available to Pepper at times like this. Instead of retreating into the peace of that deep slumber, as she did during her meltdown, I lie in bed tormented by fever, disturbing mental images, and a jaw-grinding restlessness. After digging around in the covers on the bed, I locate my phone. Except for a worried voicemail from Jean, I have not gotten a call all day. I drink a quart of orange juice and take another painkiller, and finally I am released from my misery and drift away.

When I awaken, the last rays of the setting sun are streaming through the half-opened blinds, and three cats are sleeping soundly around me. As I regain consciousness I hear Frank talking on the phone in the living room. I slide out of bed and shuffle into the front room as he hangs up and approaches me with concern.

"Are you okay?"

"Not yet, but we're betting on a total recovery."

Too weak to move anything except myself, I ask Frank to carry the large flight cages inside for the night. We step out the side door of the house and onto the patio, and I automatically glance at Pepper's and Gabriel's cages, as I have done hundreds of times every day for the past three months. Pepper is balanced on her top perch but I don't see Gabriel anywhere. Frightened something has gone wrong during my extended absence, I rush over to his cage and then do a double take. Gabriel is resting on the top perch looking at Pepper in the adjacent cage. I intercept Frank as he is carrying a flight cage into the garage.

"How long has Gabriel been on that perch?" I ask in shocked confusion.

"Who?"

"This bird." I tap the top of the cage as Gabriel looks up at me curiously with his white spot glistening in the amber sunlight. "How long has he been up on this perch?"

"I don't know." Frank shrugs, unaware of the miracle staring us in the face. "He was there when I came out to fill the feeders a few hours ago."

I look at Frank and then at Gabriel, convinced I'm having a fever-induced delusion. "How can this be?" I stare at Gabriel in disbelief. "Can you fly?" I tap the top of his cage again as he sits calmly on his high perch gazing up at me. I carry the small starter cage he has been living in for the past four months into the garage, open the side door, reach in, and touch Gabriel lightly on the chest. He flies lightly to the far perch and then turns to look at me over his shoulder as if he too is astonished. Overcome by exhaustion and the drama of the day, I sink into my chair in the garage, drop my head into my hands, and weep.

"What's wrong?" Frank asks in alarm as he muscles the large flight cage with the female black-chinned and One-Eyed Jack through the door.

"Nothing." I shake my head slowly. "Nothing at all."

After we get the birds put away, Frank and I head into the house. When I get back to bed, I have a voicemail from Nicole, a friend who is interning at Cedars-Sinai. A year earlier, the aspiring physician from France took several of my English classes at UCLA. Dreaming of landing an internship at one of the top hospitals in the country, she recruited me to help her write application essays and practice for interviews. Within six months she had the job. Since then, she has been calling me regularly and walking over during her lunch breaks to visit me and the cats, though I suspect mostly the cats. Seizing the opportunity to take advantage of her medical expertise, I call her back and describe my current condition, but before I can finish she offers a diagnosis.

"It sounds like it could be West Nile."

"West Nile?" I repeat with surprise. I had heard people talking about this virus on the news but assumed it was one of those dreaded tropical diseases like Ebola that immediately killed its victims.

"We're seeing a lot of it right now. Have you gotten any mosquito bites lately?"

I raise my pink polo shirt and check the large welt Frank drenched with hydrocortisone the night before. I describe the monstrous bite, and Nicole recommends plenty of liquids and bed rest.

"You're so healthy, it probably won't last more than a few days. But you need to take it easy for a while," she cautions.

Two weeks ago, her advice would have been laughable. But now, with only fourteen hummingbirds in rehab (five more than a wildlife specialist who called from Missouri a few days ago informed me her facility has admitted all year), the worst of the summer stress is behind me and I am on vacation. Or so I think.

Just after sunset, while lounging on the bed catching up on my intake records with three cats flattened by the late-summer, triple-digit heat, I get the most wrenching call of the year, if not of my entire rehab career.

In rapid-fire delivery, Diana describes the injuries an adult female has sustained after slamming into a picture window. From her harried description of the bird spinning in a tight circle on the ground whenever she tries to fly, I am certain she has a broken wing. Agitated and distraught, Diana insists on keeping the injured hummingbird in a cage inside her house and wants to know what kind of food to buy for her. This question is always a serious talking point. I get around twenty calls a year from people who want to keep an injured hummingbird as a pet. So I patiently explain all of the reasons why she cannot, legally or in good conscience, go down that road. But Diana is persistent, not in a pushy, arrogant manner but in a desperate, terrified way that makes me suspect some dark and menacing threat is lurking behind her hummingbird crisis.

Understandably, most callers refuse to accept the dim prospects of severely injured birds. The majority of hummingbirds with traumatic head injuries, broken backs, and broken wings cannot be saved. But nobody wants to hear that. So I have to walk callers through the five Kübler-Ross stages of grief, from denial (backpedaling on the initial diagnosis that the bird has a broken wing), to anger (which occasionally is directed at me but more often at other people and, sometimes, nature), to bargaining ("What if I . . ." questions), to depression (despondence, regrets, tears), and, finally, to acceptance (delivering the bird to rescue despite the bleak prognosis). And usually I have to get through this thorny conversation in five minutes because other callers with the same feelings and hesitations are lined up waiting to be escorted through the same exacting process. Emotionally charged exchanges like these, which are more common than I care to recall, make me feel out of my depth sometimes, as if I should have a doctorate in psychology and years of clinical experience before I plunge into such treacherous waters. But there is no time for all of that. Hummingbirds and their finders are hurting. So all I can do is aim for the heart and hope my words hit home.

"It's not humane," I finally tell Diana after five minutes of back-and-forth debate. "By keeping her, you're holding on to a disaster that's just going to get worse with time. She'll suffer for weeks until she starves to death. Try to imagine yourself locked in a cramped cell with a painful injury and no nutritious food. You don't sound like the kind of person who would put a hummingbird through that kind of torture."

My last comment nudges her over the edge and she begins weeping.

"It's just that she has always been here with us. My daughter — she's sixteen — and I have been watching her for five years. She's become part of the family. And my daughter is going into the hospital tomorrow for cancer surgery again and if our little hummingbird dies, I just have this horrible feeling—" She struggles to catch her breath.

"Diana," I say firmly, "I'm going to tell you right now, don't do this." My caveat causes her to break down into uncontrollable sobbing. Still, she needs to get the whole story on the table.

"This beautiful hummingbird has been nesting and raising her babies in the magnolia tree by our kitchen window for five years," she tells me, sobbing, "and she's been here all through my daughter's cancer, and some days we sit together and watch her feed her babies and she has been the only light . . . the only . . . hope that has kept us going. And now my daughter is devastated seeing her so broken and helpless like this and I just . . . can't—" She breaks off in breathless sobs.

"Diana, listen to me," I counsel, surprised at the tenderness in my voice. "For all of the hard things you are going through right now, the last thing you want is for this hummingbird to suffer after the joy she has brought you. Her presence in your life has been a gift, and her injury has no bearing on your daughter's situation. Think of her as the inspiration she has been rather than as a harbinger of bad things to come."

Diana continues crying so uncontrollably she can't speak. I wait patiently.

"It's just so hard," she finally says in a quivering voice. "I would feel so horrible if I had to take her to some cold animal shelter to be put down. I'd just never get over it."

"Then bring her to me. And remind yourself that you are showing your love and compassion by doing the right thing for her. Because in the end it's the most humane and unselfish act for this wondrous creature and the best thing for everyone's peace of mind and hope of moving on, including your daughter's during this difficult time."

Diana's sudden silence makes me fear she is about to go off on some enraged and defensive tirade the way callers stuck in the anger stage, who insist on keeping injured birds despite my best efforts to dissuade them, sometimes do. Finally, after taking deep breaths to regain her composure, she says, as if a curtain has lifted, "You're right. Thank you, Terry." Still, Diana wants to discuss the matter with her daughter before bringing the bird over. I tell her I'll be waiting.

By the time I hang up, I'm a nervous wreck, more stressed than I felt in my worst moments battling the afflictions of West Nile. Thinking about Pepper and how the prospect of losing her had me by the throat yesterday, I can only imagine what dark corridors Diana's thoughts are racing down with a hummingbird who has been in her heart and imagination for five years and is so closely associated with her daughter's survival.

Diana's breakdown leads me to reflect on my own experience over the past twenty-four hours. The tortured images swirling through my mind as I contemplated Pepper's possible death finally brought the hummingbird equation into sharp relief. This was the lesson that the long, lonely night on the garage floor what seems like a lifetime ago had been pointing to. I can almost hear the young Anna's voice in my head: *You cannot accept my death or that of others until you have come to terms with your own mortality, and all that entails. Remember that thing you felt slipping away as you sat holding me in the garage on that cold winter night two years ago? That was you. Watching me die, you saw your own life, and you cried as much for you as for me. Because part of what makes you who you are and guides your understanding of yourself is your connection to me.*

And this is why so many callers are coming apart at the seams when they encounter a dying hummingbird. People feel so tightly bound to hummingbirds that the birds become miniature mirrors. In urban communities throughout Los Angeles, hummingbirds are the poster children for primal innocence, both theirs and ours. They symbolize the beauty of pristine nature before human civilization came tromping into paradise with its rough, heavy boots and mucked everything up. And despite our ongoing interference, these fearless spirits continue living alongside us, serving as a reminder of what once was, and what can be. This is why their deaths, as small and insignificant as they may seem, have the power to drive the hard truth of our own mortality straight home. Because in the end, as much as we work to deny it, our fundamental condition is not so different from theirs.

This is the emotional war Diana was waging with herself when she called me. Being so closely tied for so many years to a hummingbird whose death, in Diana's mind, signaled the end of her daughter's life made the grim conclusion impossible to face. But an hour later, when Diana shows up with the hummingbird in a black-velvet-lined jewelry case, her relief is unmistakable.

"Thank you so much for taking her in." Diana snuffles with red eyes as she hands the exhausted bird over to me. "As soon as I told my daughter what you said, she insisted I bring her over immediately because she said that she understood"—I hand Diana a tissue as she struggles to explain through her tears—"what it's like to feel pain and to be frightened, and she doesn't want the hummingbird to go through that. And she said she will always carry her in her heart, no matter what happens." Diana weeps from somewhere deep inside. "She was so strong."

Going to bed that night with a sense of steadily recovering health, I realize that Diana's tragedy has delivered the last piece of the puzzle that finally brings clarity to the complex and elusive feelings I have been carrying around since my first traumatic loss. With her hummingbird's broken wing threatening to shatter everything around it, Diana's daughter, having been confronted with the prospect of her own death at such a young age, has been pushed to that same precipice I teetered at the edge of two years earlier. A precarious ledge that demands letting go of everything we think we know. And only by opening our minds and allowing our connections to these magical creatures, who have so completely taken our hearts hostage, to extend beyond our immediate physical experience with them can we make peace with our loss.

CHAPTER 27

Any Day Now (My Wild Beautiful Bird)

EXCEPT FOR A HANGOVER HEADACHE and residual fatigue, I bounce back from my battle with the dreaded West Nile virus a few days later. Pepper, too, has recovered completely, and Gabriel is flying with near-normal efficiency, although he still has some trouble going in reverse off a perch. This will come.

On Wednesday morning, in a sudden flash of insight, I decide to put Gabriel in the large flight cage with Pepper, a move that will serve the dual purpose of giving him more space and easing her fear of adult males. The second I pop Gabriel into her cage, Pepper flies to the far perch in alarm. But Gabriel, who has been eyeing the silver-feathered beauty from across the room for three months now, cannot contain his interest and follows her, landing on the same perch about six inches to her left, leaving her with ample personal space. After studying Gabriel for a minute, and likely being drawn in by his dark, handsome good looks and polite demeanor, Pepper shimmies over on the perch and pokes his chest lightly with her bill the way hummingbirds feeling camaraderie toward one another do. Gabriel returns the gesture, and the relationship

274

is officially solidified. They remain together this way for five days, pirouetting through the sunlit air by day and sleeping side by side at night. But autumn's wingèd chariot is hurrying near, and neither bird really needs the training afforded by a large flight cage. Pepper has been in rehab for three months, and Gabriel has been out in the real world for four years. And as the late-summer sun slants at a lower angle at the end of each day, I sense it is time for both to move ahead.

On Saturday I release the eight birds in the aviary. This time, seven of eight, including the UCLA hybrid, choose freedom. The only one that stays on is Powder, who hangs back warily when I open the doors. Even after she's spent three cycles in the aviary, the integrity of her primary feathers is still compromised by the sugar-water diet she endured during her deprived youth. She continues to make progress, and I agree with her decision to stay another round.

After scrubbing down the aviary and placing handfuls of freshly cut cape honeysuckle around the perches, I put Pepper, Gabriel, and the last four caged birds in it. All are mature adults, which makes for a rare and fascinating group. Unlike feisty fledglings and cocky young adults, older birds recovering from serious injuries rarely fight in rehab. There is an odd, collective sense that everyone is a survivor with nothing to prove. They all know how to catch fruit flies and mine flowers. Baths are old news, as is sleeping in a tree at night. They are by far the most self-possessed group I have seen all year. The only wildcard is Iron Mike.

Iron Mike landed in rehab after colliding with a spoke on the Ferris wheel at the Santa Monica pier. He bounced off the steel spoke and plummeted to the wooden pier below, where a pit bull on a leash grabbed him in her mouth and then obediently relinquished her prize to her pet guardians. When the young couple arrived at my house with the bird; their four-year-old son, Michael; and one of the sweetest dogs I have ever met — she licked my hands tenderly from the half-opened back window of the car — the male Anna's was nearly unconscious. As Michael's father recounted the chain of events that had brought the family to my door, the young hero could not resist adding a few critical details to the story.

"I was riding the black horse with a balloon," Michael suddenly interrupted his father's pragmatic account.

"You were riding a black horse when you found the humming-bird?" I asked in amazement as I fed the patient before popping him into the ICU.

"When he fell out of the sky and Annie picked him up," he added, twisting the front of his yellow SpongeBob T-shirt into a knot.

"What color was the balloon?"

"Red," Michael answered after a moment of reflection.

"So you were riding a black horse with a red balloon when this Anna's hummingbird hit the Ferris wheel and fell out of the sky onto the pier right in front of your pit bull, Annie?" I recounted in wonder, marveling at the whimsical world kids, like humming-birds, inhabit.

Michael looked up at me with enormous brown eyes and nod-ded in serious silence.

"He's mixing up the chronology," his father said, stepping in. "He was actually riding the black horse with the red balloon on the carousel about ten minutes before Annie picked the hummingbird up off the pier," he reported in a didactic tone.

"Well, I'm very proud of you," I told Michael. "You've done a wonderful thing bringing this little bird to someone who knows how to take care of him."

Michael studied the hummingbird in the ICU for a few seconds before nodding in complete agreement.

Within an hour of their departure, Iron Mike was up and flying, but when I put him in a large flight cage, he wobbled unsteadily on the perch, signaling a mild head injury that demanded a stint in rehab.

Iron Mike is a first-year male, but his crown and gorget are almost entirely cloaked in shimmering magenta, indicating he was born in late winter and has been hanging around the beach for several months. As the youngest male in the group, Iron Mike still has some unresolved ego issues. Iron Mike boldly claims the center perch the moment he gets into the aviary, and he lifts off every few minutes to patrol his domain, hovering in front of each cage mate with flashy bravado before moving on to impress his next subject. As I observe the brazen showoff making his rounds, I can almost see the chink in Iron Mike's armor. Any recovering bird who looks that tough and invulnerable is fundamentally dishonest. Because in the end, injured hummingbirds are all scared and under pressure. And Iron Mike's displays of self-importance are comical, as the adults ignore him with puzzled indifference. Still, I am worried that his need for recognition might prompt him to attack Pepper, which would send her screaming back to a flight cage. But Iron Mike is a perfect gentleman with Pepper and the other females. It's the rocketing rufous that drives him crazy.

The adult male rufous arrived earlier in the week. He'd slammed into a Century City high-rise and dropped onto the cement ledge just outside a window. Fortunately, the young administrative assistant who discovered him edged out onto the fifteenth-floor ledge during lunch hour and retrieved the knockout *before* calling me, thus sparing my fragile nerves from a late-summer breakdown. The stunning, scarlet-bibbed rufous had some trouble with vertical lift his first several days in a large flight cage, but the minute he got into the aviary, he came roaring back to health. Now he is one of those rare birds that can fly so fast, he's a blur. His quickness is so unprecedented that I cannot come close to following him with my eyes. For exercise, he flies laps around the aviary at the speed of light. This irritates Iron Mike, who feels inclined to pursue him during his fast-paced workouts. But because Iron Mike can go only about half his speed, the rufous keeps ending up on Mike's tail during the chase. And instead of stopping and turning around, Mike just looks aggravated and strains to fly faster in a futile effort to catch up.

Adding to the comic relief of this last group is One-Eyed Jack, a male Anna's brought in a few weeks earlier by Leslie, who gave him his name because she once worked the tables in Vegas. One-Eyed Jack lost his left eye after colliding with some unidentified flying object but is otherwise quick and sound, and he has learned to compensate for his loss of binocular vision by flying backward much of the time. I have never seen a hummingbird make such a radical adjustment, but he is mesmerizing to watch as he spins around the aviary, suddenly braking in midair to grab a fruit fly before returning to his reverse rotations. Amazingly, despite his impressive speed, One-Eyed Jack never collides with another bird or any object inside the aviary.

The antics of the adult group provide endless entertainment, but after a day I release the lightning-fast rufous so Iron Mike, who is becoming increasingly defeated by his supercharged antagonist, can get some rest. Gabriel and Pepper settle in comfortably with this refreshingly peaceful group of battered casualties that includes an adult black-chinned female who lost two wing feathers to a cat, and the still undersize but now mature Powder. Every morning, with a rush of relief, I get up at dawn to hang feeders and a freshly watered fuchsia in the aviary then head back to bed. My twenty cages sit clean and empty in the garage. The ICU has been vacant for weeks.

Free from the ceaseless demands of healing hummingbirds, I return to my ritual of taking our cat Bobo for a walk on a leash every afternoon. Bobo is the kind of feline who was born with a brain far too big for his species and he therefore requires daily excursions around the neighborhood to stay mentally stimulated. One sunny afternoon in mid-August, as Bobo and I are passing the community garden across the street from our house, I notice a prominent sign on the entry gate posted by the city that reads *Warning: West Nile virus has been detected in the area*. I smile wistfully as I recall my terrifying Sunday morning with Pepper two weeks earlier. With hummingbirds, so many things happen so fast and change so quickly that recent events always seem as if they occurred much longer ago. Bobo turns left at the end of the block and then makes another unannounced left at the next corner, and we run into Jonathon, who took in the newborn kitten from the Santa Monica shelter several weeks ago. When he catches sight of us down the block, he waves in friendly recognition.

"Max is a giant," Jonathon exclaims as we approach. "He weighed over three pounds at two months. And such a huge baby. He never got off our laps except to use the box." He laughs. "Daniel wanted to keep him." Jonathon rolls his eyes. "So I just found him a great home. Somebody with more than enough money to feed him for the rest of his life."

I thank him profusely and promise to call with the numbers of two hummingbird finders who fell in love with our cats during their visits and are looking to adopt hopelessly spoiled bottle babies like Max. Sensing my conversation with Jonathon is coming to a close, Bobo turns and then leads me home.

Later that afternoon, when I head into the aviary to fill feeders, I bring along a handful of freshly picked lavender and hibiscus. Before I can get the flowers attached to perches, Pepper, Gabriel, Iron Mike, and Powder begin mining the nectar from the blossoms in my hand with alacrity and grace.

Hummingbirds are driven by all that is light and bright. As beautiful to the human eye as they are, these fireworks of the forest inhabit an even more fantastical world in which everything shimmers and sparkles. The iridescent color on the male's head and gorget and, in many species, the circular spot on the female's throat are not only instrumental in bringing hummingbirds together but determine the flowers they prefer. Just as hummingbirds are attracted to the sequined feathers on each other, the iridescent striations on flowers such as hibiscus and the sparkling pollen on passionflowers magnetically attract hummingbirds with a vibrant glow that pulsates in the bright sunlight. In plants such as lavender, this iridescence is visible only in the ultraviolet range that humans can't see but that flashes like a neon sign for passing hummingbirds.

In the late-afternoon sunbeams streaming through the aviary bars from the west, I can feel the wind from the hummingbirds' wings on my face and arms. And in that moment, I become entranced by the divine beauty that I so often overlook in my quest to identify and address their problems. As I listen to the hypnotic hum of the dozen blurred wings buzzing around me, I am transported to a place governed by neither space nor time and feel as though I have stepped out of my body into that state of complete serenity Lao Tzu has been pointing me toward all summer. It lasts less than a minute, and then it's gone. But the memory is unforgettable.

Standing in the aviary among the spinning wings, I recall having only one other disembodied moment like this in my life. It happened seventeen years ago when Frank and I were diving off a remote island in the kingdom of Tonga in the South Pacific. For weeks we had been exploring mysterious caves and breathtaking virgin reefs a two-hour boat ride from the main island. On this particular dive, a dazzling French angelfish tagged along beside me as Frank floated several yards ahead. The shimmering blue-and-gold angelfish stayed close to my elbow through the entire dive as we drifted weightlessly above the motley coral blanketing the ocean floor. Occasionally, when I stopped and turned to admire his magnificence, my faithful escort would pause, fins still undulating, and turn one eye upward at me before returning to our silent voyage. The current carried us over luminous reefs and massive coral heads sprinkled with vivid sea anemones and inhabited by thousands of brilliant tropical fish. The dive was so tranquil and removed it seemed as if we had entered a world that had been enveloped in silence since the beginning of time. As we kicked gently under an arch through which the sun refracted in soft, celestial rays around the fronds of a giant sea fan, I was overcome by an exhilarating feeling that time moves in a circle with no beginning and no end and that somehow the enduring peace that surrounded us in this remote underwater world would, in its eternal presence, prevail beyond everything else. In this flash of insight, there was no longer a me standing apart from the sea and its multicolored inhabitants. And as the lines between me and everything else fell away, I experienced that elusive sense of being at one with nature and the universe that Eastern religions celebrate as the ideal consciousness.

Now, standing in the aviary with Gabriel and Pepper mining the flowers in my hand, I have been transported to that same enchanting place. And I finally grasp what Lao Tzu meant when he asserted, *The sage does not seek fulfillment.* By devoting one's time to repairing helpless rescues like Pepper and Gabriel and the hundreds of other radiant hummingbirds I have encountered this summer, fulfillment just happens.

At the end of the week, Deion, a sixth-*dan* aikido black belt who runs a dojo in the San Fernando Valley, brings me a young black-chinned fledgling who, since she needs to go into a starter cage, will be heading to Jean's facility tomorrow. On Deion's way out, he stops to watch the birds in the aviary and falls into awestruck silence. After a few minutes he jolts, as if waking from a dream.

"Sorry about that lapse. I just kind of went into a trance."

"No worries. It happens to me all the time."

"How did you get started doing this?"

"I found a bird once," I answer reflectively. "It was something I always wanted to do, five hundred hummingbirds ago."

"It's one of those be-careful-what-you-wish-for things, right?"

"Never have my prayers been answered so abundantly."

"So how do you know when to release them?"

"You watch their energy. It's all in their chi."

"Really?" He looks at me in amazement.

"Yeah, it's just like martial arts." I glance at him with a knowing look. "You can tell by observing their posture and the way they move who is ready for battle and who isn't. Know what I mean?"

"Absolutely! Chi is everything," Deion agrees. "Is it hard to let them go?" he asks as we watch Gabriel preen his wing feathers and Pepper mine fuchsia blossoms with graceful elegance.

Deion's question takes me by surprise, because I haven't thought about how hard it is going to be to say goodbye to Pepper and Gabriel after all this time. "It's a mixed bag. Some are harder than others." I gaze at Pepper wistfully. "But as much as you care about them—"

"Never fall in love with your inventory, right?"

"Our love for them is the reason we set them free."

"How do you decide which day to release them?"

"The weather has to be perfect." I gaze up at the sky. "Like launches at Cape Canaveral. No rain, not too cold, no wind, a lot of sun, but not too hot. Conditions have to be optimal when they take off so they don't crash and burn their first day out."

"How about these guys? When are you going to let them go?"

"Any day now."

"Too much smog today, though," Deion observes, squinting up at the hazy blue sky.

"That's the one constant we're stuck with, I'm afraid."

My conversation with Deion that afternoon reminds me of something Sensei Nishiyama had confided to me years ago while we were chatting in his office one day. Because he headed both national and international karate federations, Sensei always had stacks of letters that needed to be written announcing upcoming seminars, training sessions, and rule and schedule changes. The minute he discovered that I could write, Sensei drafted me to help him wade through the piles of correspondence forever flooding in. Invariably, during our administrative sessions, the conversation would drift to karate students and events at the dojo. One rainy winter afternoon as we were making our way through a dozen replies, Sensei mentioned a highly skilled black belt from another dojo who always became so paralyzed by stage fright during his exams that he could never finish his kata properly even though he performed impeccably during training. Despite this flaw, Sensei always promoted him to the next level. When I asked Sensei why he would pass someone who always failed so miserably on the day of the test, he waved his hand in the air and insisted that a student's performance on an exam was irrelevant.

"Then how do you know whom to promote and whom to hold back?" I asked him curiously.

"Simple." Sensei leaned back in his chair and gave me a long, thoughtful look. "Just watch how student walks."

"How he walks?"

Sensei nodded pensively. "When student stands up and walks to center of dojo, easy can tell. Everything after that"—Sensei shakes his head—"not matter."

"Really?" I asked with astonishment. "So all these hundreds of students training madly day and night are stressing out about an exam that is irrelevant?"

"Of course training is very important for posture, speed, timing, and proper technique," Sensei reminded me.

"But the test doesn't matter." I finished his thought with a sly smile.

Sensei leaned toward me and narrowed his eyes with a conspiratorial grin. "Don't tell anybody."

Watching the hummingbirds zip around the aviary that afternoon, I understand exactly what Sensei meant. Each bird possesses a unique energy that reveals his or her strength, skill, and confidence. And after years of closely observing their demeanor and flight, I know long before I open the doors exactly who is ready to take on the natural world and who is not.

That night, just after dark, Chad from Venice Beach calls about a hummingbird stunned by a window strike late in the day. Chad tells me the hummingbird is now flying around in a small cage in his living room. After describing the adult male's sudden recovery, for a minute, Chad asks if he should release him.

"Hummingbirds can't see in the dark, so keep him overnight and release him first thing in the morning."

"Is it okay if I feed him every hour, then? Because he's so cool and I stay up all night," Chad points out innocently.

"He doesn't need to eat all night."

"But I stay up all night anyway, so is it okay if I feed him every hour?" he persists.

"Feed him until ten or so, then cover the cage and let him sleep, all right? Because he has to get up and go to work in the morning, unlike us."

"Okay, Terry." Chad laughs cheerfully. "I totally see your point. And, dude, what you do for hummingbirds is so awesome!"

Awesome. How many times have I heard that word this summer? An old term that has been co-opted and converted into slang by American youth. For William Blake, it meant "inspired to reverential wonder by the sublime and majestic in nature." In reaching beyond beauty, the sublime, rather than being ornamental, overtakes reason in its pursuit of a higher perception that aims for transcendent knowledge. So what better way to celebrate this sense of wonder than by aiding these charismatic creatures in their efforts to survive in a manmade environment fraught with urban hazards? Because for all the headaches hummingbirds have caused me, when they come through the door, I am humbled by their splendor and boundless allure. And as the summer edges to a close, I realize with mounting clarity that, in keeping with Lao Tzu's description of the ideal life, the more I give to them, the more I have.

Considering all of this, then, Chad, when you said that rescuing hummingbirds is awesome, you nailed it. Totally, dude.

CHAPTER 28

What a Wonderful World

BY THE LAST WEEK in August, I have taken in one hundred and sixty hummingbirds. With the release of the final group in the aviary, one hundred and thirty-five will be reintroduced into the wild. Jean's figures run even higher. Taken altogether, the number of birds we have gotten back out there is staggering. Over the past four decades, hard-working rehabbers have released more than ten thousand healthy young hummingbirds in Southern California. Most survive and propagate for several years.

Experts estimate Southern California hummingbirds live from five to eight years. Hummingbirds have roughly the same number of heartbeats in a lifetime as humans. A hummingbird that lives eight years has about three billion heartbeats, approximately the same as an eighty-year-old human.

The main source of information on hummingbird longevity comes from banding studies, some of which estimate a lifespan of between four and six years and others of between six and eight. But examples of older hummingbirds are common, including a nine-year-old black-chinned discovered in Montana, a nine-year-old ruby-throated in West Virginia, a twelve-year-old broad-tailed, and more than one instance of a rufous living beyond the ten-year mark. And I receive numerous calls every summer reporting Anna's and Allen's females nesting in the same tree, and sometimes the same refurbished nest, for several consecutive years. So when you consider the offspring of our releases and the descendants of their progeny, rehabbers have added to the streets of Los Angeles and the broader western landscape not just ten thousand of these captivating birds but hundreds of thousands.

As I scroll through a summer of text messages and revisit the endless photos of damaged, grounded, and distressed humming-birds brought to me over the past six months, I understand that I am gazing into the cold eyes of nature, which is staring back at me with steely indifference. And only then do I realize the formidable adversary I am up against. Nature escorts you into the heart of darkness and leaves you there to find your own way out. Rehabbers enter the indifferent, irrational, and amoral world of nature and try to impose reason and morality on an environment in which perpetuation of the species takes precedence over the survival of the individual, which is essentially meaningless. This last point is what is so hard for Americans — and particularly Californians, with our overriding commitment to individuality — to accept. Whenever somebody brings me a hummingbird in need of help, the bird is, in that person's eyes, the most important bird in rehab. And while there may in fact be millions of hummingbirds flying around the Western world, when an injured or orphaned bird comes through my door, his or her particularity is all that I see.

I've answered two thousand calls this summer, and I recollect the pep talks, encouragement, and consolation I've offered. I consider the creative strategies I have devised to inform, educate, and comfort an urban public unprepared to cope with raw nature. Most of the time I am left guessing whether callers have the emotional resources to deal with the hard realities presented by a merciless and unforgiving natural world. When I sense they do not, I am forced to reframe, cajole, and, when I have to, outright lie about what is going on out there. My job is to harness callers' unchecked emotions, refine them, and turn them back out as something productive and purposeful, something that, despite man's carelessness and nature's indifference, reintroduces the beauty of life into our fallen world. Because what most callers really want is someone to listen to their concerns and fears and reassure them that making an effort to save something as diminutive as a hummingbird is not crazy, silly, or irrelevant. And by encouraging rather than dismissing that moment of compassion, I hope that I am helping people develop and evolve a more empathic consciousness that spills over into their interactions with all living things, including fellow human beings, toward whom so many callers express such abiding hostility. Because, in the end, whether we are rescuing hummingbirds or simply admiring them from a distance, their hypnotic beauty and magical flight bring people together.

On a spectacular morning in early September, under a dazzling turquoise sky half obscured by fluffy white cumulus clouds so thick and towering they look like steppingstones to the higher reaches, I head out to the patio. The hummingbirds are swirling wildly in the aviary as if they feel some special electricity in the air and sense something is up.

For a brief moment, I try to imagine what it must be like to be them. To be capable of such phenomenal speed and possess the power to execute straight verticals, fly sideways and backward, and effortlessly soar high into the sky. I visualize what the buildings,

trees, and clouds must look like passing by in a blur. What a wonderful world they inhabit and how much fun it must be to fly like
angels and dance on air as they view our constantly changing landscape from high above. Of course, their lives are not as carefree as
they appear. They have land squabbles, gender conflicts, and hard
days just like us. Still, with all of their troubles, every time I watch
the new releases buzzing and circling one another around the patio
their first day out, I suspect they have a lot of fun. When people
ask me if I think hummingbirds ever stop fighting and just play, my
answer is always the same: If you could fly like that, wouldn't you
play?

I approach the aviary and reach for the handle on the side door,
but then I hesitate with a heavy heart. After such intense emotional investment over the past four months, it's hard to imagine
life without my two shining stars. Summoning all of my resolve,
I say goodbye first to Gabriel, then to Pepper, and open both aviary doors. Without wasting a moment, Iron Mike leads the charge
out the security door, the black-chinned and One-Eyed Jack, flying forward this time, on his tail. Pepper glances at me and hesi-
tates on her perch, but when Gabriel heads for the open door, she
rises up and follows along. As soon as he crosses the threshold to
freedom, the angel Gabriel spirals in wide loops once, twice, three
times and then climbs hundreds of feet and vanishes through a
hole in the cotton-candy clouds and into the exhilarating blue beyond. Seeing Gabriel's act of brilliance, Pepper begins her spiral,
ascending weightlessly into the heavens on gossamer wings. At a
dizzying altitude, she soars over the buildings and trees, elevating
higher, faster, stronger, and fearlessly into the vast unknown.

I am flying.

Epilogue

FOR THE FOURTH TIME, Powder remained in the aviary after the other birds' release. I left both doors open, hoping she would finally muster the courage to go. A day later, she ventured out to explore the bougainvillea surrounding the patio, but before I could get the aviary scrubbed and the doors closed, she was back inside, snapping up the last of the late-summer fruit flies. For the next several days she came and went through the open security door, always returning at night to sleep in the aviary's ficus tree. After a week of this routine, I came out one afternoon to find the UCLA hybrid, who had been released nearly a month earlier, perched inside the aviary with her. The hybrid, which I'd finally concluded was a female, also came and went before vanishing a week later.

Powder slept in the ficus tree every night for three weeks, then every other night for about a week, and then finally gained the confidence to make a total transition to the wild. Her continuing presence in rehab that summer served as a powerful reminder that anybody, regardless of education and experience, can be seduced by the beauty and charm of a hummingbird. In late September, I saw the agile little flier filling up at the sugar feeder for what turned out to be the last time before her autumn migration to Mexico.

Pepper hung around the patio sugar feeders for a few weeks after her release but never retreated back into the aviary. Occasionally she buzzed me in the mornings when I came out to fill the feeders, but, to my infinite satisfaction, she never let me get too close. Then one day she too was gone, perhaps returning to her film career in Los Feliz. I never saw Gabriel again. He already knew his way around town, so I expect he went back to the prime real estate he had staked out in Beverly Hills before he'd returned to be saved by me, and with me, for a second time. And even though I have not seen Gabriel since our long summer together, I hold on to the memory. And if I ever do run into him again, Gabriel will be easy to recognize. He's the one with the white spot, the magical third eye that gave me a glimpse into that bright and shining realm that belongs wholly to hummingbirds.

In the summer of 2008, after releasing the last group of adults, I received only one more bird. Julie, who identified herself as an eagle rehabber, called in late September and asked if she could bring me an orphaned fledgling. Although I had gone back to teaching and hadn't gotten any hummingbirds for two months, I was happy to take him. In the ensuing conversation, Julie, who used to live in Los Angeles, explained that she was bringing me a young black-chinned who, thanks to an early-fall snowstorm in Idaho, could not be released until the following spring. Since making the fifteen-hour drive to LA was easier than overwintering the juvenile, Julie and her husband decided to use the hummingbird as an excuse to visit old friends in the city.

Several days later they showed up with a spirited black-chinned fledgling and a handful of paperwork from Idaho Fish and Wildlife granting permission to transport the little powerhouse over state lines. I caged the excitable male in the garage for the night and then put him into the aviary the next morning, intending to leave him there for at least a week until he got his bearings. Because of his late arrival, I wanted to keep him until he became comfortable using a sugar feeder, since flowers are in short supply by the end of September. But when I came out to check on him the first afternoon in the aviary, he was hanging upside down on the horizontal bars. Puzzled by his behavior, I slid him off the bars and let him go in the center of the aviary, but he returned to the same spot and began banging against the bars. Concerned that his long, interstate car trip may have been disorienting, I slid him off the bars again and attempted to distract him by letting him go near a fresh bouquet of honeysuckle strategically positioned in the back of the aviary. When I came out ten minutes later and found him in the same agitated state, hanging nearly upside down on the bars with his tail sticking outside, I realized he was pointing straight south, as if being physically pulled from the aviary by a magnetic force beyond his control. That same primal energy, indefinable and defying description, compels billions of migratory creatures to run, swim, and fly up and down the planet every spring and fall in pursuit of an end we can never fully comprehend. After watching the distraught fledgling cling to the bars with his tiny feet as his tail strained farther outside the aviary, I reluctantly opened the doors and invited him out. The second he cleared the threshold, he streaked thirty feet into the air and then headed south over the Beverly Center on his way to Mexico. And while his swift departure brought a wave of relief that the long rehab season had finally come to a close, it also left me cautiously bracing for the next call, another hummingbird, and a rapidly approaching spring.

Acknowledgments

WHILE WRITING A BOOK can be a lonely affair, rescuing hummingbirds is never a solitary pursuit. Before this book became an idea, Ann Lynch already invested several years helping to fund my rescue efforts through her nonprofit, South Bay Wildlife Rehabilitation. In addition to her, I would like to thank the California Wildlife Center and Linda Lindsay for their enduring commitment to rehabilitating the hundreds of helpless young hummingbirds I send their way each year.

My deepest appreciation goes out to my agent, Felicia Eth, for her unwavering faith and resolve that brought this work to publication, and to Lisa White and Tracy Roe, whose editorial expertise and laserlike precision in fine-tuning the manuscript motivated me to make this book all that I had hoped it would become. Thanks also for the contributions of Beth Burleigh Fuller, Brian Moore, Laney Everson, Taryn Roeder, Katrina Kruse, and the rest of the team at Houghton Mifflin Harcourt.

Many thanks go out to Douglas Altshuler, Chris Clark, and George C. West for generously sharing their original research, which has led to remarkable insights into the mysteries of hummingbird flight, breeding, and migration. And to Brian E. Small for capturing these miniature miracles with his brilliant photography. A special thanks to Sara Michele, Rocky Stickel, and Steve Diggins for donating their colorful and poignant photos of wild and rescued hummingbirds.

I want to express my appreciation to the Bella Hummingbird live webcam for educating people all over the world about hummingbird breeding and nesting habits and for spreading valuable information aimed at advancing our rescue efforts. Also, many thanks to China Adams for creating the original website that provided a fast connection to the public, making it possible to save countless young hummingbirds at a moment's notice.

Finally, I want to extend my gratitude to all of my friends who have offered support and assistance during my years of rescuing and writing about hummingbirds. Heartfelt thanks to Lily Sheen for her guidance and encouragement that inspired me to finish this book far sooner than I could have imagined. And to Ashley Herman, for all of the orphaned chicks she shuttled to my doorstep when I was too stretched to retrieve them myself. Also, thanks to Tara Neuwirth for giving me the flexibility to take time off from teaching over the years to save thousands of hummingbirds. A million thanks to Cameron, Yuko, and Alexandra Wood for graciously allowing my rescue project to overflow into their backyard and for being there to prop up an exhausted rehabber at all hours. My sincere gratitude goes out to my sister, Victoria Masear, for her generous support and steady supply of information on eastern hummingbirds; Dick Willis for his consistently levelheaded advice on human nature; Tom Shinmoto for his insights on all things Japanese; José Aguilar for his enlightening American Spanish lessons; Gail Borden and Kyle Voorheis for their photographic contributions to the website; and Dave and Eva Schwartz for always being there, no matter when or what the request.

Since saving hummingbirds requires a community, I want to thank all of the compassionate Southern California hummingbird finders for their willingness to invest the time and energy to deliver their precious rescues to facilities where they can be rehabilitated and released back into the City of Angels.

And, most of all, to my loving husband, Frank; although I know you don't want me to mention it, none of this would have been possible without you and our demanding crew of cats who, despite staging regular protests over being ignored, have sat up late with us, night after night, waiting to see how it all ends.

Index